D0908321

THE HOLOCAUST IN HUNGARY
FORTY YEARS LATER

Edited by

RANDOLPH L. BRAHAM and BELA VAGO

Social Science Monographs
and
Institute for Holocaust Studies
of The City University of New York
and
Institute for Holocaust Studies
of the University of Haifa

Distributed by Columbia University Press, New York

1985

EAST EUROPEAN MONOGRAPHS, NO. CXC

Copyright © 1985 by Randolph L. Braham
Library of Congress Card Catalog Number 85-50468
ISBN 0-88033-083-X

Printed in the United States of America

Holocaust Studies Series

Randolph L. Braham, Editor
The Institute for Holocaust Studies
The Graduate School and University Center
The City University of New York

Previously published books in the Series:
Perspectives on the Holocaust, 1982
Contemporary Views on the Holocaust, 1983
Genocide and Retribution, 1983
*The Hungarian Jewish Catastrophe
A Selected and Annotated
Bibliography,* 1984
*Jewish Leadership During the Nazi
Era: Patterns of Behavior in
the Free World,* 1985

The Holocaust Studies Series is published in cooperation with
the Institute for Holocaust Studies. These books are outgrowths
of lectures, conferences, and research projects sponsored by the
Institute. It is the purpose of the series to subject the events and
circumstances of the Holocaust to scrutiny by a variety of academics
who bring different scholarly disciplines to the study.
The first three books in the Series were published by
Kluwer-Nijhoff Publishing of Boston.

CONTENTS

v

PREFACE

This volume is an outgrowth of two international conferences held in 1984, on the occasion of the fortieth anniversary of the Holocaust in Hungary. The first conference was held under the auspices of the Institute for Holocaust Studies of the Graduate School and University Center of The City University of New York (March 20-21); the second under the sponsorship of the Institute for Holocaust Studies of the University of Haifa (May 14-17).

The conferences were devoted to an in-depth evaluation of one of the most controversial chapters in the tragedy that befell European Jewry during the Nazi era. Perhaps no other chapter in the Holocaust has elicited as many agonizing questions and given rise to so many heated debates as the destruction of Hungarian Jewry. Almost oblivious to the systematic destruction of the Jewish communities in Nazi-dominated Europe, the Hungarian Jewish community—though subjected to harsh legal and economic measures—survived the first four and a half years of the war relatively intact. Though it suffered 63,000 casualties even before the German occupation of the country on March 19, 1944—close to 18,000 "alien" Jews were massacred near Kamenets-Podolsk in August 1941, around 1,000 Jews were killed in and around Újvidék (Novi Sad) in January-February 1942, and around 42,000 died in labor service in the Ukraine and elsewhere in 1942–43—this community continued to live in the belief that it would somehow escape the fate that had befallen the other Jewish communities of Europe. The Jews of Hungary lived under the illusion, fostered by their national assimilationist-conservative leaders, that their patriotism and loyalty to the Hungarian nation were appreciated and that the aristocratic-gentry leadership of the country would protect them. Though these leaders, like the other Jewish and the non-Jewish leaders of the world, were fully and accurately informed about the details of the Final Solution, they kept the Jewish masses in the dark. Misguided by their naive optimism and trust in the ruling elite of the country, they failed to take any precautionary measures. Consequently, when catastrophe struck with the German invasion, the Jewish masses were helpless and totally defenseless. Because of the swiftly approaching Soviet front, the Jews of Hungary—excepting those of Budapest—were subjected to the most ruthless and concentrated destruction process in the Nazis' war against the Jews, on the very eve of Allied victory.

The studies included in this volume aim to identify and analyze the many historical, cultural, political, and socioeconomic factors that may have contributed to this tragic end of Hungarian Jewry, once one of the most prosperous and flourishing Jewish communities in East Central Europe. The first part covers the antecedents of this tragedy, beginning with an analytical article by Nathaniel Katzburg of Bar-Ilan University on the tradition of anti-Semitism in Hungary. This is followed by a literary-historical overview of the Jewish question in Hungary by György Száraz, the editor-in-chief of *Kortárs* (The Contemporary) of Budapest and the author of *Egy előitélet nyomában* (On the Tracks of a Prejudice), a highly acclaimed work on the origins of anti-Semitism. The next two essays complement each other. Professor Ivan T. Berend of the Karl Marx University of Economics (*Marx Károly Közgazdaságtudományi Egyetem*) of Budapest expertly describes the ideological and political background of Hungary on the eve of the Holocaust, while Professor István Deák of Columbia University skillfully dissects the peculiarities of Hungarian fascism, differentiating it from both Italian fascism and National Socialism. Professor Gyula Juhász, an associate of the Institute of History of the Hungarian Academy of Science (*A Magyar Tudományos Akadémia Történettudományi Intézete*), discusses with great erudition the attitude of Hungarian intellectuals to the Jewish question with emphasis on the interwar period.

The responsibility for, and the impact of, the Holocaust are discussed in the seven essays included in the second part of this volume. The first two essays in this part also complement each other. While Professor György Ránki, the well-known historian associated with the Institute of History of the Hungarian Academy of Science, focuses with great persuasion on the German responsibility for the Holocaust in Hungary, Professor Bela Vago, a leading expert on East Central Europe, documents the determining role played by the Hungarians in this tragedy. Whatever the fundamental differences in the scope and emphasis of these two essays, they jointly prove the linkage between the German and Hungarian dejewifiers: neither could have achieved their ideologically defined objectives without the help of the other. Dr. Elek Karsai, the author of numerous documentary works on the Holocaust in Hungary, discusses some interesting aspects of local and county administration with respect to the ghettoization and deportation of Hungarian Jewry. Professor Raphael Vago of the University of Tel Aviv, the author of several perceptive pieces on East Central Europe, documents the attitudes and reactions of the Jewish community of Palestine—the *Yishuv*—to the Holocaust in general and the tragedy that befell Hungarian Jewry in particular. Professor Asher Cohen, a recognized expert on the *Hehalutz* (Zionist pioneers) in Hungary, provides insight into the resistance movements that operated in Hungary during the latter part of the war with emphasis on the heroic activities of the Zionist youth. The rescue activities of Raoul Wallenberg, one of the legendary figures of the Holocaust era, are described with sympathy and admiration by Elenore Lester, a prolific author and journalist associated with *The Jewish Week* of New York. This part ends with a balance sheet of the cultural losses of Hungarian Jewry provided by Dr. Raphael Patai, a well-known scholar and prolific writer.

The third part of the volume is devoted to historical interpretations and literary reactions. The uniqueness of the Holocaust in Hungary is discussed by the editor of this volume, associated with The City University of New York. Professor Ivan Sanders of Suffolk County Community College provides a masterful overview of the treatment of the Holocaust in contemporary Hungarian literature.

The last essay, constituting the fourth part of the volume, is devoted to the lingering issue: the Jewish question in Hungary after the Holocaust. This sensitive topic is treated with great erudition and expertise by Dr. András Kovács, a sociologist from Budapest.

The interpretations and views expressed by the authors are theirs alone and do not necessarily reflect those of the editor or of the institutes and institutions that sponsored the two international conferences.

This volume could not have been completed without the cooperation of the contributors. For this I am greatly indebted to them. I would also like to express my indebtedness to the leaders of the two institutions of higher learning that sponsored the conference—to President Harold M. Proshansky and Dean Solomon Goldstein of the Graduate School and University Center of The City University of New York, and to President Ephraim Evron and Dean Lawrence Davis of the University of Haifa. I would like to express my special thanks to Professor Ayeh Grabois of the Department of General History for his valuable contributions to the publication of this volume and to Ms. Hava Gotel of the Institute for Holocaust Studies for her administrative expertise in assuring the success of the conference at Haifa University. The real dynamic force behind the Haifa conference was Professor Bela Vago. He also played a very important role in the planning and organization of this volume. For this all those interested in Holocaust studies are greatly indebted to him. Finally, I would like to express my appreciation to

the Holocaust Survivors Memorial Foundation, the primary supporter of the
Institute for Holocaust Studies of The City University in New York, and to the
contributors to the Special Holocaust Research and Publication Fund of the
Graduate School and University Center—above all, Susan and Marcel Sand
and Valerie and Frank Furth—for their generosity.

Randolph L. Braham
May 1985

INTRODUCTION

Elie Wiesel

I would like to point out a few elements that make the tragedy of Hungarian Jewry unique. I would like to demonstrate that: one, the world knew; two, the victims did not; three, it could have been prevented. A few dates: March 19, 1944—Germany occupied Hungary. I remember: it was spring, and I was still in the yeshiva in my hometown, Máramarossziget. As we were studying, somebody came in and said that the Germans had just arrived. We went into the street and saw tanks. The first Germans were polite, and we thought, "Well, this too will pass." Ten days later, on the 29th of March, the first decree was issued ordering the Jews in Hungary to wear the yellow star.

A few other decrees: Jews had no right to leave their homes except during certain hours; they had no right to use public transportation, to visit public gardens, parks, restaurants, theaters, museums. Fifth of April: another decree was issued declaring Transylvania and all the provinces of Carpatho-Ruthenia military zones, thereby enabling Eichmann and his accomplices to implement the "Final Solution." One week later the ghetto was established in my town, which was called Máramarossziget. May 16: the first transport. May 22: the fourth and last transport. I was a part of the last.

On May 18, while I was still in the ghetto, a telegram was sent from the American consulate in Istanbul to the State Department. And for the first time, the name of my town entered the history of the United States. In that long and detailed telegram, it was reported that refugees who reached Palestine had related terrible facts regarding Jews in Hungary.

According to sources in Poland there was clear evidence that mass extermination was being prepared. "The Jews in Hungary are already interned in camps and ghettos, three hundred thousand Jews from Sziget, Carpatho-Ruthenia, Marosvásárhely, Szeged, Debrecen, Nyíregyháza, Beregszász, Nagyszőllős, Nagybánya, Szatmárnémeti, Mátészalka, Munkács, Szabadka, Kolozsvár," and a few other names that have been misspelled in the telegram. Now remember, the telegram was sent on May 15 and we were still in Sziget.

It is important for us to emphasize the dates. On April the 7th—two days after the provinces were declared military zones—two Slovakian Jews escaped from Birkenau. One is called Rudolf Vrba and the other, Alfred Wetzler. To escape from Auschwitz was quasi-impossible and yet they managed to escape because they were motivated by one fact, one drive. Because they were in Birkenau, they knew that preparations were being made to "receive" Hungarian Jews. They had been in touch with the underground in Auschwitz-Birkenau, witnessed the work that was going on: the gas chambers being enlarged, barracks readied, and additional ovens being built. Therefore, Vrba and Wetzler decided to escape—to warn Hungarian Jews, who were all still in Hungary: not a single Hungarian Jew had yet been deported. The two emissaries managed to reach Slovakia, and fourteen days later, no, more—three weeks later—on April 25, Alfred and Rudolf were sipping, I quote Vrba, "were sipping sherry at the Zilina headquarters of the Jewish Council" and were telling their story to Dr. Oscar Neumann, spokesman for all Slovakia's Jews, Oscar Krasznyanski, Irving Steiner, and a man called Hexner.

Vrba says, and I quote him, "I told them one million Hungarian Jews are going to die. Auschwitz is ready for them. But if you tell them now, they will rebel. They will never go to the ovens. Your turn is coming, but now it is the Hungarians' hour. You must tell them immediately." We know that the message was communicated—to the leaders of the Jewish community in Budapest, and therefore immediately to Turkey, to the Jews of Turkey, Switzerland, the Vatican, Washington. Therefore, I do not understand why it took so long for the report to be mentioned in a telegram—in late May. Moreover, once it was mentioned, and once the telegram was sent, and once they knew, I don't understand why no action was taken.

You study the media awareness and the diplomatic documents of the time and again you are embarrassed. On its front page of March 20, 1944, the day after the occupation of Hungary, *The New York Times* of course mentions the arrival of spring, and *The Washington Post,* with a big picture reports the very important event that King Peter of Yugoslavia is getting married. The German occupation of Hungary is not mentioned at all. The war on various fronts is referred to, naturally, and the news is good. The long struggle for Monte Cassino was nearing an end, flying fortresses bombed the Third Reich, six U-boats were sunk in the Atlantic. On the eastern front, the Red Army conquered more than forty towns in the Moldavian Republic, and two hundred places in the Ukraine and Poland, including Kamenets-Podolsk and Moghilev were conquered, reconquered, liberated. What happened to

Hungarian Jews? Why didn't they know? There is no doubt that the world knew.

I remember that when we arrived in Birkenau we were met by the *Canada,* a kommando; its members were angry at us. I didn't understand it then, but now I understand. They were terribly angry at us. They said, "Why did you come?" And I remember—I think I mentioned it in my first memoir—I was angry at them. "What do you *mean*—why *did* we come? Did we have a choice?" Now I understand. They had tried to warn us. After all, for the two men to leave Birkenau, it took the involvement, the self-sacrifice of hundreds of people, Jews and non-Jews. And they came—they brought the message. And the message was not received, meaning, it was not absorbed; it did not become knowledge. The information was there, but it was not transformed into consciousness. You study the newspapers in the United States and you are shocked. Beginning in 1942, everything was known. The names Auschwitz, Treblinka were known to the readers of *The New York Times* and *The Washington Post.* Not to us. When Jews from Hungary arrived in Auschwitz, they didn't know what it meant. The Jews in Birkenau said, "Why did you come, since we warned you?" Why weren't we warned?

When I came to Babi Yar for the first time, I thought nobody knew Babi Yar, or if they did, maybe it was only because of Yevtushenko's poem or Shostakovich's music. I came home and I went back to the sources. Three months after Babi Yar, *The New York Times* had a five page, five column story on the third page, with all the details of Babi Yar. Then in '42, when the first report came from Geneva, from Gerhart Riegner, it was published in all the papers, in September. In '43, when the Warsaw ghetto was in the midst of its unique endeavor of glory, bravery, gallantry and desperate heroism—again, the newspapers reported the events, blow by blow. It was impossible not to know the intention of the Germans or the heroism of the fighters. Now we know what happened—from a book published in Israel by Professor Asher Cohen of Haifa University. It is an informative, depressing and, at the same time, encouraging story. We know what happened in Hungary, in Budapest. Apparently, many people in Budapest were informed. In 1943, for instance, refugees from Bendzin reached Budapest. These young refugees, *Halutzim,* told the story of Bendzin and Sosnovic. And they told the story of Polish Jewry. They told the story period! They told the story of Auschwitz. As we know, Budapest was still a very quiet, peaceful city until 1944. I remember I was there to see a doctor in the Jewish hospital in 1943. The war was going on. The Jews in Budapest lived as in a strange hallucination. Yeshivas were full, with many underground *bachurim* who came from Poland. And the Hasidic rabbis were travelling from Szatmár to

Sziget and Nagyvárad. The cafés were full. We had a strange sense of security there, and yet the people from Bendzin had told the story. Asher Cohen quotes one Jew from Bendzin, "I don't understand you. How many kilometers," said he, "separate Budapest from Auschwitz?"

But why go so far? In 1941, the Hungarians decided to expel all the foreign Jews from Hungary, meaning all Jews who could not provide proof of their citizenship. I remember because I was young and it made an impression on me: we worked day and night at the house of our *Dayan* who kept the birth registry. We added names but we couldn't add all of them. A few hundred Jews were expelled from Sziget too. I remember one who came back from Kolomya and told the first stories of atrocities. He simply said, "I want you to know: those Jews who left Sziget were killed. I saw them being killed." We didn't believe him. He was a poor beadle, a *Shamesz*. We couldn't believe him. So we also *knew,* but why should we believe a poor beadle? There were influential, important people who knew while the victims did not. What would have happened had we known? Let me read another short paragraph: "On the evening of May 25th, an incident occurred in Birkenau. Large groups of Hungarian Jews sensed the doom and began escaping into the woods. And the same incident occurred three days later. The SS used their flood light, caught the escapees, and shot them all." Now this happened in Birkenau when the trains stopped. Just imagine the same thing happening in Máramarossziget, Nagybánya, Szatmár, and in all the other cities *before* the trains were boarded.

Eichmann came to Budapest on March 19 with two hundred persons. And that figure included guards and typists! Just imagine, two hundred. It's true, the Hungarians had their *Vadász csendőrök* (gendarmes) and their police, and we had enough anti-Semites. And for every German there were thousands more helping. But Eichmann felt so secure that he came with only two hundred people, that's all. Just imagine what would have happened if we had known—if the first transport, the second, the third, the fourth transport of Sziget had dispersed at the railway station . . . Therefore I believe the tragedy of Hungarian Jewry is a severe indictment. Why didn't we know? I could tell you many stories because, after all, I am a Hungarian Jew. And to this day I try to understand what happened. If ever there was a tragedy that could have been prevented, it was that one. It was so late—it was already April, May—the first transport left Sziget on May 16, three weeks before D-Day, before Normandy. Germany was losing the war and knew it. And yet 450,000 Jews from the provinces were being taken in the sealed wagons of their trains. Day after day, night after night. Why weren't they stopped?

Now we are convinced—I am—that if there had been an outcry, a unified outcry, naming names, not speaking about theories or principles but a statement from Churchill, Roosevelt, and all the other leaders saying that Jews in Hungary, from Máramaros, from Nagybánya, were being threatened and carried away, it would have stopped or at least slowed down the process.

During the two days of the International Conference reports and studies were presented by great experts, including Bela Vago and Randolph Braham. I am not sure whether there is an answer unless one says that such was the indifference of the world to our fate, and therefore to its own, that it numbed people. Numbness is the only possible explanation. But why should people always be numb when only Jews are threatened?

May I end with something which is very topical? I think that March 19th happened just before or after Purim in Sziget. There is something in the Purim story which always left me puzzled. We know that the Jews in Shushan, in Persia, lived very happily then. There was a flourishing Jewish community just like the one we had in Hungary. Jews occupied positions in the highest places in government. There were bankers, teachers, professors, writers and critics everywhere. Then one man, and only one man, came along; his name was Haman, and he decided because of a whim, to kill all the Jews, men, women and children. And it almost happened. Now my question is, how is that possible? Could one man change the mentality of a whole people? What happened to the liberals? To our friends in government? To the ministers? What happened to our neighbors with whom we lived for centuries in semi-peace? How was it possible that one man could usher in a threat of such magnitude? We Jews in Hungary learned that it was possible. It was done—overnight. It was enough for the Germans to come in, for Eichmann and his two hundred accomplices to appear and the yeshivas were stopped. And the *shuls,* the houses of prayer and study were forbidden. And the universe began shrinking. First, we were supposed to leave our towns and concentrate in the larger cities. Then the town shrank to the ghetto, and the ghetto to a house, the house to a room, the room to a cattlecar, the cattlecar—well, I will not continue.

Most Hungarian Jews entered a very small room, and I as a writer feel I have no right to imagine what happened inside.

I. ANTECEDENTS

Chapter 1

THE TRADITION OF ANTI-SEMITISM IN HUNGARY

Nathaniel Katzburg

The beginnings of anti-Semitic tradition in Hungary are marked by the emergence of political anti-Semitic ideas in the 1870s. In those years traditional anti-Jewish views were given modern ideological form and attained prominence and wide publicity.

The first to propagate anti-Jewish political and social ideas publicly was a deputy of the Hungarian Parliament, Győző (Victor) Istóczy.[1] His speech, delivered in Parliament on April 8, 1875, was one of the first attempts to formulate anti-Semitic ideology in political terms. His main themes were Jewish separateness and exclusiveness, and the Jews' striving for domination. Their increasing numbers and strength gained them powerful positions and thus constituted a danger for non-Jews. Consequently, Istóczy said, anti-Semitism was a struggle of self-defense of the Christian nations against the danger of Jewish supremacy.[2] The speech was not taken seriously by Parliament and the press, but, as the British Consul in Budapest observed

M. Istoczy only blurted out his share of the general antipathy,—an antipathy which shows itself in various social phases, and which, though it is rarely expressed in public, no Hungarian gentleman is in private conversation at any pains to conceal.[3]

From the early 1880s anti-Semitism gradually gained ground, especially among students, intellectuals, and segments of the middle-classes. Many of the anti-Semitic followers were recruited from among the German bourgeoisie. One of the main aims of the anti-Jewish agitation was to make the subject

3

of Jewish-Gentile coexistence a topical issue, an open question which, contrary to accepted view, was not settled by legal emancipation. In this the anti-Semites were successful to a considerable degree. Debates on the Jewish question in Parliament were provoked several times during 1880–1882.[4]

The most acute manifestation of Hungarian anti-Semitism in this period was the blood libel of Tiszaeszlár in 1882.[5] The particulars of the case are well known and there is no need to enter into details here. From a political point of view, however, it is significant that the Catholic priest of Tiszaeszlár and Istóczy, as well as his fellow deputy Géza Ónódy, were closely involved. The investigation and the judicial proceedings caused great excitement throughout the country and were accompanied by systematic anti-Jewish agitation in the clerical and extremist sections of the press, as well as in numerous pamphlets, leaflets, handbills, and posters.[6] Following the acquittal of the defendant, serious disorders occurred in many parts of the country. Conditions seemed now suitable for the establishment of an anti-Semitic political party. Established in October 1883, the new party adopted a twelve-point program.[7] Some of the points demanded effective protection of landed interests and artisans, particularly of small businessmen. The program further demanded the restriction of the allegedly harmful commercial activities of Jews, a revision of the penal code, and the reinstitution of the Jewish Oath. The strength of anti-Semitism was clearly revealed in the 1884 general elections, when 17 members were elected on an anti-Semitic platform. They came mainly from the purely Magyar districts of central Hungary, and some were elected in constituencies with a considerable German minority. The anti-Semitic parliamentary group was one of the smallest in the Lower House of Parliament and the other parties treated it with unconcealed hostility. Furthermore, it is clear that anti-Semitism had not yet struck deep roots in Hungary, partly because the masses of Hungarian peasants were not attracted by the anti-Semitic slogans, and partly because of the emphatic opposition voiced by the government and the political parties.

Nevertheless, early Hungarian anti-Semitism was significant in the context of Hungarian-Jewish relations. Following the Jews' political emancipation, these relations appeared to be evolving smoothly, to the mutual benefit of both parties. The emergence of political anti-Semitism indicated that there were sections within society who rejected emancipation and viewed with animosity the Jews' role in national life. This in itself was not new, and ever since the idea of emancipation came up it had its opponents. But the organized manifestation of anti-Jewish ideology, and the parliamentary activities to advance these ideas and to put them into practice were certainly new. It was a reminder, and for the Jews a bitter reminder, that there was a Jewish question in Hungary, and that Jewish integration was not free from problems. This may be regarded as the point of departure of the entire set of ideas and attitudes toward the Jews, handed down by successive generations and becoming in the course of the following decades part of Hungarian political thinking.

At the turn of the century a new element was added to the ideology which evolved during the 1880s. This was the clerical-conservative ideology carried by the Catholic People's Party, supported by the Church, the pro-Habsburg aristocracy, and the great landowners. The party regarded as its main task to combat what it regarded as anti-Christian and destructive ideas, especially Liberalism and Socialism. The "heretic" Liberalism, according to clerical presentation, was closely associated with the Jews, and it was promoted by the press, almost wholly controlled by them. Liberalism, in this view, led to materialism, to unscrupulous ambition and decay in moral values. Jewish intellectuals, the charge went, lacked tradition and had no sense of attachment; they disseminated such "destructive" ideas as cosmopolitanism and intellectual rationalism which were alien to the Magyars and deeply resented by the conservative elements in society. These themes were to be repeated and presented as historically valid during the 1920s and 1930s, when charges that the Jews were cosmopolitan and were exerting a baneful and corrupting influence on the morals and on the spiritual life of non-Jewish society were to figure prominently in anti-Semitic thought.

The Jewish question and anti-Semitism occupied a dominant position in Hungarian politics and the public mind during the interwar period. The root of the problem was that the balance of coexistence between Jews and Hungarians became disturbed. Actually this was already evident during World War I, when non-Jewish society became increasingly conscious of the Jewish problem.[8] This process was accelerated by the revolutions of 1918–1919, and reached critical proportions after the overthrow of the Soviet republic and the establishment of the counterrevolutionary regime. With relation to the Jews the new regime initiated a reevaluation of the Jewish position. This resulted in two major conclusions: First, that the corrupting influence of Jewry in national life and culture had reached such proportions that it should be eliminated, or at least severely limited, and secondly that Jewish integration was a total failure and no more desirable.

Regarding the destructive influence of Jews in national culture, this was, to repeat, already a main motive in anti-Jewish ideology before the war. Now there were steps taken to put ideology into practice by the *Numerus Clausus* Law, which was enacted in 1920. It restricted the admission of Jews to institutions of higher learning to six percent—the percentage of Jews in the population.[9] Beyond the very act of restriction, a precedent was established by the Law. Jews were now to be treated as a separate group. At that time no one could foretell where this would lead, but the very principle that the Jews were separate, became deeply rooted during the interwar period. It was a direct outcome of the conception referred to before—that Jewish integration was no longer desirable. And if the Jews were a separate group, there was only one logical step to the next conclusion: Jews were aliens. This notion also became a basic tenet of anti-Semitic conception of Hungarian Jewry.

Closely connected with the view of the Jews as a separate entity was the emergence of racial ideology in Hungary—a new phenomenon. In prewar, multinational Hungary, where almost half the population were non-Magyars, racial exclusiveness was out of place, because national interest demanded the absorption of alien races, turning them into Magyars. It was probably for that reason that Hungarian anti-Semites in the 1880s did not adopt German racial doctrines, although otherwise they were deeply impressed by the German ideas. Jewish identification with Magyar nationalism was highly valued, and assimilation was encouraged as the most effective means for integration. But in the situation produced by the unitary national complexion of postwar Hungary assimilation and integration lost their political significance. In these circumstances conditions were now favorable for the introduction of racial ideas. They first appeared in the 1920s, when writers and scholars began to produce theories about a Magyar race. These were a mixture of ancient Magyar history and mythology, and modern, allegedly scientific racism.[10] But the application of racial theories in Hungary presented grave difficulties and contradictions. The Magyars were themselves hardly a "pure" race, having intermingled with the ethnic groups in whose midst they had lived throughout their thousand-year-old history. Moreover, the Magyars were not at all concerned with preserving any race separateness or exclusiveness; on the contrary, they strove to assimilate other ethnic groups who lived in the Kingdom of Hungary; in the case of the Swabian Germans, Slovaks, and Croatians they succeeded to a large degree.

In these circumstances racist theories gained ground only slowly, and until the late 1930s Jews were still classified as a religious community and not as a racial group. But in 1939 race distinction with regard to Jews became official policy. Its most eminent exponent was Prime Minister Pál Teleki (1939–1941). His approach to the subject was not only that of the politician but also—and primarily—that of the scholar (Teleki was Professor of Geography at Budapest University). In his view human groups differ from each other biologically and mentally.[11]

The Jews are not all of the same origin, but their groups in Eastern and Western Europe, and anywhere else developed and lived for long-long centuries in absolute seclusion, not intermarrying with the people, in the midst of which they were living. In consequence they form biological groups which are distinct from the surrounding people. . . . You can in eight or nine cases out of ten recognize the Jew. This proves that they form what we call a race. But the biological race and the blood is not so important. What is important is much more the ideological age-old seclusion, their own code of moral and the whole ideology and behaviour in all the forms and actions of life which are thoroughly different from those of all the European peoples.[12]

Basically these ideas bear much similarity to those voiced by Istóczy 60 years before, when he spoke on Jewish separation and exclusiveness. Teleki's views, however, bear the stamp of his time, when attempts were made to relate racial-biological conditions to mental characteristics. It should be pointed out that, unlike most of Hungarian racist politicians, who were pro-German, Teleki was not only anti-German but also detested the Nazis.

Another exponent of racial ideas, less known than Teleki, was the author Dezső Szabó (1879–1945), who had a great influence on intellectual youth in the interwar period. In his many writings he propagated racist ideas combined with anti-Semitism, but he was a strong opponent of German imperialism. The same can be said of many of those who belonged to the group of "populist" writers in the 1930s, who advanced racist ideas and propagated the exclusion of Jews.[13] Thus, Hungarian racist ideology was to a great extent an original Hungarian product, an intellectual current which occupied a prominent place in interwar political thinking.

The theory of race was put into practice by the Second Anti-Jewish Law of 1939, in which Jews were defined not by their religious affiliation but by their racial origin. Consequently, many Christians of Jewish descent also came under the provision of the Law; their number was estimated at about 100,000. A further step in the direction of racial exclusion was taken in 1941 when the so-called Race Protection Law was enacted, for "the protection of the racial purity of the Magyar nation." The main provision of the Law was the prohibition of marriage between Jews and non-Jews.[14] The Law had but little material influence on Jewish position, because the Jewish community as such viewed with disfavor marriages outside their community. The significance of the Law was in the context of Hungarian-Jewish relations. It marked the final departure from the basic concept in favour of Jewish assimilation.

The international connections of the anti-Semitic movement are also of interest. Hungarians were closely connected with anti-Semitic movements and leaders in foreign countries, and they played a leading role in the international congresses of anti-Semites. The notorious blood libel case of Tiszaeszlár gave prominence to Hungary in the international anti-Semitic community.[15] There were especially close ties between the Hungarian and German groups and their leaders. Among the first contacts were those between Istóczy and Wilhelm Marr, the leader of the extreme anti-Semites in Germany. He gave wide publicity in Germany to a speech by Istóczy in Parliament in 1878, in which he proposed reestablishment of the Jewish state in Palestine, so that Jews who were unable or unwilling to assimilate could settle there.[16] Istóczy was most impressed by the support he received in Germany, while at home the interest in his ideas was rather moderate. In his correspondence with Marr, Istóczy expressed the hope that the success of the anti-Semitic campaign in Germany would also help him in his efforts in his own country.[17] Istóczy also fostered links with leaders of other groups of German anti-Semites, including Bernhard Förster, a leader of the conservative *Deutscher Volksverein,*[18] and Ernst Henrici, the leader of the *Sozialer Reichsverein.*[19] An aide of Henrici, Julius Ruppel, visited Budapest on the invitation of his Hungarian comrades and had lengthy discussions with Istóczy.[20] Thus German anti-Semites of various shades became comrades-in-arms with Hungarians in the struggle against Jewry in the 1870s and 1880s.

Over 50 years later German-Hungarian anti-Jewish cooperation was renewed under entirely different conditions. The nascent National Socialist movement in Germany, and the Hungarian extreme Right established contacts with each other, which developed into operational collaboration. In 1923 a plot was discovered, directed against the Hungarian government by the Association of Awakening Magyars *(Ébredő Magyarok Egyesülete),* the main group of the extreme Right and the most notorious anti-Semitic group of the 1920s. The plot was to be carried out in collaboration with the Bavarian nationalists led by General Erich Ludendorff and Hitler. According to information by the British Minister in Budapest, the plot appeared "to have aimed at overthrowing existing 'anti-Christian' regime and exterminating Jews."[21] What was meant in 1923 by the phrase "exterminating the Jews" is not clear; it is certain, however, that the conspirators were considering measures against the Jews much stronger and perhaps more effective than those stipulated under the *Numerus Clausus* Act then in force. The significant point is that the links between the Hungarian extreme Right and the Nazi movement laid the foundations for future cooperation. Two men who attempted to establish a mutual rapport in 1923, the Hungarian racist Gyula

Gömbös and Hitler, came to power in their respective countries at the same time, the former in September 1932 and the latter in January 1933, and their understanding was then renewed. In greeting Hitler on his appointment Gömbös refers to the exchange of ideas between them ten years before.[22]

The Germans were not the only foreign associates of Hungarian anti-Semites. Istóczy was also in contact with the French anti-Semitic leader Edouard Drumont;[23] Hungarian activists participated in the assemblies of the Austrian Christian-Socialists, who came to Hungary to meet with their friends there. In the early 1880s attempts had been made by the anti-Semitic movements in various European countries to obtain cooperation on an international level and to establish an international anti-Jewish organization. Hungarians took a leading part in these activities. The "First Anti-Jewish International Congress" was assembled at Dresden in September 1882 and was attended by a Hungarian delegation of four members, which included Istóczy and two of his fellow members in the Hungarian Parliament. This was the most distinguished of all foreign delegations to the Congress. The *Manifesto to the Governments and Peoples Menaced by the Jews,* adopted by the Congress, was compiled by Istóczy.[24]

During the 1920s the Association of Awakening Magyars made great efforts to promote their international relations, directed particularly to the Western countries, under the slogan of protecting Christianity.

> Antisemitism in Hungary means the protection of Christianity against progressing Judaism and does not aim only at local circumstances, sad as they may be—but embraces the interests of all Christendom in every part of Europe and of the world where Christian civilization is or should be established! Therefore Hungary claims the aid of every Christian people of whatever nationality, to help her in the mutually vital struggle against Judaism.
>
> The danger being international—defence should be international too![25]

Of all the foreign contacts of Hungarian anti-Semites, it was the German connection which proved to be the most durable throughout the 70-year history of Hungarian anti-Semitism. It was an integral part of its tradition.

In concluding these observations on Hungarian anti-Semitic tradition, reference should be made to some of its implications, as seen in the perspective of Hungarian-Jewish relations. In the eyes of many Jews these relations were based on the solid ground of emancipation. This, so they believed, had settled the Jewish question. Many non-Jews shared this belief, which appeared to be well founded from the point of view of contemporaries. At the latter part of the nineteenth century emancipation was seemingly justified. Assimilation appeared to be well under way, cultural integration was making great progress, and this was combined with deep loyalty to the state and sincere attachment to Hungarian national ideas.

This process, however, was put into question with the emergence of political anti-Semitism, and has been kept on the agenda of the nation ever since. The anti-Semites voiced disappointment at what they regarded as the slow progress of assimilation. They claimed that Jews were still clinging to their exclusiveness—that they constituted a separate body within the nation, and were unable or unwilling to assimilate. In this view Jewish separation was the gist of the problem, implying that sincere and complete assimilation was the solution. At a later stage, however, assimilation was rejected by the anti-Semites altogether, and was declared to be undesirable. And if assimilation was undesirable, cultural integration was even more so, because it had harmful effect on the spirit of the nation. These views were rejected by a considerable section within the non-Jewish society, but their very existence, and propagation, was a strain on Hungarian-Jewish relations. And with the progress of anti-Semitism in the interwar period this strain became increasingly heavy. The brute and unrestrained anti-Jewish propaganda infected the atmosphere and injected public opinion with an intense anti-Jewish venom. It succeeded in persuading a considerable, if not the greater part, of the nation that Jews had to be excluded from the fabric of national life. This became a fundamental principle of Hungarian anti-Semitism in the 1930s, and was adopted as official policy from the end of the decade on.

And here anti-Semitic tradition comes in. Anti-Semitic propaganda at that time could point to its historical past in the nineteenth century, it could justify the anti-Jewish struggle of the present on historical ground and thus give it historical legitimation. Thus the "old" anti-Semitism became an honorable tradition and a source of inspiration. The main significance of this tradition was that it constituted a constant reminder of the problematic nature of Jewish existence in Hungary.

Notes

1. Istóczy (1842–1915) was a lawyer and civil servant. He served as a member of Parliament between 1872–1895. For further details on Hungarian anti-Semitism

see Jacob Katz, *From Prejudice to Destruction; Anti-Semitism 1700–1933,* Cambridge, Mass.: Harvard University Press, 1980, chapters 20, 24.

2. *Istóczy Győző országgyülési beszédei . . . 1872–1896* (Parliamentary Addresses of Győző Istóczy), Budapest: The Author, 1904, pp. 1-14.

3. *Public Record Office,* London, File FO 7/857 No. 55 (April 20, 1875), as quoted in Nathaniel Katzburg, *Antishemiyuth B'hungaria 1867–1914* (Anti-Semitism in Hungary 1867–1914), Tel-Aviv: Dvir, 1969, p. 222.

4. On January 28, 1880, Istóczy spoke in the debate on the street riots which occurred in Budapest that time; Istóczy, *op. cit.,* pp. 72-75. On March 11, 1880, he participated in the debate on the Jewish School Fund; *ibid.,* pp. 76-81. On March 3, 1881, he put a question in Parliament on the ban against a meeting of anti-Semitic students in Budapest; *ibid.,* pp. 82-103. On February 18, 1882, he spoke for the adoption of a petition requesting the repeal of emancipation; *ibid.,* pp. 104-117. On May 24, 1882, Istóczy brought up in Parliament the Tiszaeszlár affair; *ibid.,* pp. 118-127.

5. See Andrew Handler, *Blood Libel at Tiszaeszlár,* Boulder: East European Monographs, 1980, Several new publications on the subject, issued in Hungary in recent years, indicate that the case still holds its fascination.

6. Some of these are reproduced in Katzburg, *op. cit.*

7. On the program of the anti-Semitic party see Gyula Mérei, *A magyar polgári pártok programjai (1867–1914)* (Programs of Hungarian Bourgeois Parties, 1867–1914). Budapest: Akadémiai Kiadó, 1971, pp. 145-146.

8. *A zsidókérdés Magyarországon* (The Jewish Question in Hungary). Budapest: A Társadalomtudományi Társaság kiadása, 1917.

9. See Nathaniel Katzburg, *Hungary and the Jews 1920–1943,* Ramat-Gan: Bar-Ilan University Press, 1981, pp. 60-79.

10. For details on racial theories and conceptions, especially in the 1940's, see Gyula Juhász, *Uralkodó eszmék Magyarországon, 1939–1944* (Dominating Ideas in Hungary, 1939–1944). Budapest: Kossuth Könyvkiadó, 1983, pp. 173-199.

11. Teleki dwelt at length on his concept of race when addressing the Upper House of Parliament in the debate on the Second Jewish Law on April 15, 1939. *Gróf Teleki Pál országgyülési beszédei* (Parliamentary Addresses of Count Pál Teleki). Budapest: Studium Kiadás, n.d., pp. 122-123.

12. Teleki's letter to John A. Keyser (London), February 13, 1939. *Soviet Jewish Affairs,* London, no. 2, Nov. 1971: 109.

13. Asher Cohen, "Racism and Anti-Semitism in the Populist Left in Hungary: The Writer and Politician Péter Veres." *In: Dappim L'cheker T'kufat Hashoa* (Studies on the Holocaust Period). Vol. 1. 1978, pp. 176-188.

14. Katzburg, *Hungary and the Jews,* pp. 158-183.

15. Joseph S. Bloch, *My Reminiscences.* Vienna and Berlin: R. Löwitt, 1923, p. 30.

16. Wilhelm Marr, *Vom jüdische Kriegsschauplatz,* Bern: R. Costenoble, 1879, pp. 42-44. For the text of the speech see Istóczy *op. cit.,* pp. 42-63. The speech was motivated by the forthcoming Congress of Berlin on the Eastern Question. Istóczy urged Austria-Hungary's support for a Jewish state in Palestine should this come up at the Congress.

17. Katz, *op. cit.,* chapter 24.

18. Győző Istóczy, *Emlékiratfélék és egyebek* (Reminiscences and Other Things). Budapest: (The Author?), 1911, p. 41.

19. Mór Szatmári, *Husz esztendő parlamenti viharai* (Twenty Years of Parliamentary Storms), Budapest: Amicus, 1928, p. 26.

20. The discussion was reported in the *Berliner Ostend-Zeitung* and repro-reprinted in Istóczy's monthly *12 Röpirat* (Twelve Pamphlets), July 15, 1881, pp. 13-16.

21. *Public Record Office,* London. File FO 371/8856 C 11878 (July 6, 1923).

22. Gy. Ránki, E. Pamlényi, L. Tilkovszky, and Gy. Juhász, *eds., A Wilhelmstrasse és Magyarország* (The Wilhelmstrasse and Hungary). Budapest: Kossuth Könyvkiadó, 1968, p. 43 (Minutes dated February 6, 1933).

23. According to Istóczy it was Drumont who initiated the contacts; Istóczy, *Emlékiratfélék,* p. 41.

24. The minutes of the Congress were published in *Schmeitzner's internationale Monatschrift,* vol. II, May 1883.

25. *Anti-Semitism in Hungary. Monograph. Edited by the Association of Awakening Hungarians.* Budapest: Bethlen Gábor Society, 1920, p. 20. For British and American comments on this pamphlet see N. Katzburg, *Hungary and the Jews,* pp. 44-45.

Chapter 2

THE JEWISH QUESTION IN HUNGARY:
A HISTORICAL RETROSPECTIVE

György Száraz

Among the many letters from Jews and non-Jews alike after my book—
Egy előitélet nyomában (Tracing a Prejudice)—was published in 1976, only
one or two can be considered offensive. One was that of a critic of an
American paper, who described my calling the murderers of 1944 the
carefully selected scum of my people as an "apology in bad taste." This seems
peculiar, for I did not narrow down responsibility to the direct perpetrators,
since someone had to carry out the careful selection, and not only were
murderers needed but also the opportunity and the right atmosphere.

I do not deny that I was led by a twofold aim: to make whatever small
amends I could to Hungarian Jewry, and at the same time to defend
Hungarians against the frightful accusation of being "a Fascist people."
However, I have not attempted to deny or minimize responsibility. It is also
important to point out that searching for excuses is not alien to me. Neither
is that so often provoked disillusionment or anger on the part of Jews, which
is not always a symptom of a cynical rejection of responsibility, but one of
a troubled conscience clutching at every straw. The need to exculpate oneself
is a powerful temptation, one does not easily escape it.

I caught myself in the act when I took part in a press debate over the Poles
who found refuge in Hungary in 1939. The question arose how many such
refugees actually existed. The sources contradict each other, and estimates of
their numbers differ widely—between 35,000 and 165,000. We all know that
for various reasons the precise number of Hungarian Jews who perished in
the succession of catastrophes in 1942–1944 is also unascertainable. The only

13

thing we can be sure of is that the number is most likely about 560,000. I emphasized in my book that the numbers are really immaterial from the point of view of responsibility. Considering the nature of the crime, it would be as monstrous even if there had been only 50,000 victims.

I could have said the same of the Poles. Perhaps 35,000 had been saved, perhaps 165,000. But that was precisely the point at which I caught myself: my heart told me to accept the lowest possible figure for Jews killed and the highest for Poles saved; and only my sense of reality forced me to settle for the arithmetic mean that appeared most likely. But should I feel ashamed of this? Certainly if I were capable of a kind of distortion, but certainly not if I kept to the level of hope. For when I *hope* that the lower figure is correct in the first case I am not identifying myself with the crimes of Fascism; nor am I seeking credit for the regime guilty of war crimes when I should like to believe in the highest figure in the other case. My humanity, my Hungarian spirit is hoping, really illogically: since I am well aware that however high the number of Poles saved may have been, it cannot counterbalance the murder of 565,000 Jews.

There is a sentence in the judgment of the court trying the men most guilty of war crimes in Hungary: "These criminal acts left a stain of shame, hard to remove, on Hungarians, and even those Hungarians, who were not in the least involved in these acts will be forced to carry this stain of shame against their will and intention."

The truth of this sentence is beyond doubt. Even if direct responsibility is extended from the actual murderers and their accessories to include the merely indifferent.

At the time, I borrowed the motto of the documentary novel of a fellow writer, Mária Ember's *Hajtükanyar* (Hairpin Bend): "What is discussed here is not only the fate of Jews, but also Hungarian history." I believe this is true also in the broader sense, beyond the reference to the year of 1944. What I will state hereafter, I will state in this spirit, for I am convinced that if we are trying, after all, to understand what a sane mind can barely comprehend—the horrors of 1944—then it is impossible to avoid the examination of Jewish fortunes and Hungarian history together.

I will go on in the spirit of this recognition.

Jewry in Hungary formed a separate, but not isolated ethnic and religious community during the early centuries of shared history. The medieval state was powerful, the conditions secure. Hungarians were relatively late in embracing Christianity, and it took some time for the new religion to permeate the masses. This was one of the reasons why Jews lived peacefully in Hungary, while in Western Europe the Jews were subjected to ritual-murder trials, plunder, murder, forced conversion, and expulsion. Royal acts merely regulated their legal status in Hungary; they could trade and own land. Even in 1279, a declaration of a synod stated disapprovingly that the Jews in Hungary "are not discriminated against among Christians, they live together with them as in one family." Religious bias began to infiltrate the country from the West later, and this was reinforced by the economic anti-Semitism of traders and merchants in the towns: provisions of codes of German origin attest to a growing intention to exclude Jews. That the first expulsion in 1362 was the work of an Anjou King was not mere chance either: the new foreign dynasty brought in different attitudes and different methods of governing.

The first expulsion marked a turning point in the by then almost 400-year history of Jews in Hungary: the old legal foundations were shaken, and the fortunes of Jews became dependent on the friendly or hostile disposition of the ruler of the day. The position of Jews became stabilized again under the strong hand of Matthias Corvinus; but soon after his death, in 1494, the first ritual murder trial took place in Hungary, in the town of Nagyszombat. A typical traumatic situation prevailed: external—Turkish—threat, a wavering central power, a weak ruler, greedy barons, growing general penury. The Jews were suitable not only for plunder, but also for the role of scapegoats: for it was possible to imagine that they were allies of conquering Islam, secret spies, agents of the decay of the country. It was almost natural that after the Turkish victory at Mohács (1526), the widow of the fallen King, who bore the prejudices of her Spanish origin, gave permission to the towns to expel the Jews.

The fall of the independent, strong medieval state also signalled the end of the Jewish communities in Hungary. Part of the country, what was left of the kingdom, fell to the Habsburgs, another part was occupied by the Turks, a third became a principality tributary to the Sultan. And when the Turks were expelled, the whole country became part of the Habsburg Empire. Only the feudal constitution of the country preserved relative independence, but constant battles had to be fought with the centralizing Austrian power even for that. Hungary was home to many nationalities even in the Middle Ages; now mainly Slav, Romanian, and German settlers came to revive the districts depopulated during the wars; the administration of the Empire filled even the capital city, Buda, with German settlers. Thus the ethnic composition changed further to the detriment of the Hungarian elements. Later, when the age of national awakening dawned, the national minorities demanded linguistic and cultural rights first, then political ones, while the feudal Hungarian nation—which was fighting for similar rights with Austria—insisted on exclusive Hungarian supremacy. Now the "ethnic expropriation" of the common past began in the spirit of nationalism: history became reflected in the minds of the antagonists as "exclusive Hungarian glory" on the one side, and as the chronicle of the sufferings of "captive nations" on the other.

There were hardly 4,000 Jews in Hungary early in the eighteenth century. That was the time when increasingly rapid immigration began at first from Bohemia and Moravia, later from the Eastern Slavic territories, to which the pivotal point of the persecution of Jews shifted in the meantime from the more progressive West. But this also signals the beginning of a new "Jewish history" in Hungary.

The backwardness and semicolonial status of the country initially offered opportunities to the newly settled Jews. The Austrian administration gave no favor to them, and the overwhelmingly German burghers excluded them from the towns; they were protected by the county authorities and lived on the estates; the raw materials of the estates—hides, wool, grain—turned into money in their hands, and they also leased feudal privileges: inns, slaughterhouses, distilleries. Their activities damaged the interests of the guilds, but also laid the foundations of the *narodnik* (populist) antipathy, since they became the "direct" exploiters in the eyes of the peasants.

According to the late-eighteenth-century ideas of the Enlightenment, emancipation of the Jews really meant their assimilation to "enlightened humanity." But nationalism and the national state soon replaced those of *étatism* and the Enlightenment. For the Jews, who had already begun to assimilate, after many internal struggles, there was no other alternative to assimilation. This process took place relatively simply in the case of Western Jewry. In the East, however, things happened differently because of specific circumstances.

By that time a Jewish question already exiated in Hungary. It was centered on the struggle for emancipation fought by the "reforming nobles" on the one side, and by the "reformist Jews" on the other, one at the diets against the ruler and the forces of conservatism, the other within Jewry, against isolationist orthodoxy. The diet of 1790 opened the towns to the Jews, and guaranteed their civil rights. The two principal reasons why the reformist nobles supported the cause of emancipation were that they considered Jewry as a constructive element from the point of view of patriotism, and that they hoped the Jews would increase the number of Hungarians in the multinational country.

Certain peculiarities become apparent here. The settlement of Jews in urban areas meant—apart from its reinforcement of the burghers' antipathy for the competitors—that the assimilation of the masses, which mostly found themselves in a German environment and which anyhow spoke Yiddish, was oriented toward the Germans, thus arousing the suspicion of Hungarian nationalists. Later, in the second half of the nineteenth century, when the Magyarization of towns began in the wake of progress, this superficially Germanized stratum was forced to yet another switch, and its consequent "diluted Magyarism" provoked national irritation again at a critical stage. But the formula is even more complicated. The politically most active urban stratum recognized early on that it could expect emancipation only from an independent Hungarian state; therefore it assimilated in that spirit. At the same time, the majority of the Jews continued to live in the countryside, thus they adopted Hungarian ways without the "German detour." But the country did not necessarily mean a Hungarian ethnic medium; on the other hand, the administration and the landowners were overwhelmingly Hungarian even in areas with a national-minority population. Thus the Jews living there also took their cue from the "boss-people." This is the reason why simultaneous charges were brought later—of course from two different directions—against Germanizing and Magyarizing Jews.

The very active participation of Jews in the 1848–49 revolution, and the national resistance that followed its collapse put the final seal on the Jewish-Hungarian brotherhood. Then the *Ausgleich* (Compromise) with the Habsburgs followed in 1867: the Austrian Empire became the Dual Monarchy. The regime made scant efforts toward compromise with the national minorities; it entertained the illusion of a "thirty million strong Hungarian empire." But Magyarization was a vain effort: new nation-states came into existence beyond the borders and they exerted a powerful attraction on their kin within; the principle of maintaining the politicoeconomic unit became questionable; and the demand for the integrity of Hungary based on that principle became hopeless.

Yet the emancipation was a joint victory of Jewish progressives and liberal-nationalist Hungarian leaders. It is understandable that the Jews of the time shared the interests of the regime, and secured a great role in its rapid economic progress. It is even more understandable considering that—except the German burghers—they alone were trained in commerce and finance; besides, they were free of feudal conventions and formed a mobile, democratic society. Jews soon became a presence in industry, trade, and banking. Yet this emancipated Jewry—soon emancipated also in respect of religion, and identified as "Hungarians of the Mosaic persuasion"—found themselves in a traumatic position as a result of these successes.

The crisis of agriculture was concurrent with industrial boom. Jews well provided with capital bought up a large number of the decaying estates of the nobility, and the capitalization of the large estates also took place with their cooperation. Masses of peasants flocked into towns to become industrial workers: their rudimentary anticapitalism was spiced with anti-Semitism. And since the bankrupt nobility dominated the civil service, ambitious young Jews went to work in the private sector or turned to the professions. The clergy turned against the emancipated Jewry in the wake of religious emancipation and mixed marriages, but the question of immigration also reinforced anti-Semitism: Eastern Jewry, mostly destitute, fleeing from persecution in the Pale, flooded across the borders at the time of the agricultural crisis, just when the emigration of the peasant masses to America was gathering speed. To make things worse, the immigrants were not like the emancipated Jewish Hungarians, and the unassimilated masses posed a new problem to a government involved in problems with national minorities.

Besides the hostility typically attracted by a successful group, scapegoating also emerged, mainly in the context of impoverishment of the landowners and in immigration. Political, economic, and religious antipathies coalesced to form political anti-Semitism, which was, by 1880, an obviously sociopathic phenomenon—a mirror of contradictions and disturbances of the age. Proof of its scope was the wave of anti-Semitism that swept through the country in the wake of the ritual murder allegation of Tiszaeszlár. The trial was not a cause of anti-Semitism but a result of the temper of the times.

This form of anti-Semitism, however, soon collapsed; the spirit of liberalism won out again, closely related to the abatement of the crisis and the economic stabilization of the country. But anti-Semitism with political, indeed racial overtones, remained a factor from then on.

The more affluent Jews—the industrialists, bankers, and landowners— took advantage of the opportunities emancipation offered. The working class was more responsive to social questions. They more easily grasped the ideas of the age precisely because of the internal democracy of the Jews. They were active in great numbers in civic radicalism, the working-class movement, and different kinds of revolutionary art. As a result, the historical classes regarded Jews with growing hostility. They felt themselves threatened both by the plutocracy and the revolutionaries. They saw Jews as prominent in the front lines of both. The myth of the secret alliance between the Jewish banker and the Jewish labor leader, which played such an important part in the ideology of racism, is likely to have arisen in that way and at that time.

The First World War followed, then the disintegration of the Habsburg Monarchy, and with it of historic Hungary, at the peace treaty of Trianon. Hungarian imperialism lasted no more than 51 years, from 1867 to 1918. Yet the accusing finger of Trianon pointed back a thousand years—to the medieval state, the generations of Hungarians who had fought the Turkish conquerors and the Austrian domination. All were condemned as barbarian powers that had suppressed other peoples, so that a cumulative sentence was passed for the crimes of several centuries. The fact is that Hungary was the most harshly punished victim of the Paris peace treaties. While only one out of twenty Germans came under foreign rule, as many as seven out of twenty Hungarians were caught outside the new borders. The trauma was terrible: it seemed absurd that territories that had belonged together for a thousand years could be suddenly separated; that all of the people who were born as citizens of a Great Power and had lived some part of their lives as such would have to realize that they were now citizens of a tiny country. Even though the economy also sustained terrible damages from the amputation, and hundreds of thousands of refugees fled across the borders, the basic question was ultimately not whether the territory of the state, having narrowed down to 92,000 square kilometers, could maintain 8.5 million people, but whether the nation, having lost its vigor and self-confidence, could survive.

The situation was typically one where a scapegoat was needed. And there were certainly people who badly needed such scapegoats to deflect attention from their own guilt.

In order to ward off the responsibility of the historical classes, and simultaneously feed an illusory national self-esteem and find diversion for social discontent, the counterrevolutionaries—having established themselves thanks to the Allies—invented the myth of the nation-destroying Jewish plot. They also exploited the fact that Jews were prominent in the leadership of the defeated 1918–1919 Communist and democratic revolutions. Defeat in war and the disintegration of the body politic were thus presented as a consequence of the machinations of Jewish war profiteers and defeatist propagandists.

Count István Bethlen, the Prime Minister, consolidated the situation. In essense he restored the rule of the historical classes, restraining white terrorism—which he called "white Bolshevism"—calming the waves of murderous anti-Semitism. He knew that the country could get access to Western credits needed for consolidation only if law and order prevailed. Nevertheless, political anti-Semitism was present as a force from that time on.

A national self-examination did not take place, Trianon became the source of all of Hungary's troubles, and the panacea was the restoration of the historical frontiers of Hungary. The most tragic consequence was, however, that the cause of the nation and that of progress were separated. The masses were cut off from liberalism and radicalism "compromised" during the revolutions of 1918–19 as well as from the Communists, who had been forced underground. Thus the slowly accumulating dissatisfaction with the conservative regime eventually found a way out in ideologies that jointly offered nationalism and socialism. The ideology of racism (according to which there could be but one refuge for Hungarians: the cleansing of foreign elements) increased its effect. When the danger of German expansion increased, many simply added the Germans to the list next to the Jewish, Slav, and Romanian enemies. Thus, even the anti-German racists did not become the genuine allies in 1944 of Hungarian Jews chosen as scapegoats.

Political anti-Semitism welded together anti-Jewish feelings of racial, religious, and social origin, and exploited the gentlemanly antipathy to Jewish capitalism. The effect was increased first by the misery of Trianon, later by the great economic crisis hot on the heels of short-lived consolidation. The swollen army of public servants and the educated middle classes could earn only a meager living given the truncated area of the country, and competition was most murderous in the professions. Professional people left the ceded territories in the greatest numbers, and the ratio of Jews was also highest in the professions. The anti-Jewish legislation that was to come was inherent in these developments.

The ideology, which was again a reflection of the disturbances in the thinking of the whole of Hungarian society, was composed of this mixture. The parties distinguished by this or that kind of cross, had ideologies also inspired by Nazi ideas that filtered through the borders.

Discrimination in the early 1920s caught assimilated Jewry unaware. They had faught in the war, and some of them had done their bit not only in the revolutions, but also in the counterrevolution. These Jews were given satisfaction following the Tiszaeszlár trial, and this was the first time after emancipation that they again found themselves facing the question of "we" and "they." The younger generation were already living fully assimilated lives, devoid of Jewish group-consciousness. Faced with discrimination they mostly reacted individually. But the continuously provoked Jewish sensitivity became oversensitive. As a result some Hungarian Jews (whose self-esteem was offended) and some progressive Hungarians became mutually suspicious and inflicted injuries upon each other. The poet István Vas was unfortunately right, when he wrote: "The organism was attacked by an illness, in which the virus also dictated the rate of defense."

The fatal notion of using anti-Jewish measures to ease dissatisfaction with the government by winning Hitler's support for the revision of the Trianon borders on the one hand, and checking the power-hungry Right on the other was conceived in the mid-1930s, when Gyula Gömbös held office. Gömbös's successor, Kálmán Darányi, also implemented this policy: He locked up Ferenc Szálasi, the leader of the Arrow Cross Party, and at the same time proclaimed the settling through legislation of the Jewish question. No matter how desperately the Jews argued, regardless of Bethlen's warnings, or the protests of Hungarian writers and artists, legislation cleansing the professions of Jews was soon enacted. The First Vienna Award (November 1938), which returned the Hungarian-inhabited areas of Czechoslovakia, soon followed. A few days later came the German *Kristallnacht,* and the Hungarian far Right considered the soaring flames of the German synagogues as signals.

The new Prime Minister, Béla Imrédy, assessed matters similarly: he introduced the draft of the Second Anti-Jewish Law in late December. Another change of government took place: Count Pál Teleki formed a new administration, which followed Darányi's policies. He banned the Arrow Cross Party, but presented the Bill again, for as he said, he hoped that it would lessen tension. The new Act came into force in May 1939, and barred Jews from the public service, restored the *Numerus Clausus,* and extended it to all.

But the far Right was still dissatisfied; it demanded an even more radical law, and campaigned in the elections of 1939 on that platform. Teleki did not want to carry on the game. He declared that no one should count on a Third Anti-Jewish Law, and that even the earlier ones would be "enforced in the Hungarian way." But the Arrow Cross candidates obtained 750,000 votes, and their elected representatives clamored for the Third Anti-Jewish Law.

The war broke out. Hungary was neutral for a time. Teleki refused to allow German troops to use a stretch of the Hungarian railways and opened the border to Polish refugees. His Minister of the Interior made some quiet gestures of goodwill toward the Jews. Then came the Second Vienna Award (August 1940). Northern Transylvania became Hungarian. But the Romanian regime changed in the wake of the decision, and the far-Right Iron Guard *(Garda de Fier)* became an important factor of the new regime. German-Romanian relations became alarmingly cordial. Teleki quickly released Szálasi from prison, where he had languished since 1939, and promised to prepare a Third Anti-Jewish Law. But he did not submit this

Bill to a vote. The end was in the barrel of a pistol; he committed suicide early in April 1941.

The Bárdossy government then took office, and war followed with Yugoslavia and with the Soviet Union. The "final," the "German Solution" proceeded unmercifully in the meantime in Slovakia, in the newly born Fascist state of Crotia, in Transnistria (occupied by the Romanian army), in the Bohemian-Moravian Protectorate, and in the Polish Government-General. László Bárdossy secured acceptance of the Third Anti-Jewish Law in August 1941, and that defined being a Jew in racial terms.

Yet another change of government: Miklós Kállay was next, of whom Hitler demanded the Final Solution in October 1942. The Prime Minister had no intention of complying. He took measures for the sake of appearances, abolishing the equality of the Jewish faith and passing several acts further aggravating the position of the labor servicemen. But these latter measures adopted turned out to be the introduction of the final phase, the death sentence of 42,000 Jewish members of the forced labor service system.

In October 1942, the Germans again demanded preparatory work for the deportation of the Jews.

Kállay refused again, and requested the Jewish leaders to come and meet with him. He asked for patience, his sole aim was to win time by misleading the Germans. In March 1943, Hitler demanded that Horthy dismiss Kállay— after Stalingrad, the Don disaster for the Hungarian army, and Rommel's defeat in Africa. But the peace of the "Jewish island" in Hungary remained undisturbed for nearly another year.

The game was not only forced, but also cynical. And it was not only cynical, but also fraught with danger in a trauma-ridden society systematically infected by anti-Semitism. The masses could not see behind the scenes. They could perceive only that there was one issue on which "moderate" governments agreed with the Right: that the time had come to "cleanse" the country of "anti-national," "traitor" Jews, who were strangling the lives of Hungarians. How were they to know that Teleki had introduced the Second Anti-Jewish Law against his own wishes, in order to keep the Germans at bay? That Kállay's measures only played for time?

In reality it was a cruel game of chance, not a race against time. When Russian troops crossed the Dnieper in February 1944, and approached the Hungarian border, Kállay again held discussions with the Jewish leaders: he asked for their help in starting negotiations with the Allies. But by then Adolf Eichmann's *Sonderkommando* was already gathering in the Linz area. And when the occupation came, and the Hungarian Jews were concentrated in ghettoes by Hungarian gendarmes, the masses believed—and what else could they believe?—that what they had seen was the direct continuation of the previous anti-Semitic legislation.

1945 was simultaneously liberation and the creation of a national trauma, one more severe than Trianon. After 1920 the young still learned to have faith in the phantom of "national greatness"; illusions no longer existed in 1945, even the realistic sense of identity of a small nation was damaged. The First World War was fought for imperialist aims on both sides, and Hungary had drifted into the conflict as a member of the Austro-Hungarian Monarchy; however severe the punishment, the injustice of it soothed the pain and also fed the hope of getting justice. But this cannot be said of the Second World War: one side represented justice, the other side evil. And Hungary had been on the wrong side. There were no honors won in battle. Hungarians paid in blood for the restoration of territories lost at Trianon. And there was no proud resistance record, such as was claimed by neighboring nations. And there were no Jews to be blamed and used as scapegoats.

The 25-year-long counterrevolution and the horror of 1944 had compromised everything. Hungarians could not protest in earnest even against the lost rights and expatriation of Hungarians from the lands their ancestors had settled since Újvidék massacres, the anti-Jewish laws, and the trains taking Jews away were there in the immediate past. It did not matter that Miklós Horthy's regime had not sprouted from the soil of the people, that it had been forced on the nation by foreign arms, and that Szálasi's rule was the end-product of that regime. It seemed pointless to refer to past achievements to counterbalance the recent memory of the Arrow Cross Party. Hungarians had to accept that theirs was the first pre-Fascist regime in Europe and that they were Hitler's last satellites. Their sense of history seemed to have grown false. It alsmost seemed that it was better to throw it all onto the rubbish heap, forgetting the lot.

What was left of Jewry was divided against itself and confused in its thinking. They had been forced to negate assimilation since 1938, and now everybody was forced to decide for himself what course to follow—weighed down by terrible memories and the pain of personal losses. Many did not bother to return; others did so, only to depart again. Still others decided to put an end to Jewishness within themselves. The situation was the most traumatic for those who stayed put: they had to fit into a non-Jewish environment on which they were dependent for their livelihood. Yet they could also feel the hostility from time to time. The poison that during the war had been absorbed in huge doses seemed intolerable when meted out daily in small portions.

The desire to find scapegoats was spontaneous this time, not prompted by the state. It was evident among the more simpleminded, and a rather sizable part of the old middle classes could be classified among them. During the immediate postwar inflation, for instance, there was talk of "wheeling and dealing" and "black-marketeering" Jews. These attitudes had murderous manifestations, such as the Kunmadaras pogrom of May 1946.

The Jews—unless they were ultimately tied by bourgeois prejudices—could see a twofold liberator in the Soviet Union and the Communist Party—the only guarantee that the horrors of 1944 would never be repeated. Thus the Jews provided reliable and enthusiastic cadres to the Party, and later to the state machinery.

But there was also another way out: internationalism. But, this alternative to assimilation again created peculiar traps. Mátyás Rákosi recalled the image of the revolutionary Jew in the masses opposing the Communists, even though the same Rákosi had expelled the Jew Béla Kun from Hungarian history. And gossip started about a general Jewish retaliation when Jews began to make their presence felt in the state machinery. Eventually, this would cause a Catholic priest to advise a Jewish colleague to ask his co-religionists to quit the political peace to counter the spread of anti-Semitism.

Jews working in the Party or state machinery also found themselves in a trap. They were able to accept the methods of the increasingly distorting Rákosi regime as alternatives to the ghetto, the persecutions, and the death camps, perhaps believing that there was no other way to reeducate a "Fascist people." But Rákosi himself also was in a trap: aware that a large part of public opinion looked on him as a Jew, he behaved from time to time as an anti-Semite.

Finally he took a peculiar course; the "termination" of the problem. Nothing should be said about the past, "ex" Jews, and "ex" anti-Semites should unite in the building of socialism. It was not all that hard to gain acceptance for this policy: the solution may seem desirable not only to internationalists of conviction, but also to those who want to put an end to their own Jewishness; and it brings relief not only to the guilty but also to those who are not. Thought if it is true that Erik Molnár called on society to clarify the question of anti-Semitism at the political academy of the Communist Party in 1945, the subject, which had been going on in fits and starts, completely disappeared from public discussion in 1949. The Jewish-Hungarian dialogue ceased. National self-examination, which should have began then, failed to take place.

Naturally, we cannot examine the covering up of the "Jewish problem" in isolation either. If the whole of Hungarian history appeared to be useless around 1945, there was still need for some sort of history; so a certain populist-*narodnik* view evolved. It was unhistorical, though apparently justified to counteract earlier interpretations, which were for gentlemen only. Kings, princes, and counts found themselves expunged from the pages of history, in favor of tales of peasant uprisings and revolutions. But since certain elements of nationalism could seep into even the populist concept, anxiety gave birth to the notion that it was not a new phase of Hungarian history that started in 1945, but *history* itself. The Jews could feel themselves party to an honest bargain: since everything that could lead to the revival of the past was thrown out with "bad" history, and the ideologies relevant to it; it was therefore certainly worthwhile giving up further dialogues—all the more so, since damaging views, otherwise destined to be forgotten forever, might emerge in the course of the debate.

This narrowed-down concept of history also had some frightening distortions. The 1919 proletarian dictatorship, the leaders of which were considered as traitors to the workers' class, and the 1941-44 Hungarian resistance movement, the surviving Communist organizers of which were picked as victims for show trials, could hardly be properly studied. It was the Rajk trial (1949) which provides the example of manipulation for all that was behind the endeavor to cover up the past.

The information published about the arrests pointed out that "there were no workers, and working peasants" among the members of the "gang of spies." A small, irritated exchange of words developed at the trial, when the judge enquired about the original family name of László Rajk: was it true that his ancestors were called Reich? Then, in the case of another accused, György Pálffy, it was established that he was of German extraction, his grandfather was a "kulak," his father a "bank manager." But a small interlude took place at the end of the questioning of Pál Justus:

"*Presiding Judge:* Tell me, Pál Justus, were you not a member of some Zionist conspiracy?

Justus: Never.

Presiding Judge: András Szalai! You were, weren't you? I did not ask you a short while ago.

Szalai: Yes, I was."

The presiding judge naturally knew that Szalai was and Justus was not. But had he only asked Szalai, then the "Jewish race" of Justus would not have been made clear to the listeners, while this way the matter was unambiguous. And thus every group of the heterogenous Hungarian society of 1949 could find enemies to suit their own taste, since a "Jewish—German—Horthyst" gang was in the dock. Did anybody care that the whole thing was a little bit of a monster born of Arrow-Cross phraseology, reminiscent of the Judeo-Bolshevik–plutocratic conspiracy?

A disturbed sense of identity was characteristic at the time not only of the Jews. Its "embedded" nature must not be neglected. Thumbing through resumes submitted in the fifties, one would find that the families were made up mostly of day laborers, smallholders, industrial workers, and miserable clerks. Horthy's army was made up of the rank and file and deserters. And each family had its own outstanding personality: a grandfather who took part in the harvesters' strike, a cousin who served in the Red Army in 1919, an uncle who was a trade unionist.

Gendarmes, policemen, members of the Arrow Cross Party, highly decorated ex-servicemen were rare, and the same went for nuns, estate stewards, wealthy farmers, stockbrokers, instructors in the pre-military organization, or even scoutmasters, housekeepers of priests, or shopkeepers. It is ironic that homogeneity was made possible precisely by the heterogeneity of the families. There was someone to pick from in most families. After all, no family could consist entirely of Communist youth workers or Arrow Cross uncles.

The roots of his homogenization are to be found in the early thirties, when well-to-do tradesmen turned their whole families into members of the middle classes by magic, and middle-class people pretended to be of the nobility. Self-interest, then fear, become bedfellows of vanity later: it was useful to be a full-blooded Turanian Hungarian even with a German grandmother, later it was advisable to appear a pure Aryan with a Jewish great-grandfather; still later the Slovak mason granddad graduated to a German masterbuilder of Szepes County, to prove links with the German race. The face-lifting continued after 1945, before the political screening committees, with changed emphasis. Some relatives—say a 1919 red soldier, an emigrant Octobrist—were quickly brought back into the family, while others were erased. Then it came to pass around 1950 that the great-grandfather of Jewish extraction whom the family took back into grace would have to be made to disappear again, since he was a capitalist, but the German grandmother could be brought back in exchange, as a working peasant woman.

Of course, all of this also reflected the disturbances in the sense of identity. But there was a logical continuation: if everybody "was good" always, that involved everything: the whole of the people, of society, and history—and naturally, also of anti-Semitism. This peace remained, however, only an appearance in reality, bitterness and prejudice lived on in the souls. The village cadre "picked" from the Tisza District, convinced of the guilt of the Jews and at the same time revering Mátyás Rákosi, was a good example of split consciousness. One can still meet traces of that split consciousness today. Inherited opinions are still voiced. Some say Rákosi's "rule" meant "Jewish suppression" of Hungarians, while others contend the "wise leader" was an anti-Semite. Witness the Zionist trials, or the relocation of some Jewish families in 1951. The matter is dangerous: for one of the views can only be expressed surreptitiously, since racial agitation is against the law; but the other can be freely expressed as part of the criticism of Rákosi. Yet the appearance is that racial agitation is suppressed not because of its own absurdity, but in the face of Jewish opinion.

The process could be called historical self-examination or, preferably, taking possession of the whole of our history. It began in earnest in the early 1960s—in close relation with the broadening of the mass basis of the regime. Naturally, the process was not uninterrupted. Some preferred the strengthening of the cementing force of historic community consciousness, while others feared that internationalism would suffer from a flareup of national pride, illusions, and dangerous ideas.

Both camps received reinforcements, one from the ranks of nationalism, the other from that of cosmopolitanism. And interestingly enough, each gained support from the ranks of sectarian dogmatism. This was the time of seesaw works in literature, the authors of which idealized some historical characters in such a way that in they dragged into the mud other sacred cows. Writings which presented the people of the country sometimes on this, at other times on that side of the fence—as "the last satellite" here, or the firm basis of anti-Fascist resistance there—were characteristic products of this schizophrenic era. Reception of Cold Days *(Hideg napok)*, a film on the carnage of Újvidék perpetrated by the Hungarian army in 1942 was typical of the public mood. The people were divided about whether it was better to remain silent and not indulge in self-accusation or whether it was better to confess their sins. Eventually Hungarians arrived at a clearer view by exploring their "cold days."

If we see the events of the past in the context of the Jewish tragedy of 1944, extremes were evident there too. Some people saw the embodiment of the nation in the priests of Zirc who saved Jews while others were inclined to cite Father András Kun, the mass murderer. Debates that would have been unimaginable in the Rákosi era flared up several times: Was General Otto Winkelmann obviously trying to find excuses, when he said that Hungary was a country of "Gestapo agents and informers"? The statement that the Horthy regime had an imposing network of informers even before 1944 was also cited as an argument. But this very argument, or rather its reverse, indicates the vulnerability of such reasoning: let us just imagine how powerful and extensive the resistance organization had to have been in a country whose government was forced to use such machinery to defeat it. Of course, this is not true either. But it demonstrates that the statement that Hungary is a country of informers is at most useful only as rhetoric. And debates of this kind tend, by their nature, to bypass the essence. They whip up emotions instead of clarifying and awaken the instinct to ward off responsibility.

On the other hand, just as over- or undervaluation of the Hungarian resistance is not a good thing, neither is overemphasizing the number of those who saved or hid Jews in 1944. Reality becomes distorted also when the press publishes too many articles about such heroes, however true the stories may be.

Establishing a real order of historic values, filling the gaps left by schizophrenia is no easy task. And these gaps do not run exclusively between Jews and non-Jews. Emotions still run strong, particularly concerning the relatively recent past. It is understandable that people who became acquainted with the regime in the interrogation cells of the Horthy era are infuriated when some politicians of that regime are not condemned outright. It should be understood, however, that it is not possible to differentiate according to viewpoints; it is not possible to mete out half-judgments. For the real responsibility may disappear in the shadow of general facelifting, as in that of general condemnation; and the contours of the real crimes may be erased. We must be careful, for historic perspective does not always lead to sober objectivity; it can often create the possibility of misrepresentation. Fairness must not be allowed to beautify things.

The long, "funny war" of Hungarian writers, historians, publicists was not only ultimately unavoidable, but also necessary: it helped clarify public thinking. Surely that the process has not yet finished. At least, Hungarians have not always experienced its results. Kings, princes, and counts have been rehabilitated over the years. And those left unrehabilitated are judged in the context of their own age. Self-esteem and critical self-knowledge slowly begin to coexist with each other, and the merger will create a healthy attitude.

There was a period when if one read only Hungarian publications it seemed that Jews lived there until 1945, and then disappeared. When mentioning them was unavoidable, they were called "persecuted persons." This has come to an end.

To demonstrate the relationship between "Jewish" and "non-Jewish" subjects, a comparison of two films is helpful.

One of the films is *Magyarok* (Hungarians). Ten poverty-stricken peasants set out for Nazi Germany to do volunteer work. There they come face to face with the "modern" horrors of history, as an isolated, and even self-isolating "minority," exposed even in their favored situation. The work carried within it all of the possibilities of a great film: it could have been the symbol of the eternal tragedy of the people without history, living apart from the political nation, and it could have become a film of historic self-knowledge. It was neither. A single sequence shows why not: a peasant youth is staggering across an otherworldly land wearing long boots and a short jacket. His frightened cries stir the stillness of the forest: "Hungarians, where are you?" Then (the whole film is the vision of a dying young man) he stumbles upon the "old man of folk-tales," who tells him in a shaky voice about the "death of the nation": "I am, my son, the last of the Hungarians . . ." But the same young man does not know who Hitler is, who is at war with whom.

It was a mixture of self-pitying mysticism, and concrete reality that prevented *Magyarok* from becoming what it could have been: a Hungarian tragedy. Somehow it became stuck halfway between self-knowledge and folklore. People who lived without history were not made to exist without history and outside the political nation only by the fact that they knew nothing about the world, but that they mostly "knew something wrongly"; their existence did not exclude participation in history, since they were means and object at the same time: objects of murderous impulses and historic crimes, and they manipulated means of such impulses and crimes.

The other film depicts deserters hiding in a reedy marsh with military police hot in pursuit of them. It is called *Job Lázadása* (Revolt of Job). A small boy is wandering in a foggy meadow in the last scene of this film, shouting angrily and desperately: "Messiah, hey, Messiah, where are you?" The story in a nutshell is this: in the sixth year of the anti-Jewish laws, in 1943, Job, the old peasant Jew trader adopts a Christian boy with the help of the authorities. It is an absurd psychological situation propped up by the absurdity of the fact. The upper Tisza region is not a land of idylls, but that of the alleged ritual murder of Tiszaeszlár. One must wonder, could there be a "village" Jew at the time, however simple, who would not have been frightened away from such inconsiderate adoption plans by that fact?

There would be little use of listing all of the absurdities. One will suffice: During the deportations, there were people who watched from behind fences and drawn curtains. But there was also indifference and filthy passion. There was *not*, however, a sad band playing a farewell, conducted by a Christian priest.

The Jewish folk world is beautiful in the film: showing the enchantment of Sabbath candles, the cup of Elijah, the pebbles of remembrance on tombstones in cemeteries, the tales of the Hasidim and also the balladic dream-world of the poetry of József Kiss about the "Hungarian peasant Jews." But this way an idyll was born of the tragedy. for the film knows only guilty people, who came from outside, and sympathizers, who almost became one with the victims. The makers of the film simultaneously flatter Jewish and the Hungarian vanity. They paint an idyllic picture that is equally acceptable to both parties—although it is false. They compensate the Jewish public with a beautiful Jewish fairy-tale world, and dish up glossed-over psuedo-"reality" for Hungarians offended by the accusation of their being a Fascist people. Ultimately the filmmakers offer a Jewish-Hungarian-Gypsy folklore—an exotic, lachrymose story to the foreign public.

I would like to conclude with another example—with a short story I read in a periodical. The story is about a dying old woman who, when the nurse rolled up her sleeve to give her an injection saw tatooed on her arm her concentration camp number, and mistaking it for her Hungarian identification number, said "What a funny idea you had!" Naturally, the nurse was horrified by the hostility of the woman and the friend who was looking after her.

Was the nurse insensitive, or only ignorant? This particular ignorance is only part of the *general* one; today's youth know hardly anything about history, and it may easily happen that—with their analytic, scholarly skill— they would classify the cynical inscription above the gate of concentration camps: "Work makes you free!" as a poetical thought. A few quiet sentences of explanation at the bedside of the dying woman could have, perhaps, been a more serious lesson in history to that young nurse than a library of obligatory reading.

The Passover Haggadah prescribes the answers to be given to the questions of the wise, the evil, the good child, when he enquires about the reason for the feast. But it also obliges adults to start talking to those children, who cannot even ask a question yet.

Chapter 3

THE ROAD TOWARD THE HOLOCAUST.
THE IDEOLOGICAL AND POLITICAL BACKGROUND

Iván T. Berend

The segregation and the subsequent mass extermination of the Jews during World War II and following the German occupation of Hungary, can by no means be regarded as a "natural" consequence of Hungarian social and political processes. However direct the role that Nazi Germany played in this tragedy and however palpable and demonstrable the discontinuity of the historical processes after 1938 or in 1944, it is indisputable that there are also strong continuities that connect the 1944 tragedy with the political processes that took place in Hungary during the preceding quarter of a century. It is this historical background and the major interconnections that this essay aims to explore.

The major point of departure is the emergence and evolution of the "Jewish question" and of political anti-Semitism. The question is well-known and closely connected with the frequent distortions of socioeconomic development in the countries of East Central Europe. The weakness and the segmented character of the modern capitalist economy and society found vigorous expression in the economic power retained by the aristrocracy, which together with the gentry played a decisive sociopolitical role. The retrograde anti-capitalism of the elements of one-time nobility, their peculiar upper-class status, ensured by right of birth and institutionalized in the military-bureaucratic elite, made it impossible for the new bourgeoisie to incorporate on any appreciable scale even the lower strata of the old nobility. As a result the peasantry, although freed from its feudal bonds, nevertheless continued to be excluded from the nation—the usual lot of the peasantry in societies ruled by the landowning nobility. The road to the bourgeoisie, together with the chance for a good education and a high paying job, was—with few exceptions—generally closed to the peasantry.

Thus, the exclusive character of the former aristocratic societies made it virtually impossible for a new bourgeoisie to evolve and grow out of the internal social forces—from the upper and lower strata of society. This social vacuum could be filled—since as early as the eighteenth century—only by elements external to the given society. These "gap positions" of society, to cite Marx, came to be occupied in Hungary, just as in Poland and Romania, by foreign—that is, Greek, German and later increasingly by Jewish commercial and industrial entrepreneurs. The Jewish population of Hungary, capable of a relatively fast assimilation and growing in numbers owing to the influx of immigrants from the eastern parts of the Austro-Hungarian Monarchy, occupied, so to speak, a substantial part of the niche of the petty bourgeoisie created by capitalist development. Although 35 percent of the Jews in Hungary were manual laborers, in the villages the term "shopkeeper" became synonymous with "Jew." The situation was similar in the so-called intellectual professions, which were not controlled by the state. One third to one-half of all doctors, journalists, and lawyers were recruited from among the Jews. An increasing number of Jews, who had invested their capital accumulated by trading in flour mills and other commercial undertakings, got rich and rose to the upper levels in the unfolding large-scale industry and modern banking system. Thus, the weakness of "embourgeoisement" and the unique features of a "noble-society" linked in a well-known way the process of an emerging capitalist economy and society to the birth of the "Jewish question." Around the turn of the century, anti-Semitism increased all over Europe. The Dreyfus Affair in France, humiliated in a lost war, and the evolution of the pre-Fascist ideology of a *völkisch* anti-Semitism in Germany and its transformation by Karl Lueger into a political program in Vienna were the milestones of the process. In Russia, bloody pogroms took place. In Romania, the peasant rising of 1907 turned against Jewish merchants and tenants. In Hungary, the Tiszaeszlár charge of ritual murder and the foundation by Győző Istóczy of the short-lived Anti-Semitic Party were indicators of these tendencies. But anti-Semitism at that time had not yet got hold of the masses in Hungary and for the most part did not become government policy.

But all this underwent a radical change after World War I, after the revolutions following it, and the victory of the counterrevolution made possible by foreign intervention.

We could witness the emergence and strengthening of ideologies turning anti-Semitism into an organic constituent of their theories and also influencing government policy. There were equally present in them tendencies of a *völkisch*-oriented traditionalism, classic conservatism and a national right-wing radicalism all in touch with one another at several points but especially regarding anti-Semitism.

Dezső Szabó published his moral novel *Az elsodort falu* (The Swept-Away Village) in the spring of 1919. A rebellious social thinker, he unfolded in it a peasant mythology and connected it with the glorification of racial purity. With overwhelming passion he attacked the city as the root and cause of corruption—the world of aristocracy and foreigners—as well as capitalism, the Germans and the Jews, and the revolutions conceived in the spirit of a conspiracy to destroy the Hungarian people. The author, an eccentric rebel, was a pioneer in making known in Hungary the fashionable ideas of French and German philosophical and literary thinking and in introducing to the country the *völkisch* racial mythos. A decade later, his ideas gave rise to a large-scale movement.

It was roughly at the same time that Gyula Szekfű, a prominent historian, worked on his essay which was to exert a huge impact on his generation: *Három nemzedék. Egy hanyatló kor története* (Three Generations. The History of a Declining Age). He condemned in it not only the revolutions but also liberalism and set national traditions against foreign ideas. His conservativism also rejected "foreign capitalism" and emphasized that "there are definitely anti-capitalist peoples . . . and our Hungarian is an anti-capitalist talent."[1] The foreign order of capitalism was represented by the equally foreign Jews, but the urban proletariat that evolved in the process of capitalist development was for the most part also of foreign origin. It was with these foreign elements, ideas, and institutions that Szekfű confronted "the building up of really national traditions" and held the view that the force maintaining the nation was able to survive on the basis of the traditional, historical "genteel" classes grown out of, and remaining on, the domestic soil, and on the untouched basis of the peasantry.

Szabó, the eccentric writer and political thinker, and Szekfű, a prominent and able university professor who was sensitive to politics, agreed, for all their substantially divergent ideas and attitudes, on the condemnation of corrupt foreign capitalism, of the Jews, Marxism, liberalism and of the "corrupt city," as well as on programs of renewal that would take place on a traditional, national, racial, and populist basis.

Similar ideas permeated the political-intellectual leaders of the military-gentry circles gathering around Miklós Horthy in Arad and later in Szeged. The peculiar gentry-style Right radicalism taking shape in their circle was compatible with a kind of transformed traditional capitalism. But they formulated the social issues in a way also well-known from German examples which distorted them into typically racial ones. Their anti-Communism was associated with a unique, distorted "anti-capitalism": it was not private ownership but "Jewish capitalism" that they attacked and proclaimed a "rebirth" and a "new era." Or, as Gyula Gömbös put it: "I will be led by two guidelines. The one is the Christian thought, called in brief the protection of the race, the other is the agrarian idea."[2]

Proclaiming the slogan of "racial protection," they set themselves the task of occupying the economic positions held by Jewish capitalists and forcing back Jewish intellectuals—a policy which came to be called the "changing of the guard." It was about the same time that the German Gottfried Feder, a spiritual father of Hitler's, confronted Aryan, industry-creating capital *(schaffendes Kapital)* with Jewish, money-grabbing financial capital *(raffendes Kapital)* and misled thereby the instinctive anticapitalism of the masses into the blind alley of anti-Semitism. This idea was expressed in Horthy's circle by placing the historical agrarian economy, based on large estates, against foreign, antinational, speculative capital. "Industrial, commercial, and mainly banking capital," wrote Endre Bajcsy-Zsilinszky in the summer of 1921, "made efforts in the recent past to gain control over Hungarian lands and to force them into an overall dependence. In the future just the reverse will have to be done: capital must be harnessed to the carriage of Hungarian lands."[3]

A few years later, looking back upon the time following the victory of the counterrevolution, the same Endre Bajcsy-Zsilinszky wrote with utmost clarity: "The new generation was dreaming about a new comprehensive reform policy which coalesced the social, racial and national ideas . . . the old politicians wanted restoration, a return to the past in everything. . . . Our generation . . . wanted force, determination, purposeful action. . . . The desire of the dictatorship swam in the air like gossamer threads in autumn."[4]

With the consolidation of the Horthy régime, the programs realizing the linkup of racial and social policies by the dictatorship, together with the pogroms accompanying the rule of the white terror, were curtailed. Article 25 of Law No. XXV of 1920, the so-called *Numerus Clausus Act,* which limited the number of the Jewish students studying at the universities, institutionalized the "changing of the guard" policy with respect to intellectuals, and it was effectively complemented by the social movement of university "Jew-bashings" organized by the "Turulist" movement. Rightist radicalism, however, primarily after Count István Bethlen had been appointed Prime Minister, was pushed back into the opposition. Gyula Gömbös, Tibor Eckhardt, Endre Bajcsy-Zsilinszky, Horthy's most influential supporters in Szeged, who had founded the independent opposition Party of Racial Protection in 1923, were virtually excluded from exercising power at the level of government policy until the end of the decade.

In view of the European peace settlements dictated and financed by the victorious Western Powers, the Hungarian counterrevolution, too, could be consolidated only if it adopted a policy of liberalization. The conditions were not yet favorable to right-wing radicalism. Hitler's rash attempt to gain power resulted in his imprisonment. The Hungarian counterrevolutionary system, however, managed under the cover of its so-called Christian-national program, to preserve and raise irredentism and anti-Semitism to the level of governmental policy, which at that time was not yet accompanied by practical limitations.

But by the autumn of 1929 the world changed dramatically. The economic collapse also threatened political instability. Moreover, even where this instability was more apparent than real it appeared real enough in the East Central European countries which had managed, with no small difficulty, to get over their postwar revolutions just a decade before. It is commonly known how this helped Hitler to power with the support of the lower middle-class, the big business, and the army. Count István Bethlen's era of consolidation also suffered a conspicuous collapse, and a similar change of political direction took place within the Horthy régime. In 1932 Gyula Gömbös, who had been forced in 1923 into the right-wing opposition of the system, was appointed Prime Minister.

The increasingly strengthening alliance with Hitler's Germany also paved the way for a triumphant right wing. The pro-Nazis hoped by such measures to overcome Hungary's serious economic collapse and to secure a revision of the Versailles-Trianon peace treaties through the alliance with Nazi Germany.

Agriculture was especially severely afflicted by the crisis. Grain prices fell to one-third of their former levels in the world market, and exports dwindled catastrophically. In addition, the credit crisis caused further insolvency. As a result, the agrarian supplier and debtor countries of Central and Southeastern Europe had to find a way out of this situation as well as to eliminate the unfavorable competitive conditions of the world market. Such measures, they hoped, would create, by means of contractual agreements, a protected and closed regional market. Were they to succeed they would be able to avoid the difficult task of making structural changes in the world economy.

Nazi Germany realized at once the possibilities open to it. The policy measures of agrarian protectionism applied since 1925—the so called Bülow tariffs—which were further strengthened after 1929, were replaced during the first months of 1934 by the opening of the German markets to food and raw-material imports from Eastern Europe. The first agreement relating to the new policy measures, which was regarded subsequently as a pattern, was concluded with the Hungarian government in February 1934 (in the form of an amendment to the 1931 trade agreement). This agreement contained provisions for significant import quotas for Hungarian agricultural supplies and also ensured prices, in the form of customs disadvantages (to the debit of the claims against the mark—frozen in Hungary in the summer of 1931) which were much more favorable than the world market prices. As a result, Hungarian exports to Germany doubled between 1933 and 1934, and increased from 11.2 percent of total export in 1933 to 24.1 percent in 1937. Imports from Germany rose during the same years from 19.7 percent to 25.9 percent of total imports, by which Germany became the most important trade partner of Hungary. Simultaneously, German capital investments also increased, and by 1938 about half of the invested foreign capital in the Hungarian industry, all together around 13 percent of all stock capital, were in the ownership of German financial groups. Similar processes also took place in neighboring countries.

With this trade policy Germany attained a dual objective. Germany was now able to make methodical preparations for a *Grossraumwirtschaft* (Grand Space Economy) to ensure, in the case of the expected blockade, that the greatest possible proportion of her food and raw material supplies could be imported by land from nearby countries. In addition, by means of political pressure, promises, and blackmail, Germany drew the countries already linked to it by economic ties ever more into its alliance system. In several cases this objective was fully attained by 1937–38.

The statement made by the American historian D. Kaiser was equally true for what the Germans called *Süd-Ostraum* (Southeastern Space) and for Hungary. He said that by restricting the influence of the Western Powers and by expanding his own sphere of influence Hitler "won the first battle of the Second World War already in the years between 1934 and 1938."[5]

Another motivation for the Hungarian government policy to undertake and even to initiate the integration into the German *Lebensraum* (Living Space) and alliance system was the hope of achieving thereby a territorial revision. The Horthy régime regarded the powers endeavoring to invalidate the peace dictates as its natural allies. Thus it was not accidental that after the conclusion of the alliance agreement with Italy even Count Bethlen, a leader among the conservatives not sympathizing with Nazi-type totalitarianism, saw in the German alliance the most promising possibility of the assertion of Hungarian foreign policy. In March 1933, a few weeks after Hitler came to power, Bethlen went "unofficially" to Berlin. The former Prime Minister, the most distinguished politician of the Government Party and one of Horthy's closest political advisers, gave lectures in Berlin, Munich, and Hamburg against the Little Entente. He called for the support of the Hungarian revisionist claims and also met with the secretaries of state and defense of the Nazi cabinet and even with Hitler himself. A month later, on May 21, Prime Minister Gömbös told Hans Schön, the German Minister in Budapest, that he wanted to pay a visit to Hitler as soon as possible. The next day he sent a letter to Hitler asking him for political and economic cooperation. "We, old comrades in race protection, who profess the same world outlook," wrote Gömbös at the end of his letter, "understand and will help each other."[6]

From 1935 onward, more significant differences began to appear among the dominant political groups of the Horthy régime. These became evident, among other things, also in the Bethlen-Gömbös controversy. Bethlen, however, held it necessary to demonstrate unity in the question of the German alliance. While in 1935 he declared the Italian-Hungarian alliance to be "the foundation of Hungarian foreign policy," he also added that Germany was "the dynamic force that wishes to put an end to the injustices of the peace treaty," and therefore the country must pursue a pro-German policy.[7]

From Hitler's rise to power, the revisionist policy of Hungary was built upon two pillars. As formulated by Gömbös, reliance was placed on Mussolini's support against Yugoslavia in the south and on the alliance with Hitler against Czechoslovakia in the north. Although this "equalizing" line of setting Mussolini against Hitler was recognizable in the endeavors of Hungarian foreign policy almost as far back as 1940 after 1936, when the Italian situation had undergone a radical change, the Hungarian policy began with increasing one-sidedness to adjust to Nazi Germany gaining an incessantly growing weight.

Hitler's overt preparation for war alone strengthened the growing orientation of the Hungarian foreign policy toward Germany. It helped swing the Horthy régime farther to the right and reinforced its shift to extreme right-wing endeavors of a fascist type. This could be observed in a double sense at the level of policy-making: first, the government policy itself shifted to the right; second, the ultra-right-wing opposition of the government also strengthened. And very soon even a Nazi-type mass movement and mass party also made their appearance.

The political move toward the right took a perhaps excessively abrupt and vehement form under the Gömbös government. It was especially Gömbös's visit to Germany in September 1935 that brought about a rapid change. Almost simultaneously with the change in the German-Italian relationship, the government increasingly subordinated its foreign policy to the German ideas—all the more so as it had already become clear by then (as also formulated by Foreign Minister Kálmán Kánya at the time of his German colleague's visit to Budapest) that we "shall fight together in the war to come."[8] In connection with all that, Gömbös committed himself in his talks with Hermann Göring to introduce a Nazi-type totalitarian system within two years. An intimate friend of his, Miklós Kozma, noted on Gömbös's visit to Berlin: "I have stated unambiguously that a Hungarian-German agreement was concluded between Gömbös and Göring which is of much greater scope than anybody in Hungary—including Kánya—would think. This agreement extended over the political system, the totalitarian issue and over the Jewish and Catholic questions."[9]

The nonparliamentary system, the organization of a Nazi-type mass party and the solution of the "Jewish question" alike were included, together with the demand for an immediate implementation, in the political plans of Gömbös and his circle.

But the conservative-ruling elite, along with Bethlen's more moderate policy was supported by the majority of the capitalists and landed gentry, whose infuence on Horthy was great. A significant role was also played by the abrupt death of Gömbös in 1936.

Recent Hungarian historical literature has revealed and demonstrated in detail[10] the peculiar tendencies that asserted themselves in the politics of that time. These studies have shown how the conservative-moderate groups occasionally managed to prevent the government from extreme right-wing radicalization. But this proved to be a short-lived success; the adherence to the German alliance and the shift of the country's internal policy to the Right proceeded irresistibly, despite the relative moderation of the governments of Kálmán Darányi and Béla Imrédy.

Without outlining the political paths of the Gömbös, Darányi, Imrédy, and Teleki governments, an attempt will be made to briefly outline the causes of this shift to the Right. A decisive role was obviously played in it by the success of Nazi Germany against the Western appeasement policy, as well as its aim to channel German aggression toward the East. It was, after all, by an alignment with the Germans that Hungary could gain some of its lost territory. The successful result of this policy led to an extraordinary consolidation of the regime. Of no less importance, however, was the role played by the strengthening rightist opposition of the Horthy system.

The old right-wing opposition pushed back earlier was restored first by means of Gömbös and his circle after 1932 and then again after 1935. At that time a new rightist opposition, much larger in number and more vigorous and more threatening in character, came into being. Along with the earlier, rather insignificant groupings, Ferenc Szálasi organized in 1935 the Party of National Will *(A Nemzet Akaratának Pártja),* which promised both the introduction of a Nazi-type system and the restoration of a Hungarian Empire. Following Szálasi's visit to Germany, the Fascist movement, based so far on the genteel middle-class, began its propaganda among the workers and tried to become a mass movement. As a result of the fusion of the various Fascist factions, the foundation of the Szálasi-led Hungarian National Socialist Party *(Magyar Nemzeti Szocialista Párt)* was declared in the Buda Concert Hall in October 1937.

Although the government from time to time made hesitant efforts to liquidate Szálasi's Nazi movement even by means of the police, and Prime Minister Darányi had announced on taking office that he would end the opposition of both the extreme leftists and the extreme rightists, he was never able to do so. Szálasi's Arrow-Cross Party *(Nyilaskeresztes Párt)* gained a firm footing among the petty bourgeois, lower middle-class, and *lumpen*-elements; and even made headway among the inexperienced, mainly young, working masses. With 25 percent of votes gained in the 1939 election it ranked as the largest opposition party. Moreover, the largest strike of the Horthy period, a nationwide miners' strike, was organized by the demagogic Arrow-Cross Party.

The Hungarian Arrow-Cross movement was less able to profit from the social discontent of the peasantry. In the case of landed peasantry, social discontent provided a mass basis rather for the "national democratic" line of the Smallholders' Party *(Kisgazda Párt),* which had reorganized and built up its independence since the early 1930s. Discontent ensured a social background primarily for the populist movement, which experienced a new upswing at that time. But this movement, which was based on the peasantry and rejected both capitalism and Marxian socialism and proclaimed a "third route," was not homogeneous either. While its left wing brought into prominence the basic social questions of Hungarian society, its right wing, in consonance with general political developments, increasingly shifted to the Right and professed a common platform with rightist radicalism. Influenced by József Erdélyi, János Kodolányi, Lőrinc Szabó, and others, the adherents of the movement found that the solution to the social problems lay in settling the "Jewish question." Expressing the views of this group, Gömbös clearly pointed out at the Szárszó Conference in 1943 that in Hungary it was not the class struggle but the struggle of races that was destined to solve social problems. The corruptive substance of anti-Semitism penetrated into, and spread in, the society and politics of the Horthy régime from various directions.

The alternating governments were much more content to take the wind out of the sails of the merely partially restricted extremist right-wing. By their hesitant measures, they themselves proclaimed its demands and competed with it in their implementation. The catastrophic policy of the revisionist foreign political endeavors and the competition with the extreme left led, by the time World War II broke out, "the hesitant satellite"—(in György Ránki's phrase)—to close ties with Nazi Germany. Most characteristic was the Darányi government, which began with a containment policy. It banned on April 15, 1937, the Party of National Will and had Szálasi arrested. It declared three days later that a Jewish question did exist, but that the government wanted to solve it in a "constitutional way." On April 3, 1938, Horthy took a stand in his radio speech against the extreme rightist incitements, but five days later the government submitted to Parliament its draft resolution for the First Anti-Jewish Law.

The Teleki government, which was most intent on asserting the independent policy line of the conservative circles and which succeeded the Imrédy government—(turned out of office on February 16, 1939, on account of its excessive advocation of the policy of German alliance and the process of internal fascization)—hardly more than a week after its inauguration signed the Fascist Anti-Comintern Pact. Three months later Teleki's government issued Law No. IV of 1939 "On the Limitation of Jewish Participation in Public Life and the Economy"—the so-called Second Anti-Jewish Law, which laid the "Jewish question" on a racial instead of a religious basis. Then, in November 1940, Hungary joined the Tripartite Pact—the German-Italian-Japanese Agreement—less than a month after its ratification.

True, in view of Western protests, Teleki did not want to take individual responsibility for the war waged on the side of Germany and chose instead to commit suicide (April 1941). But his gesture could not stop the further political shift of the Horthy system to the extreme right.

It was the natural consequence of these political and ideological processes that less than a week after Teleki's suicide Hungary joined the war against Yugoslavia with a subsequent further swing to the Right. Other consequences were the extermination of the Jewish population through the institutionalization of the forced labor service about two weeks following Teleki's suicide, the declaration of the Third Anti-Jewish Law in August of the same year, which, ignoring even the traditional policy line of the Horthy régime, was followed, after the German occupation of the country and with direct German participation, by the deportation of the Jews of the countryside. The process was crowned by the bloody tragedy of the Arrow-Cross rule of terror that followed the coup of October 15, 1944.

Deportations and the mass murders on the Danube embankment cannot, obviously, be regarded as an "organic" continuation of the political processes of the preceding 25 years, but they certainly could not have happened without the ideological and political processes of that period.

Notes

1. Gyula, Szekfű, *Három nemzedék. Egy hanyatló kor története* (Three Generations. The History of a Declining Age.) 2nd ed. Budapest, 1922.

2. *Országgyülési Napló* (Parliamentary Records). Dec. 17, 1923.

3. *Szózat* (Appeal). Budapest, June 19, 1921.

4. *Előörs* (Vanguard). Budapest, June 13, 1929.

5. D. Kaiser, *Economic Diplomacy and the Origins of the Second World War. Germany, Britain, France, and Eastern Europe 1930–1939.* Princeton: Princeton University Press. 1980.

6. *National Archives (Országos Levéltár),* Budapest, Pol. Dep., Ministry of Foreign Affairs, Nos. 158, 21/7, 206/1933.

7. Report of the Hungarian News Agency, Mar. 24, 1935. *National Archives,* Kozma Documents, No. 5.

8. *National Archives,* Min. of Foreign Affairs, Res. pol. 47, 4/7. 796 res. Sept. 20, 1936.

9. *National Archives,* Kozma Documents, No. 7. Berlin visit.

10. Cf. Gyula Juhász, *Magyarország külpolitikája* (Hungary's Foreign Policy). Budapest: Kossuth, 1969, 374 p., *Magyarország története* (Hungary's History). Vol. VIII. Edited by György Ránki. Budapest: Akadémiai Kiadó, 1976, 1393 p.

Chapter 4

THE PECULIARITIES OF HUNGARIAN FASCISM

István Deák

Antecedents of Hungarian Fascism

By their very nature, all fascist movements are peculiar, or particular, in character. Unlike Bolshevism, the other great totalitarian movement of our times, fascism has never been truly universalist: it has not given rise to an organization even vaguely approximating the Communist International. Nor did Mussolini or Hitler aspire to a role similar to that assumed by Stalin, as the undisputed leader of a worldwide movement. This is because fascism has always been intensely nationalistic; indeed, it might well be viewed simply as the ultimate expression of nationalism. The German or Italian Fascists sought to conquer, to dominate, even to annihilate other nations; they had no desire to export their own particular brand of fascism. In fact, such a notion would have been inherently contradictory, for it would have invalidated the very essence of fascism as a modern political religion based on the idea of conquest. By definition, it could not be extended from the conquering nation to the conquered. The latter, after all, had just proven unworthy of fascism by allowing itself to be defeated. This, perhaps, is why conquering fascism has always ruled by terror, whereas conquering Bolshevism has made use of a far more clever combination of indoctrination and terror.

Yet, if the fascist model has never been imposed by one state upon another, it has always been able to influence and inspire. The fascist movement in Hungary was, at least in part, a product of such inspiration. The Italian model, especially corporatism, undoubtedly inspired some Hungarian counterparts, but this influence had declined by the 1930s; the true model was

German National Socialism. Because Hungary was geographically so close to the Third Reich, because it was so pitifully weak in comparison to Germany, and because the rulers of both states shared a common hostility to the Treaty of Versailles and Bolshevism, German National Socialist influence played a more important role in the development of fascism in Hungary than in some other countries. In addition, anti-Semitism was rabid in both countries, Hungary was economically and socially backward compared with Germany, and there was a large German minority within Hungary's borders. Finally, whereas the West had nothing to offer economically, Nationalist Socialist Germany pulled Hungary out of the economic depression in the 1930s.

Nonetheless, Hungarian fascism, particularly in its Arrow Cross variety, was also a genuinely domestic product, the extreme manifestation of an already intensified Hungarian nationalism. Hence the great dichotomy—one of many that characterized the movement: Hungarian fascism was both a native and a foreign-inspired movement; it was simultaneously chauvinistic and bent on slavish imitation of an external model. While xenophobic, it tended to idolize Germany, German National Socialism, and the Führer. Individual Fascists were perfectly able to admire Germany on the one hand and to fear German expansionism on the other. Small wonder, then, that some Hungarian Fascists hailed the superiority of the Aryan race (to which the Hungarians do not belong), while others upheld the superiority of the heroic Hungarian "race," and still others dabbled in Turanianism, which preached the mythical kinship and historic mission of all Turkic peoples (to which the Hungarians do not belong either).

This lack of unity on the question of relations with Nazi Germany, and by extension with the Germanic-Aryan race, was further complicated by the presence of a German minority in Hungary. Again, some of those Hungarian Fascists who idolized Germany did not hesitate to preach or practice oppressive policies toward the German-speaking inhabitants of their own country. Simultaneous contempt for the *Schwaben* and adulation of the Reich were characteristic manifestations of the East Central European inferiority complex vis-à-vis Germany. Local *Schwaben* were seen as East Central Europeans, a not-too-attractive race of local peasants, while Germans of the Reich were perceived as the quintessential West Europeans—better educated, technologically more sophisticated, and socially more progressive than the East Central Europeans.

There were two other reasons for the ambiguity of Hungarian Fascists' sentiments toward German National Socialism: religion and the Regent. Scores of Hungarian Fascists were practicing Christians, or at least perceived

Hungary as a Christian country. They could only resent the pagan ideology and practices of National Socialism. Characteristically, some Hungarian Nazis argued that, unlike such outspoken pagan ideologists as Himmler or Rosenberg, Hitler was secretly a practicing Catholic. As for the Regent, Admiral Miklós Horthy, his prestige was so great—or most Hungarian Fascists were so unrevolutionary—that only a minority among them conceived of a Fascist Hungary without him. Even the radical Arrow Cross leader Ferenc Szálasi, whom the Horthy regime had thrown into jail, saw himself as a prospective Duce, ruling alongside Horthy, and it took Horthy's surrender attempt in the autumn of 1944 to convince Szálasi to go along with the German plan to overthrow the Regent.

We can, then, state with some confidence that one of the main peculiarities of the Fascist movement in Hungary lay in its complex and often contradictory relationship with National Socialist Germany. Other peculiarities were of domestic origin, stemming from the particular historical experience of the Hungarian nation.

The Historical Factors

Where to begin? The complexities facing any historian in search of the origins of fascism in general apply equally to the Hungarian case. While there would seem to be little value here in going all the way back to Luther, as some experts are wont to do, it does appear that the meaningful origins can be traced back at least as far as the period before World War I, much as, according to Andrew Whiteside and others, the origins of National Socialism must be traced back to the peculiarities of the Austro-Hungarian situation. These, then, are some of the pre-1914 developments that influenced the development of Hungarian fascism:

The first was the presence of large and increasingly dynamic and politicized national minorities in the pre-1914 Hungarian Kingdom. The political demands of the minorities led in turn to a heightening of Hungarian national consciousness and the spread of Social Darwinism as a justification for Magyar predominance. Seeing the development of a life-and-death struggle between the national minorities and their powerful foreign backers on the one hand and an isolated Hungary on the other, extreme Magyar nationalists advocated the systematic assimilation of the minorities, and even violence to prevent the "death of the nation." They accused the nation's liberal leaders of weakness toward the minorities, and rejected not only the liberal government but liberalism itself as a valid solution to the country's problems.

A second domestic influence was Hungary's awkward and ever unclarified relationship with Austria in the Dual Monarchy, accompanied as it was by a complex sense of both superiority and inferiority. The Hungarian elite's self-perceived superiority in warfare and state-building ability contrasted markedly with an obvious economic backwardness compared with the western, Austrian partner. Radical Hungarian nationalists saw the solution to the dilemma in complete national independence and the building of an expansionist Great Hungarian Empire (especially toward the Balkans).

Another factor determining the character of Hungarian fascism was the peculiar social composition and ideology of pre-World War I Hungary's political and administrative elite, made up largely of the landed nobility or people who modeled themselves after it. While presiding over a rapidly developing and increasingly urbanized society, a substantial segment of the political and administrative elite continued to uphold its traditional, agrarian value system, leaving the development of business, industry, and finance to foreigners—primarily Jews. The result was the growth of a separate economic elite, which was intensely loyal to the state and grateful to the nobility and did not even attempt to add political power to its domination of the economy. This division of labor between the two elites functioned smoothly, but only so long as Hungary continued to be a large country with a dynamic economy—that is, until the Great War.

After 1918, in a truncated Hungary with a devastated economy, more and more members of the former political-administrative elite found themselves neglected by their former benefactor, the state, and were forced to seek a livelihood in business and industry. Here, however, they were confronted in hopeless competition with the entrenched and far more skillful non-Magyar bourgeoisie, particularly the Jews, many of whom were also desperately in need of work. The inevitable result was the clamor of many declassé Christian gentlemen for state intervention on their behalf, through laws limiting the economic activity of the Jews.

The growth of a new stratum of radical intellectuals, recruited generally from among the children of the Jewish bourgeoisie, was also important. These intellectuals repudiated not only the extreme nationalism, authoritarianism, and antisocial policies of the nobility and the gentry, but also the perceived materialism and political sycophancy of their bourgeois fathers. The radical activity of the young intellectuals, often brash and supremely irrational, facilitated the outbreak of the left-wing takeovers in 1918–1919 and triggered, in turn, the counterrevolutionary, anti-Semitic backlash of the postwar years.

Furthermore, the catastrophic developments of the Great War helped to create a very special type of fascism in interwar Hungary. The enormous suffering and bloodshed caused by the war was aggravated by the widespread conviction, carefully cultivated by the nationalist press, that the Hungarian people were sacrificing more than were the other peoples of the Monarchy. Hence the growing contempt for such "non-war-like" peoples as the Czechs, Romanians, and especially the Jews, who, it was stated again and again—with little justification—were shirkers. In a society where such traditional noble ideals as honor, sacrifice, courage, and faith were held to be far more valuable than bourgeois thrift, hard work, and business success, the Great War increased the Hungarian nationalists' sense of ethnic-racial superiority, as well as their frustration and bitterness.

There followed the unfortunate experience of the October 1918 Károlyi Revolution, which promised democracy, social justice, and Allied sympathy for the Hungarian cause, and achieved none of those goals. Worst of all, the Károlyi regime was forced to preside over the dismemberment of Greater Hungary.

As if some evil scenarist, calculating how best to create a Fascist movement in Hungary, were directing the course of events, the Károlyi regime was replaced by Béla Kun's Soviet Republic in March 1919. This was a crucial event, for it led to the emergence of a number of paramilitary detachments which, in their violence and nebulous ideology, paralleled the German Free Corps and the Italian Fascist gangs. This is all the more important if we remember that, before 1914, Hungarian society was religiously tolerant and ideologically liberal. Anti-Semites and extreme nationalists had never had the final say. Now, however, the wild social experiments and even wilder ideology of the Soviet Republic had caused a panic among the old political and administrative elite. In the hysterical atmosphere created by a lost war, foreign invasion, impoverishment, and inflation, it came to be widely believed—and not only by the old elite—that there was a great conspiracy to destroy the gentry, and with it the nation as a whole. Since almost all the Hungarian Soviet leaders had been Jews, it was all too easy to label the "conspiracy" as one hatched by Jews in the interest of international Jewry.

The completely false notion was diligently disseminated that, while the Hungarian nobility and, by extension, the Gentile middle class, were patriotic and respectful of national values, the Jews—and not only the handful of Peoples' Commissars—were the enemies of the nation. In this hysterical atmosphere, it was possible to ignore the fact that it was the vocally internationalist Soviet Republic which had fought what amounted to a national crusade for the recovery of lost territories, and that it was the counterrevolutionary movement, led by Admiral Horthy and Count István Bethlen, which had consorted with such enemies of Hungary as the Romanians and the French.

A Rightist Country

In August 1919, the counterrevolutionary movement filled the vacuum left behind by the defeated Soviet Republic. The new regime discarded not only democracy and socialism, but also the liberal ideology of the prewar decades. A new ideology was proclaimed, advocating "Christian" values and the return to a rather mythical pre-liberal state of affairs, allegedly characterized by respect for authority, martial qualities, and a strict social hierarchy. From then until 1945, Hungary was a counterrevolutionary country, although certainly not a Fascist one. Its basic political orientation was that of the Right, and all major political issues were settled within the counterrevolutionary rightist camp. But as it turned out, to be of the Right and to oppose freemasonry, free thought, Bolshevism, and cosmopolitanism was not enough to create even a modicum of political unity. To be of the Right was a precondition for a political career, but it still left one with a vast number of political choices. Following the 1918–1919 revolutions and the conterrevolution, Hungary had to face the problems of extreme poverty and runaway inflation, the influx of refugees from the lost territories, the inequalities of vast landed estates and a landhungry peasantry, lawlessness in the streets, and Allied pressure for "consolidation" and a representative parliament. The result was the development of two basic factions within the rightist camp which, for want of a better designation, may be called the moderate Right and the oppositionary Fascist radical Right. While the former moved increasingly in the direction of traditional prewar tolerant conservatism, the latter, or at least parts of it, flirted with the idea of social revolution. In other words, there were many in the counterrevolutionary camp whom we call rightists only because they themselves insisted on such a designation. After all, the moderate Right stood for genuine parliamentarism, human rights, social welfare measures, and equality before the law even for Jews. On the other hand, the radical Right advocated not only a corporatist or totalitarian state and the elimination of the Jews from national life, but also a drastic land reform and a general redistribution of wealth.

Some in the counterrevolutionary camp abhorred Hitler, admired the British, and defended the capitalist system; others called themselves followers of Hitler and mobilized workers and day laborers in vast strike movements.

The moderate Right regarded the radicals as Reds in Nazi uniform; the latter regarded the moderates as reactionary hirelings of the large landowners and Jewish capitalists. In a country where to be a Communist was a felony, and a chastened Social Democratic Party was forbidden to organize among the peasantry, civil servants, or other state employees, the far-right Arrow Cross was a viable alternative for the poor and the politically alienated. Invective flowed freely between the radical Right and the moderate Right, and violence was not a rarity; only on national feast days was a very uncongenial unity celebrated in opposition to the "real" enemy—the Left.

Each faction actually hampered the other's development. The moderate Right was always trying to take the wind out of the sails of the radical Right by talking social reform, using superpatriotic phraseology, introducing laws against the Jews, and appropriating the trappings of Fascist militarism. The radical Right was always able to outshout the moderates; it was also far more successful among the masses. Yet the radical Right was prevented from making a revolution by police power, and by the patriotic appeals and sundry accusations emanating from the moderate side. In a supremely clever move, the moderate rightist government seated the radical Arrow Cross faction on the far left of the National Assembly, next to the Social Democratic deputies. And, when all else failed, the government could always accuse the radical Right of being in the pay of a foreign power. However, since this foreign power, Nazi Germany, was an ally of Hungary, the charge of treason could never be exploited to the point of completely destroying the far Right.

Ironically, Horthy the man who presided over all this, combined in himself the aspirations as well as the dilemmas of both factions. As an anti-Semite, a fanatical anti-Bolshevik, and an extreme advocate of territorial revision, he had every reason to ally himself with Nazi Germany and with the domestic far Right, in whose ranks marched some of his closest accomplices from early counterrevolutionary days. He himself had been indirectly responsible for the murders, in 1919 and 1920, of leftist politicians and of Jews. But Horthy also hated Nazi ideology and the Arrow Cross mob that threatened not only his own class, the gentry, but the whole social order as well. As a navy officer he admired the British; as a former adjutant to Emperor Franz Joseph, he was familiar with political fair play and administrative impartiality. He had some rich Jewish friends, and he was surrounded by aristocratic advisers who constantly reminded him of his responsibility to an ancient and sacred constitution. Last but not least, his own family, particularly his two sons and his niece, were sworn enemies of Hitler and all Fascists. Hence, the Regent vacillated throughout the 1930s and early 1940s, regularly appointing moderate political leaders whom he encouraged to cater to the wishes of Nazi

Germany, only to dismiss them when they went too far in appeasing Hitler and the local Nazis. As a result, Hungarian politics moved from the moderate Right toward the radical right and back again, never achieving either genuine parliamentary liberalism or genuine fascism. At least not as long as Horthy was in power.

The political leaders under Horthy seldom displayed more consistency. There were, of course, those like Count István Bethlen, who never budged from the moderate side, but there were also those, like Count Pál Teleki, who, though an anti-Nazi and a genuine moderate, introduced anti-Jewish legislation, and those, like Gyula Gömbös, who, though a radical by temperament, tempered his politics when Prime Minister. Finally, there were those on the far Right who, though absolute Fascists in temperament and ideology, could be bought off or lured over to a less radical stance.

The alpha and omega of the Hungarian counterrevolutionary ideology was "Christian nationalism," a euphemism for anti-Semitism, but there was a world of difference between the aristocratic anti-Semitism of a Count Bethlen and the raw, plebeian Jew-hatred of the Arrow Cross. In fact, some of the most steadfast and efficient protectors of the Jews emerged from the moderate rightist faction, while the most efficient killers of the Jews were not necessarily Nazis, but also included more reactionary members of the moderate Right.

Thus, the spectacle unfolded: national flags and Church banners flying; men, women, and children sporting fancy uniforms or pseudo-folk costumes; sabers rattling; the Nation marching confidently toward a "new Hungarian resurrection" and a "better Hungarian future." Meanwhile, the people remained generally poor, social problems remained unsolved, the much vaunted army pitifully weak, and the lower classes politically indifferent, unless they sympathized with the far Right. In rightist Hungary Fascist slogans were incorporated into the official ideology when Hitler was still a complete nonentity, but in Hungary, too, native Nazis languished in internment camps at a time when the German *Wehrmacht* ruled over Europe. Rightist Hungary prided itself on having introduced the first anti-Semitic legislation in post-World War I Europe, but in Hungary, too, more than 800,000 Jews were still living in relative freedom and dignity when close to three million Polish Jews had already died in the gas chambers. In Hungary, Fascist slogans were on the lips of those in power, but also on the lips of some of those whom the government had put in jail.

The supreme peculiarity of Hungarian fascism was that it had always been popular but that it never really triumphed on its own. By 1939 the Arrow Cross had managed to mobilize up to one-third of the population, from generals and high officials down to factory workers, day laborers, and the rabble, but by 1944 its membership had declined by almost two-thirds. When the Arrow Cross came to power, at last, on October 15, 1944, it was only because the Germans had seen no other choice; in any case, by then one-half of the country was in Soviet hands. And when it was all over, and the whole country had fallen to the Soviets, it was a final twist of irony that thousands upon thousands of radical rightists were allowed to join the Communist Party, while many of the most decent moderate rightists were thrown into prison.

Chapter 5

HUNGARIAN INTELLECTUAL LIFE AND THE "JEWISH PROBLEM" DURING WORLD WAR II

Gyula Juhász

The least dealt with and elaborated part of the persecution of Jews in Hungary is the attitude of the Hungarian intelligentsia to the Jewish problem and the persecution of Jews, although one cannot say that there was nobody who would face this difficult problem: It is dealt with from different aspects in memoirs, interviews and autobiographies. An outstanding example of it is István Vas' autobiography *Miért vijjog a saskeselyű?* (Why Does the Vulture Screetch?). György Száraz also refers to this problem in his essay *Egy előitélet nyomában* (In the Track of a Prejudice).

When establishing our responsibility for what had happened, in his excellent essay of 1948 István Bibó considers the stand of the Hungarian intelligentsia decisive.[1] In his posthumously published study on the populist *(népies)* movement he outlined the movement's attitude to the "Jewish question."[2] According to Bibó the Hungarian intellectual life played a major role, because the Jews experienced "the hostility, indifference, narrow-mindedness and cowardice" of the Hungarian society.

There has been only one similar attempt to face the facts—15 years later, not without errors, but with the best intentions, the debate of Vilmos Juhász and Imre Kovács was published in *Új Látóhatár* (New Horizon).[3]

"There are questions," writes Vilmos Juhász, who initiated this debate, "which are rooted in reality but have long become mythologies; their truth is a mythological one, therefore they are dangerous. Such a question was the Jewish question in Hungary, just as in East Central Europe in general. To some extent the literary people were responsible for its becoming bloody mythology. In the Nazi era the writers *as writers* were silent in general. . . .

53

As people they were often honest, sometimes even heroic. But this was a private affair, and the public usually did not know about it."

Imre Kovács protests "in the name of the accused" against this generalization. According to him, it cannot be said that the writers kept silent about the Jewish question, since some of them were openly anti-Semitic and others fought against it in self-defense bravely and outspokenly. There were others who "tried to be impartial or objective if it was possible at all," but then it had nothing to do with the deportation and mass murdering of Jews.

This essay will attempt to offer a response to the above question—calmly and impartially. Perhaps this may be possible in a historical perspective.

When in the spring of 1938 the adoption of the First Anti-Jewish Law was on the agenda of the Darányi government, in the ensuing debate there was no argument in favor of the law that had not been formulated before. The more so since only intellectual occupations came within its provisions, thus evoking arguments already expressed in two of the most influential works at that time: Dezső Szabó's novel, *Az elsodort falu* (The Swept Away Village) published in 1919 and Gyula Szekfű's *Három nemzedék* (Three Generations) published in 1920.

Szekfű devoted a whole chapter to the demonstration of his concept: during the second half of the dualistic era "besides the financial control the intellectual one also fell into the hands of the Jewry who were in an excellent financial position." Although later on disagreements arose between Szekfű and Szabó, here Szekfű's arguments are very similar to Szabó's. Both demonstrated the intellectual leadership of Jewry—one from the point of view of the press, the other of Budapest theaters—but with the same emotions.

In the supplementary chapter *Trianon óta* (Since Trianon), which Szekfű wrote after Hitler's coming into power, he listed five antinomies, whose solution seemed possible only by means of urgent reform. The third one was the "Jews-Magyars" antagonism. Regarding the solution, he gave the following advice:

1. It is also the interest of the Jewry that the Magyars gain ground in every field of the capitalist mode of production.

2. The Jews who immigrated after the war should seek the solution in Zionism and minority organizations until their emigration since "the relationship between the Magyars and the Magyarized Jews who adopted the Hungarian culture" would be relieved this way.[4]

When the extreme, anti-Semitic Right called for anti-Jewish laws using the above arguments, Szekfű had taken a different stand, and during the German occupation he bravely stood up to the catastrophe and helped many of the persecuted. Nevertheless, his *Három nemzedék* played a part in that the spirit of racism broke loose.

Szabó's views had also altered somewhat by 1938. The first significant position he took in connection with the racial law was in his essay *Az antijudaizmus birálata* (The Criticism of anti-Judaism) published in 1938.[5] As is indicated by the title, he did not simply revise his former views concerning the Jewish question. It was this essay that helped reinforce the tendency to strengthen the positions of middle class Magyars against those of German origin by taking advantage of the anti-Jewish laws, and in general it contrasted a kind of Hungarian nationalism with German expansionism.

The essence of Szabó's argument was that out of the three means of German expansion in Hungary—legitimism, irredentism, and the Jewish problem—only the third one was still applicable by 1938. Jews had become the source of all the economic, social, and cultural problems because "anti-Judaism is without doubt the easiest way of making a tool of the masses, and of averting the people's attention from the other problems of life and the injustice that determines the nation's destiny. It is the most effective way of influencing people, he states, because the Christian-Jewish antagonism leaves no room for the notion of *Magyarság* (Hungarianism) in the political, historical and public life.

Again he expressed all his objections against Jewry, but he emphasized that the German threat is "more deadly" since at least "behind Jewry there is not the horrible armed forces and the horrible racial chauvinism of a hundred million people." He, too, wants to put an end to Jewry's predominance in the economy, the professions, and the press, but he feels that the anti-Jewish law is no solution, since it has no social significance for the Magyars. Szabó even elaborated a far-reaching program, which goes beyond the scope of this essay. However, unlike one of his followers, he did not maintain that, at any cost, the elimination of Jews must begin.

On May 5, 1938, when the Parliament was debating the draft of the First Anti-Jewish Law, in the *Pesti Napló* (Diary of Pest) there appeared a declaration signed by a gorup of Hungarian writers, artists, and scientists addressed to the Hungarian society and the members of Parliament in the defense of the citizens' equality before the law. The declaration pointed out that the Law promised a guarantee of the social equilibrium but offered no proposals to improve the situation of the poor; that it offended those belonging to the Christian middle class when it assumed that they could make a living only if others were outlawed and dismissed from their jobs; that it would be unscrupulous to differentiate between the dates of baptism. The declaration stressed that the Jewish citizens were unquestionably Hungarians and, it made a misplaced reference to the dissimilationist tendencies among those of German origin in the upper strata.

The declaration called upon the legislative bodies, trade unions, and institutions—the "sound and patriotic people of the whole country"—to give proof of their self-respect and stand up against the law. "Every one of our contemporaries should think of the responsibility that rests on them if the law goes into effect against their protest, the law that every Hungarian will be ashamed of one day." The declaration was signed by: County György Apponyi, István Bárczy, Béla Bartók, József Berda, Sándor Berecz, Aurél Bernáth, Mária Blaskó, László Bóka, Imre Csécsy, István Csók, József Darvas, Jenő Erdős, Jenő Eszenyi, Imre Győri Farkas, Noémi Ferenczy, Géza Féja, József Fodor, Gyula Földessy, Lula Földessy (née Hermann), Zoltán Gáspár, István Hertelendy, Béla Horváth, György Pálóczi-Horváth, Aurél Kárpáti, Károly Kernstok, János Kmetty, László Dernői Kocsis, Zoltán Kodály, Erzsébet Kozma, Zsigmond Kun, Márton Lovászy, Miklós Makay, Ödön Márffy, Ferenc Mátyás, Ernő Mihályfi, Farkas Molnár, Kálmán Molnár, Zsigmond Móricz, József Zugligeti Pintér, Ödön Polner, Gusztáv Rab, Gusztáv Rados, Margit Reidl, Zsigmond Reményik, Aladár Schöpflin, Pál Simándy, Artur Somlai, Géza Supka, Zoltán Szabó, Árpád Szakasits, Zoltán Szász, Count György Széchenyi, Lajos Szimonidesz, Jenő Tersánszky J., Aladár Tóth, János Vaszary, Béla Vikár, Tibor Vilt, and Lajos Zilahy.[6]

The declaration attracted notice, but gained no adherents. However, it had a negative reception in intellectual circles and did not make them realize that the citizens' equality of rights cannot be the subject of a debate: that the Anti-Jewish Law was a concession to the extreme Right, the proof of the Nazi penetration, and that its consequences would effect the whole of the intelligentsia. There was also no reaction to what Count István Bethlen set forth most explicitly during the debate: "Those who press for this Law will soon realize that this in fact does not solve the problem and they will urge the government, who thinks that public order will be established by this Law, to go much farther."[7]

It was held in intellectual circles that the 20 percent quota—which was four times the ratio of Jews within the whole of the population—was rather reasonable. It was stressed not only by newspapers and articles but also at the speaker's platform in the Upper House by the Calvinist Bishop László Ravasz: "In the case of any minority group, either religious or ethnic, it is not the most unfavorable solution if the proportionate share it is allowed in a certain public sphere is four times the ratio it constitutes of the population as a whole."[8]

The signers of the declaration were attacked violently, and not only from the extreme Right. To be sure it was no surprise in intellectual circles that the *Napkelet* (Sunrise) began its protest as it follows: "We are not happy to see the Hungarian writers on the occasion of the unpleasant but necessary debate of the Anti-Jewish Law and the connected press-law as the pseudo-humanist champions of justice." It accused the signers of being irresponsible to the community.

The weekly periodical *Magyar Ut* (Hungarian Way) which was the organ of the pure-born—mainly Protestant—intelligentsia sympathizing with the populist ideas, could hardly get over its surprise after the declaration was published. It deplored most that Béla Bartók, Géza Féja, Zoltán Kodály, and Zsigmond Móricz had also signed the declaration. The author, Dániel Fábián, also found the explanation in the business connections of the signers.[9] The next issue in the form of a letter to the editor described the signing of the declaration as treason.[10]

Géza Féja denied the charge, stressing that he would sign it again because he refused to narrow down the Hungarian question to Jewish question.[11]

Zsigmond Móricz was also attacked because of his article *Zsidótörvény* (Anti-Jewish Law) published in *Pesti Napló,* which was unusual in tone and in which he told how the Jews had helped him as a young journalist to form his attitude to society.[12]

After the declaration was published, many people found it strange that Mihály Babits and Gyula Illyés were not among the signers. Both of them soon gave an explanation.

Mihály Babits, who was recovering from a serious illness, published a long article in *Pesti Napló,* whose title was *A tömeg és a nemzet* (The Masses and the Nation) and gave proof of his opposition to the discriminating ambitions, the public opinion, and the policy which was dominant in the spring of 1938. The press law, which was passed with the Anti-Jewish Law, endangered the real literature, he wrote, since "it wears away with limitations." He emphasized that the racial question was unimportant to him; but much more was at stake: the Christian religion, and whether we believe in moral truth independent of time and space, or only in the trends of our time. Instead of unburdening his conscience by signing the declaration, he had chosen to write this article.[13]

Gyula Illyés published his opinion in the May issue of *Nyugat* (West) in 1938. His tone was vehement and bitter, for the "yammering of the threatened" is misleading: culture is not found in the institutions that the antidemocratic régimes want to regulate. Then he enumerated the literary toadies, the writers of romances, and publishers of cheap literature: those who called for the protection of culture. Because of this approach Illyés did not see what Babits realized: real culture was endangered since the popular publications would adapt to the new situation. Illyés first of all expressed his reservations when he stated: he would fight for the freedom of the press as he knew the enemy but did not know where to find him. The fighting line lay beyond where the enemy should be able to go because "that is the land of my treasures and my gods." [14]

During that summer, six representatives left the Smallholders' Party *(Kisgazda Párt)* and founded a new extreme rightist party, the so-called National Peasants' and Workers' Party *(Nemzeti Földmüves és Munkáspárt).* A group of the smallholder and agriculturalist members of the Smallholders' Party and three writers—Pál Szabó, István Sinka, and Péter Veres— published a pamphlet titled *A magyar parasztság levele a müvelt fiatalsághoz* (The Letter of the Hungarian Peasants to the Educated Youth).

The pamphlet begins by noting that some intellectuals from the party had joined the national socialist movements. It extensively deals with the Jewish question, which transcends all other questions involving the nation's destiny. It emphasized that the peasants did not have to compete with Jews for jobs and incomes, but were being suppressed by the bank and cartel policy and by middlemen and traders. The policy of interest rates would not change if more Christians worked in the banks, nor would the price of manufactured goods decrease if Christian agents sold them in the villages. "The peasantry continues to be poor, and you can't expect a strong intelligentsia to come out of the poor peasantry." [15]

As was foreseeable, after the Munich Agreement and later the First Vienna Award (1938) the anti-Semitic propaganda did not cease, and the reannexation of the *Felvidék* (Upper Province) from Czechoslovakia provided the momentum for its flaring up again, since among the one million inhabitants who had become Hungarian citizens, there were 78,000 Jews. Prime Minister Béla Imrédy introduced the draft of the Second Anti-Jewish Law on December 23, 1938. It established a six percent provision concerning admission of Jewish applicants to institutions of higher education; Jews were prohibited from occupying positions as civil servants; editors, editors-in-chief, or publishers of any periodicals; as well as producers, directors, artistic directors, or leading actors of plays or films.

The six months that had elapsed since the First Anti-Jewish Law had also brought changes in the public opinion of the intelligentsia. There was hardly any word of equal rights, and since the Imrédy-government had promised to introduce, together with the Second Anti-Jewish Law, the draft of the Land Consolidation Law (which promised to parcel out about one million acres of land), there were less confrontations between "social reform" and the Anti-Jewish Law. Instead the major question was: How could the true-born Magyars profit from the new anti-Jewish Law? To contrast the racist legislation with the Magyar racist conception was a trap, and most of the Hungarian intellectuals fell into it.

During the Horthy era there were different intellectual associations, some younger, some older; there was even an organization established to coordinate their activities. One of these was *Honszeretet Egyesület* (Patriotic Association), whose secret society was the *Magyar Közösség* (Hungarian Community), which, on September 28, 1938, recorded the following about the major goals and the ways to achieve them: "We want to exclude from any kind of control over Hungarian life those races and ethnic groups, first of all Jewry, which are harmful to both the Magyars and the nationalities living here." [16]

The periodical of *Honszeretet*, the *Magyar Élet* (Hungarian Life), took a stand on the Second Anti-Jewish Law in this spirit, although it published Dezső Szabó's article in which he noted that the greatest threat to the Magyars would come in the form of increasing anti-Semitic fanaticism which diverted attention from the most pressing claims of the Magyars. He did not agree either with the law or with the periodical on the definition of "Jew." He put the question differently: who is Hungarian? Anyone who has one non-Jewish parent, he answered. [17]

To fill the vacancies created by the new law was the organizing principle of a new intellectual group, the *Törzsökös Magyarok Tömörülése, Sárkányos Mozgalom* (Association of True-Born Hungarians, Dragon Movement). According to them, if the Second Anti-Jewish Law was necessary then not only should the opportunities of Jews be restricted but also those of the assimilated Germans. The *Törzsökös* Movement exercised a great influence on the Hungarian intelligentsia for some months and its ideas attracted great attention. [18]

Is assimilation possible? Can an assimilated person be regarded as Hungarian? Who is Hungarian at all? These were the questions most of the Hungarian intelligentsia were interested in when the Second Anti-Jewish Law was passed. Not only the newspapers, but also the better literary and sociological periodicals focused on the question of assimilation.

There were few people who realized the danger posed by the racial approach to the middle class mixed up with the anti-Jewish laws. Aladár Schöpflin saw it clearly in his *Asszimiláció és irodalom* (Assimilation and

Literature) published in the April 1939 issue of *Nyugat.* He pointed out that the mutilation of the civil rights of the Jews logically led to the anti-assimilationist tendencies and under favorable conditions it might develop into powerful policy which might result in a major social crisis.[19]

Gyula Szekfű was also interested in this topic. In the May 1939 issue of *Magyar Szemle* (Hungarian Review) he wrote about the necessity to lay down the basic principle of the *Törzsökös* (True-born) movement in order to avoid "the forced dissimilation of thousands of good Hungarians."[20] Among those who would be able to lay down such a principle he also named László Németh who immediately answered with his essay: *Kissebségben* (In the Minority), which created a sensation among intellectuals and left them still preoccupied with the debate on assimilation when the war broke out.

László Németh, although not from a traditional aspect, treated the problem of assimilation from a racial point of view and expressed his ideas concerning Hungarian Jewry. That these were similar to those of Dezső Szabó in many respects he did not deny, although in this very essay he criticized Szabó, who had become popular again as a result of the working of "Jews and clericals"—according to Németh. The most important thing Szabó did, wrote Németh, was to release "the Hungarian radicalism of the Jews." According to Németh, the post-1919 Hungarian Left was nothing else but the "cautious but persistent organ of Jewish interest representation."

He gives an overview of the twenties and thirties through the relationship between Hungarian radicalism and Jewry, and thus arriving at 1938 he draws these conclusions: "1938 separated not only the Jews from the other 'immigrant-Hungarians' but also the Habsburg-Swabians from the dissimilant Germans." Among the latter Hungarians might also be found, wrote Németh. Even more so, if the Magyarization of Budapest continued by the decrease of middle-class assimilations and the decrease of the birth-rate of Jews. It was here he expressed his idea that the Jewish question would have been solved without the anti-Jewish laws, owing to a decrease in the birthrate.[21]

A heated and complex debate followed, but there was hardly any mention of the anti-Jewish laws or the discriminatory measures, as if the intellectual common knowledge had gotten over it. A discussion continued as if nothing had happened, on whether Jewry was able to assimilate.

The outbreak of World War II brought about the establishment of censorship in Hungary. The censors reacted especially to matters concerning foreign policy, but also scrutinized criticisms of social conditions or government policy. However, it was not obligatory to write: the time had come when remaining silent was in itself to take a stand. Most of the writers remained silent or kept within the scope of "pure" literature. They did not speak about problems such as the "Jewish question" either, which the extreme Right, especially the Imrédy-wing, very much deplored and, during the 1940s, after the French capitulation, gave voice to several times.

No major writer—with one or two exceptions, including the poet Kálmán Sértő—joined the extreme Right, let alone the Arrow-Cross movement.

From the autumn of 1940, when Imrédy's party—the *Magyar Megujulás Pártja* (Party of Hungarian Renewal)—was founded, István Sinka and, more often, József Erdélyi, who became correspondent of the periodical *Egyedül Vagyunk* (We Are Alone), appeared at the meetings. With the German victories, however, came a renewal of racist ideology among the intellectual circles, and its effect was particularly felt on those proposing a third solution: men who believed the German hegemony in Europe would be a lasting one and sought to find a place for Hungary in the given international situation. There were writers who, as a consequence, underwent spectacular changes in their outlook; others, who failed to see the need for national unity—for a popular front policy against fascism—used their old tactics when sounding the call for "Hungarian radicalism." Instead of thinking in terms of cooperation they kept thinking in terms of exclusion.

In January 1940, László Németh attempted to draw up a program in his essay *Magyarok kibékülni!* (Hungarians, Make Peace!), he considered the hour propitious: the Prime Minister was a Hungarian scientist, the various alien groups were squabbling:

"Religion separates Pan-Germans from Habsburg-Swabians; the capitalist Jews turn to Otto, the small Jews to Stalin, those who read the *Magyar Nemzet* (Hungarian Nation) together occupy one another's place owing to the anti-Jewish law. The Hungarian minority is no longer a minority if it sticks together." Németh added that the assimilated groups should not be mistaken for the aliens since "if we are the more determined, they [the former] will adapt to us." And those who can demonstrate their sincerity in wishing to become Magyars should not be excluded.[22] He had expressed the requirement of sincerity before in his *Kisebbségben.* According to him, one should deny the anti-Magyar tendencies of one's race and acknowledge "the authority of the real Magyar spirit over cultural issues and in questions involving the nation's destiny."

At the same time János Kodolányi wrote about "radical conservatism,"[23] and in December 1940 László Németh again summed up his ideas in *Magyar radikalizmus* (Hungarian Radicalism).[24] In this essay he attacked the group around *Magyar Nemzet* (Hungarian Nation), which he considered the most important beside the government and the Arrow-Cross movement and which, according to him, held together as a result of the two anti-Jewish laws.

Then, he outlined the solution to the "Jewish question" which had been rejected by Hungarian Jewry and which "we writers consider to be the solution after our own heart." He advocated the nationalization of big business and banks, and humanity toward the small Jews. He, like many other writers, artists and scientists, claimed that it was because of the anti-Jewish laws that the organization of national resistance had fallen into the hands of Jewry. He has more than one objection against them; their "viewpoint is not a Hungarian one" and also "from the Hungarian point of view, they unnecessarily and unreasonably violate the laws of adaptation."

He persistently repeated his views, sometimes calmly, sometimes vehemently until 1941, when the movement of the populist writers began to break up and when Gyula Illyés' article—*Veres Péter utja* (The Way of Peter Veres—appeared in *Magyar Nemzet* and in the same newspaper Zoltán Szabó published *Központi gyülölde* (Central Hating Place).

In April 1941, László Németh wrote that "The Great Antipathy"—whose invisible influence was being felt on four-fifths of the periodicals, publishers, university departments and pulpits—is looking for the writer who would repudiate the writers with "third route" ideas.[25] In a lecture some weeks later he said that "the Jews would have liked to recruit a Hungarian Jewish front.[26]

The ideas of the 1939–1941 concept of "Hungarian radicalism" soon found response among young intellectuals and became vulgarized. The ideological catechism of the *Turul Szövetség* (Turul Association), which appeared in June 1941, recognized as Hungarian only those whose parents were Hungarians or those who were at least partially descended from a Euroasian ethnic group and were recognized as Hungarians by the descendants of Hungarians. One of its "Ten Commandments" prohibited intermarriage with aliens.[27]

This "Commandment" was soon imposed by law so far as Jews were concerned. On October 10, 1941, the Third Anti-Jewish Law came into effect. It prohibited marriage as well as sexual intercourse between Jews and non-Jews. This law was passed after heated debate—the representatives of the churches especially raised objections. In the Upper House, the measure passed by a 65-53 vote. Thus "criminal miscegenation" became a legal term, and procedures were instituted against offenders—names of whom some papers were happy to publish.

By that time the characteristic form of resistance was to keep silent, but there were opportunities for the Hungarian writers and artists to demonstrate that they were guided by intellectual values and not by racist legislation. The volume dedicated to the memory of Mihály Babits which was edited by

Gyula Illyés, comprised 76 authors, many of them legally discriminated against.[28]

The volume was abused not only by the extreme rightist publications but the *Magyar Élet* also published an inflammatory article against it. "More than half of the 76 people are Jewish or half-Jewish, or have Jewish interests: Jewish wives, Jewish newspapers, Jewish money." According to him, in this volume, taking advantage of Babits, Jewry had once again launched an attack for the control over the Hungarian intellectual life.[29]

Illyés not only edited this memorial volume but the *Magyar Csillag* (Hungarian Star) which appeared first in October 1941, was the forum of every Hungarian writer. Among its authors were Gábor Halász, Miklós Radnóti, and Antal Szerb.

There were others, however, who continued writing anti-Semitic articles, and some devoted themselves to anti-Jewish propaganda with neophyte rage. The metamorphosis of Géza Féja was apparent in May 1940 when he took up a new post as department head in the *Magyar Nemzetbiológiai Intézet* (Institute for Hungarian National Biology). In the following years he wrote vehemently about the "urbanites" *(urbánusok)* and social democratic leaders. Any criticism of the "Magyar line" he identified with the interest of the Jewish capitalists or petty bourgeois.[30]

In 1942 he published an article in *Egyedül vagyunk,* in which he made reference to the *Történelmi Emlékbizottság* (Historical Commemorative Committee): "Nobody should believe that the Jewish capitalists and intelligentsia may be, even if for a short time, our allies despite the wide gap between Magyars and Jews.[31] As the correspondent of *Magyarország* (Hungary) he published a series of articles on the subject for some time. On February 24, 1942, he published *Öngyilkosság* (Suicide) which caused general consternation. It was a strange necrology on the occasion of Stefan Sweig's suicide. From the example of this personal tragedy he derived the destiny of all the immigrant Jews who were recognized as aliens within Christian society. He called them rootless cosmopolitans who "disturb the life of the community that admitted them," and when they are held responsible by history, they run away. Féja did not ponder much the responsibility of the literati when he added: "There is an end to all the lies and hypocrisy and no one can run away with them." Then he went on about the problems of writing an unbiased criticism on the Jewish question (in 1942!) because Jewry was "unwilling to recognize its faults." He advised the Jews to draw a lesson from the past, since "Stefan Zweig's doom is a characteristic example of the consequence of yesterday's Jewish behavior."[32]

The *Ujság* (News) published a commentary on March 1, 1942: Féja "in his neophyte overzeal has 'committed' a strange necrology on the occasion of Stefan Zweig's suicide."[33] There appeared other criticism as well and Féja complained that he was being persecuted, that those who declare themselves "complete Hungarians" had launched an attack against him on the grounds of their international solidarity.[34]

He continued publishing articles on the subject. He went back to the subject of Stefan Zweig many a time and made oblique hints to the Eszter Solymosi—Tiszaeszlár blood libel case. He was so carried away that he wrote about the police raids on Duna-Korzó, which cleared the "Mecca of persecutees" and thus made room for the "Hungarian public."[35] He did not know that by the time he had written his article the Wannsee Conference had worked out the details for the liquidation of European Jewry.

At that time some believed that the populist conception had prevailed at last, but others considered it only the beginning of "Hungarian radicalism," especially since it did not fight against Jewry with proper force and at the proper time. This concept was expressed by Gyula Gombos in his *Álom az országról* (Dream About the Country). "The radicalism of *Válasz* (Response) was not directed against Jewry." He denied the possibility of assimilation, even in Németh's sense, since the Hungarian orientation in Hungary's destiny was a matter of instinct and even the best intentions were in vain.[36]

The need to conform to the new Order arose most forcibly in the realm of history, especially in "ethnic history" *(népiségtörténet)*, a leading advocate of which said that the notion of peoples' nation *(népi-nemzet)* was "based on the separation of those who did not belong to the people," that is, on the effort to "exclude Jewry from the nation, to let all those who, deep in their hearts, are not totally Hungarians go peacefully, and then we who remain should reorganize our lives so that they would be our way at last."[37]

A milestone in the exclusion of Jewry from the intellectual life occurred in 1942 with the establishment of the *Magyar Irodalompártoló Társaság* (Association of Hungarian Patrons of Letters). An editorial in *Magyar Út* was enthusiastic about the statutes accepted at the Association's organizational meeting, as a counterweight to the Baumgarten foundation which, according to the editorial, was furthering the interest of "the Jewish race-protection." The proof of it was the foundation's fundamental principle itself: "The writer or scientist to be rewarded should be free from all kinds of racial prejudices."

There had been hardly any literary works that expressed racial hatred since the publication of József Erdélyi's ill-famed poem *Solymosi Eszter vére* (Eszter Solymosi's Blood). In Kálmán Sértő's writings (he died in 1941) and in István Sinka's autobiography—*Fekete bojtár vallomásai* (Confessions of the Black Shepherd Boy)—one can find outspoken declarations of anti-Semitism. Among the arts, the cinema was the chief victim of racism and social demagogy. Films such as *A harmincadik* (The Thirtieth) and *Őrségváltás* (Changing of the Guards) are good examples of the new trend.

With the victories of the Allies and the battle at Stalingrad came a reappraisal of Hungary's future, and consequently of the Jewish question. More and more intellectuals were afraid of the consequences. In February 1943, László Németh wrote: "Our age is buried with us. Now we have to demonstrate that the word we addressed to the nation is not idle talk, it is worth a life. The few years or months to come are ours, the guards of today. Be worthy of it! Hold out so that the youth whose eyes rest on us will be given a good example of noble behavior." [38]

To be sure, there were different kinds of behavior. "Hold out" did not have the same meaning to everyone. József Erdélyi, for instance, was true to himself. Not only did he write anti-Semitic articles as the correspondent of *Egyedül Vagyunk,* but the organizational principle of the second part of his autobiography published in 1942—*Fegyvertelen* (Unarmed)—in which he wrote about his literary career, characterized his attitude toward Jews. [39]

Gyula Gombos did not give up his ideas either. In the July 1943 issue of *Magyar Élet* he emphasized the possibility of the third route, he wrote about the "two-sided Hungarian radicalism which clearly sees the enemies." He stressed that Jewry which, when rowing against the stream, was conservative and loyal to the constitution, might become aggressive and revolutionary again. [40]

At the second meeting in Szárszó, which was held after the Allied landing in Sicily, when preparations were made for Italy's capitulation and the end of the war seemed to be very close, László Németh was apparently very much afraid of the consequences of the persecution of Jews. The Jewish question, he said, "is brought back by history and it is more serious than ever before," which was probably a reference to the likely victory of the anti-Fascist powers. He repeated his views about the anti-Jewish laws and said: "The newspapers of the national resistance could be organized only with Jewish money. Former legitimists, racists, clericals were forced under their supervision. And now peace comes and they will be the advisors and may be the appointed saviors."

He emphasized that he had never generalized in connection with the Jewish question and said: "The Jewry, which is lacking self-criticism and is revengeful, must have become extremely strong during the past four or five years as against those who modestly respect culture; and those who do not realize that Shylock wants the heart have no ear for the sharpening of the knife."

László Németh's speech had a powerful impact, and the Jewish question was discussed yet again; others also spoke on the subject, among them Gyula Gombos and Géza Féja. It became one of Szárszó's major topics. According to Gombos, in Hungary "behind the social conflicts there are racial conflicts" which cannot be solved by social regulations. He set forth the idea, prevalent throughout the war, that the aristocracy and middle class was not Hungarian by origin but mostly German, the bourgeoisie was Jewish, therefore the Hungarian workers' and peasants' opposition to the oppressive classes "is not only social in its character but also racial: the opposition of Magyars to the exploiting aliens." Féja warned the participants: "A historical occasion may arise when, under cover of democratic slogans, Jewry will launch a new attack against the Hungarian intelligentsia in order to take the lead."[41]

However, there were other kinds of attitudes. There was the staging of Lajos Zilahy's play *Fatornyok* (Wooden Towers) in 1943; it was withdrawn after German forces occupied Hungary. Its great success was due to a scene in which the main character rejects his brother who has suggested that, considering the difficult situation, he should divorce his Jewish wife. This scene was always greeted with applause during the performances.

The noncommital attitude of the majority of writers and artists concerning the Jewish question irritated the extreme Right. In his 1943 book Mihály Kolosváry-Borcsa lamented over the alarming symptoms of the turning-point of the age: "Most of the Hungarian authors who have made their name are expediently cautious or uncomprehendingly indifferent as far as the world historical changes and most importantly, as far as the Jewish question is concerned."[42]

Zoltán Bosnyák sought an explanation for Zilahy's play in the latter's past.[43] He, too, was complaining: "There are people in the forefront of our intelligentsia who still do not understand the spirit of our times, who are not interested in the great internal war of independence of the Magyars." The explanation, according to him, lay in the fact that they were still many intellectuals who, outspokenly or not, sympathized with Jewry. He proposed the exclusion of these people.[44]

The German occupation of Hungary on March 19, 1944, threatened the existence of the last large European Jewish community, that is, of around 825,000 people (725,000 of the Jewish faith and about 100,000 Christians then identified as Jewish). A double burden weighed heavily on these people: the German occupation and the Hungarian state power. Discrimination, deprivation of rights, deportation, annihilation were in store for them due to the cooperation between the German occupants and the Sztójay government. If it is true in general that the population was unaware of Jewry's humiliation and fear of the racial laws, we may add that the majority of the Hungarian civil servants were positively anti-Semitic, or—with the exception of some brave people—faithfully enforced an avalanche of decrees issued by the government, either on the advice of the Eichmann-*Sonderkommando* or on its own, in order to "solve" the Jewish question.

A great many anti-Jewish decrees and regulations were issued before the beginning of the deportations in connection with the cultural role of Jewry. An April 29, 1944, decree prohibited publication and distribution of Jewish authors and the list of authors whose works were banned was made public. A complementary list was issued on June 24. The list contained 45 foreign and 240 Hungarian authors, among them Tibor Déri, Milán Füst, Lajos Hatvany, Jenő Heltai, Oszkár Jászi, Frigyes Karinthy, György Lukács, Ernő Osváth, Károly Papp, Miklós Radnóti, Zoltán Somlyó, Ernő Szép, and Zoltán Zelk.[45]

At the same time the *Otthon Irók Köre* (Circle of Home Writers) was banned and the *Fészek Klub* (Nest Club) transformed into *Magyar Müvészek Háza* (House of Hungarian Artists), from which not only the writers and artists of Jewish origin were excluded but also the philo-Semitic ones—those who were accused of denying the "national idea," among them Zsigmond Kisfaludy-Strobl, Oszkár Glatz, Lajos Zilahy, István Csók, and István Szőnyi. But even this was not enough. The *Egyedül Vagyunk* called for the removal of sculptures, monuments, and other pieces of art created by Jewish artists from public places and museums; their list contained sixty of them, among others the monuments to Széchenyi, Vörösmarty, and Anonymus in Budapest. The article pressed for an "artistic consideration" in making the decision: which of the sculptures and monuments had to be removed and destroyed? It also thought of the future of these pieces of art: "If they are made of bronze they will serve as weapons of the Hungarian self-defense; if they are made of marble or stone, they should be given to our talented Hungarian sculptors."[46]

Lists were drawn up about the "writers who, although Hungarian by origin, were poisoned by Jewish spirit," and demanded that their works be banned. The books written by Zsigmond Móricz and Endre Ady were also to be pulped. This was too much even for such a racist paper as *Az Ország* (The Country)."[47]

The brutal "purificators" were very much annoyed to see that the writers were not at all enthusiastic. "A rather large number of the Hungarian writers—reads an article in the abovementioned paper—still does not understand what has happened, what changes occurred on March 19. They are still speculating, they are still silent and with this silent sabotage they do almost more harm than if they outspokenly stated their opinions." It deplored the silence of the populist writers most saying that, apart from the book-day, there was no sign of their presence.[48]

On the book-day of 1944 there appeared works by Pál Szabó, Gyula László, Sándor Karácsony, and József Nyirő. A little later László Németh's volume of essays appeared: *Az értelmiség hivatása* (The Mission of the Intelligentsia) which was specially depressing since, at the time of deportations, it contained his speech at the second conference in Szárszó, where he wrote about the future revenge of Jewry. However, he left out the line about "Shylock wants the heart."

There were hardly any new writings. From August 1944 a new paper was issued, the *Magyar Ünnep* (Hungarian Holiday); the first editorial—*Magyar szellemiség* (Hungarian Intellectuality)—was written by József Nyirő who triumphantly stated: "The deliberate and regular poisoning of the Hungarian soul and intellectuality has come to an end." We find István Sinka and Dezső Szabó among its authors, the latter started a series: *Csendes szavak* (Silent Words). It is sad that this well-known poet sank to a low unparallelled in Hungary, or anywhere in the world. József Erdélyi not only published his *Solymosi Eszter vére* again, but after the deportation and annihilation of hundreds of thousands of Jews, he published a new poem: *A zsidókról* (About the Jews). It was a twelve-verse anti-Semitic abuse, which began like this:

> I've told the Jew many a time /not to be so stuck-up/
> Now he can wear/his yellow star.

And it ended:

> No one will take it off him/Until he leaves, if he can/
> he would leave, he would run/but at present he cannot/
> he would love to run away but he is not allowed . . ./
> I may be sorry, but we reap as we sow.[49]

The column where his poem was published was called *Irás és lélek* (Writing and Soul).

József Erdélyi, too, must have known about the Holocaust of Hungarian Jewry—if not elsewhere then from the very periodical that published his poems. *Az Ország,* like other periodicals, printed the United Nations' protest—accompanied with indignant or sarcastic comments—against the brutal persecution of the Jews in Hungary. Roosevelt's statement, and a broadcast by the Archbishop of Canterbury were also published.

These protests were in the background of Gyula Gombos' *Az eszközök becsülete* (The Honor of the Means), which was published in *Magyar Út* and in which he dissociated himself from the inhumanity. The means may elevate or denigrate the goals, since it is always disputable whether the prevalence of a man or a group over another man or group is lawful; only the means can be an excuse as well as justification. The utmost a small nation can do in a war is to preserve its honor. The fairness of means is the real weapon of the small nations. "When this is forgotten, everything is lost. If we are able to preserve our dignity, we preserve the most for posterity, whatever the peace would be like."[50]

But can one talk about "fair means" in connection with a racist policy? "Dignity" could be preserved only in opposition: through resistance, sabotaging the decrees, helping the persecutees; every legal or illegal form of protest was a fair means—or at least it could have been.

There were writers, artists, scientists—both Jewish and Christian—who lived illegally after the German occupation and participated in the resistance. Most of the writers and artists kept silent; they renounced the world or lived in half-illegality. Many writers, artists, and scientists of Jewish origin were mobilized for labor service and even those who were not, and were not taken to concentration camps because living in Budapest or because they were exempted by the Regent, had to hide during the Arrow-Cross era. Among them many were helped and taken in so that they were able to live through this horrible period. It was possible because, as Vilmos Juhász put it, many *individuals* chose not to adopt the "none-of-my-business" attitude at the risk of their own life. Writers too. As to the society, only elements of the Catholic and Protestant clergy and their orders and the closely cooperating laymen saved thousands of people.[51]

For a great many writers, artists, and scientists of Jewish origin there was no escape. They were killed together with more than half a million others, in labor service, concentration camps, and as a result of "individual actions." Such was the fate of about a hundred writers, artists, and scientists, including György Bálint, Andor Endre Gelléri, Gábor Halász, Károly Papp, Miklós Radnóti, György Sárközi, and Antal Szerb.

In the end of this overview, the question has to be put again: Did the Hungarian intelligentsia face this tragedy after the war? Again, the answer is no; only individuals did, cautiously, shifting the responsibility. The writers of that generation were silent—to quote Vilmos Juhász again—they "who, during and before the tragedy were the apostolic leaders of the country's intellectual life or at least wanted to be. The writers did not confess, either in their own name or in the name of the community." It is no wonder, one may add, that a large part of the Hungarian society was not willing to undergo this purification.

The explanation is not so simple as to refer to the revenge after 1945, to the prejudices of some of the survivors, or the composition of the Communist Party or of the officers of *Államvédelmi Hatóság*—AVH (State Security Authority). We have to establish our own responsibility. Imre Kovács, when he entered into debate with Vilmos Juhász in 1965, found more plausible explanations for the silence in 1944; the democratic writers took part in the resistance as *individuals,* and those who fought against the Germans, Nazis, and Arrow-Cross men fought for the Jews, too. "It was the age of individual actions, united actions were technically impossible." But he was not completely satisfied with this explanation, and in the end he went so far as to state: when talking about responsibility, the right order is to ask: "what did I do?" He questions himself: why didn't he do more, why wasn't he more heroic against the Germans, the gendarmerie, the authorities, on behalf of the Jews. "Now I know why. I was a coward! That's why I don't blame anyone else for my negligence."[52]

Yes, this may be the right way, "For we can do nothing against the truth, but for the truth."

Notes

1. István Bibó, A zsidókérdés Magyarországon 1944 után (The Jewish Question in Hungary After 1944). *Válasz* (Response), Budapest, no. 4, 1948: 778-877. Reproduced in *Bibó István összegyüjtött munkái* (The Collected Works of István Bibó). Bern: Európai Protestáns Magyar Szabadegyetem, 1982, Vol. 2, pp. 391-505.

2. *Ibid.,* Vol. 3, 1983, pp. 825-829.

3. Vilmos Juhász, Az apák helyett. A mai magyar irodalom egyik aspektusáról (Instead of the Fathers. On One Aspect of Contemporary Hungarian Literature). *Új Látóhatár* (New Horizon), Budapest, no. 2, 1965: 164-175; no. 4, 1965: 357-362. Imre Kovács, A vádlottak nevében (In the Name of the Accused). *Ibid.,* no. 6, 1965: 357-362. Vilmos Juhász, A vádlottá előlépett bűnrészes nyilatkozata (The Declaration of an Accomplice Who Rose to Be an Accuser). *Ibid.,* no. 6, 1965: 555-460.

4. Gyula Szekfű, *Három nemzedék és ami utána következik* (Three Generations and What Follows After Them). 6th ed. Budapest: Királyi Magyar Egyetemi Nyomda, 1940, pp. 440-450.

5. Dezső Szabó, "Az antijudaizmus birálata" (The Critique of Anti-Judaism). *In his: Az egész látóhatár* (The Entire Horizon). Budapest: Magyar Élet, 1940, pp. 249-294. On Szabó's position, see Péter Nagy, *Szabó Dezső.* Budapest: Akadémiai Kiadó, 1964, 604 p., and Gyula Gombos, *Szabó Dezső.* Munich: Aurora, 1969, 392 p.

6. The text of the declaration can be found in Jenő Lévai, *Fekete Könyv* (Black Book). Budapest: Officina, 1946, pp. 26-27. Lévai left out the names of Géza Féja, László Dernői Kocsis, and Gusztáv Rab. In István Vas's autobiography—*Miért vijjog a saskeselyű?* (Why Does the Vulture Screetch?). Budapest: Szépirodalmi Könyvkiadó, 1981, Vol. 2, pp. 261-284—one can find an interesting account of his own and his friends' views of, and reactions to, the declaration.

7. *Pesti Hirlap* (Journal of Pest), Apr. 24, 1938.

8. 67th Session of the Upper House of the Hungarian Parliament, May 24, 1938.

9. Dániel Fábián, "Tiltakozunk lelkiismeretünk minden erejével . . ." (We Are Protesting With All the Strength of Our Conscience . . .). *Magyar Út* (Hungarian Way), Budapest, May 12, 1938.

10. Még ők is? (They Too?). *Ibid.,* May 19, 1938.

11. Géza Féja, Vállaltam, vállalok és vállalni fogok (I Assumed, I Assume, and I Shall Assume). *Ibid.,* May 26, 1938.

12. *Pesti Napló* (Diary of Pest), May 8, 1938.

13. *Ibid.,* May 15, 1938. This is reproduced in *Babits Mihály művei. Esszék, tanulmányok* (The Works of Mihály Babits. Essays, Studies). Vol. II. Budapest: Szépirodalmi Könyvkiadó, 1978, pp. 568-573.

14. *Nyugat* (West), Budapest, May 1938. Reproduced in *Magyarok* (Hungarians). Budapest: Nyugat Kiadó, 1939, pp. 276-277, and in Gyula Illyés, *Itt élned kell* (You Have to Live Here). Vol. I. Budapest: Szépirodalmi Könyvkiadó, 1976, pp. 419-420.

15. *A magyar parasztság levele a művelt fiatalsághoz* (The Hungarian Peasantry's Letter to the Educated Youth). Miskolc, 1938, 11 p.

16. György Donáth, Az Egyesülteközi együttmüködés (Cooperation Among the Allies). *Magyar Élet* (Hungarian Life), Budapest, June 1941 as quoted by Gyula Juhász *Uralkodó eszmék Magyarországon, 1939-1944* Dominant Ideas in Hungary, 1939-1944). Budapest: Kossuth, 1983, p. 12.

17. Dezső Szabó, Querelae Magyarorum. *Magyar Élet* (Hungarian Life), Budapest, Jan. 1939.

18. For further details on the *Törzsökös Movement* see Juhász, *op. cit.,* pp. 13-18.

19. Aladár Schöpflin, Asszimiláció és irodalom (Assimilation and Literature). *Nyugat,* Budapest, Apr. 1939.

20. Időszerű történelmi munkák (Contemporary Historical Works). *Magyar Szemle* (Hungarian Review), Budapest, Mar. 1939.

21. László Németh, *Kisebbségben* (In a Minority). Kecskemét: Első Kecskeméti Hirlapok, 1939, 92 p.

22. *Kelet Népe* (The People of the East), Budapest, Jan. 15, 1940.

23. János Kodolányi, "Volt-e kompromisszum?" (Was There a Compromise?). *In: Husz év a magyar politika szolgálatában. A "Honszeretet" beszámolója* (Twenty Years in the Service of Hungarian Politics. Report of the "Love of Homeland"). Budapest, 1940, pp. 5-14.

24. László Németh, Magyar radikalizmus (Hungarian Radicalism). *Kelet Népe,* Budapest, Dec. 1, 1940.

25. László Németh, Egy műfaj haldoklása (The Dying of a Genre). *Magyar Élet,* Apr. 1941.

26. László Németh, "Faji hibáinkról" (About Our Racial Mistakes). *In: Kisebbségben* (In a Minority). Vols. I-II. Budapest: Magyar Élet, 1942, pp. 174-175.

27. *Magyar Káté* (Hungarian Catechism). Budapest: Turul Szövetség, 1941. Published in detail in the July 1941 issue of *Magyar Élet.*

28. *Babits Mihály emlékkönyv* (Mihály Babits Memorial Book). Edited by Gyula Illyés. Budapest: Nyugat Kiadó, 1941, 311 p.

29. *Magyar Élet,* Oct. 1941.

30. Géza Féja, A Márciusi Front hiteles története (The Authentic History of the March Front). *Magyar Út* (Hungarian Way), Budapest, Apr. 10, 1941.

31. Géza Féja, Szociáldemokrácia és agrárdemokrácia (Social Democracy and Agrarian Democracy). *Egyedül Vagyunk* (We Are Alone), Budapest, no. 3, 1942.

32. Géza Féja, Öngyilkosság (Suicide). *Magyarország* (Hungary), Budapest, Feb. 24, 1942.

33. Röpdém előtt (Before My Aviary). *Ujság* (News), Budapest, Mar. 1, 1942.

34. Géza Féja, Farizeusok (Pharisees). *Magyarország,* Budapest, Apr. 8, 1942.

35. Géza Féja, A "terrénum" (The Terrain). *Ibid.,* Apr. 14, 1942; — —, Razzia "Mekkában" (Raid in Mecca). *Ibid.,* May 20, 1942.

36. Gyula Gombos, *Álom az országról* (Dream About the Country). Budapest: Bolyai Akadémia, 1942, pp. 79-89.

37. Elemér Mályusz, *A magyar történettudomány* (The book was first serialized in *Egyedül Vagyunk,* beginning with the No. 53, 1941, issue of the periodical.

38. László Németh, *Az értelmiség hivatása* (The Profession of the Intelligentsia). Budapest: Turul Kiadó, 1944, p. 43.

39. József Erdélyi, *Fegyvertelen* (Unarmed). Budapest: Turul Kiadó, 1942, 204 p.

40. Gyula Gombos, Magyar politika (Hungarian Politics). *Magyar Élet,* Budapest, July 1943.

41. Szárszó. (The Papers and Discussions of the Group Around *Magyar Élet* at Balatonszárszó in 1943). Budapest: Magyar Élet, 1943, 232 p. A second edition of this work was published by Kossuth Kiadó in 1983, excluding the contribution by Gyula Gombos.

42. Mihály Kolosváry-Borcsa, *A zsidókérdés magyarországi irodalma* (The Hungarian Literature on the Jewish Question). Budapest: Stádium, 1943, 311 p.

43. Mi az igazság a "Fatornyok" körül? (What Is the Truth Around the "Wooden Towers"?) *Egyedül Vagyunk,* Budapest, Feb. 25, 1944.

44. Zoltán Bosnyák, *Harc a zsidó veszély ellen* (Struggle Against the Jewish Danger). Budapest: Új Európa, 1944, p. 44.

45. The lists and the provisions of the law are reproduced in *Vádirat a nácizmus ellen* (Indictment of Nazism). Edited by Ilona Benoschofsky and Elek Karsai. Budapest: Magyar Izraeliták Országos Képviselete, Vol. I, 1958, pp. 276-281; Vol. II, 1960, pp. 323-325. The lists are also reproduced in Randolph L. Braham, *The*

Politics of Genocide. The Holocaust in Hungary. New York: Columbia University Press, 1981, pp. 1202-1204.

46. László Balázs Piri, Mi lesz a zsidó szobrászok emlékműveivel? (What Will Happen to the Monuments by Jewish Sculptors?) *Egyedül Vagyunk,* Budapest, May 19, 1944.

47. Adyt is a zuzómalomba (Ady Too Into the Smashing Mill). *Az Ország* (The Country), Budapest, June 24, 1924.

48. Miért késik a szellemi arcvonal? (Why Is the Spiritual Battle Line Delayed?) *Ibid.*

49. *Ibid.,* July 8, 1944.

50. Gyula Gombos, Az eszközök becsülete (The Honor of the Means). *Magyar Út,* Budapest, July 13, 1944.

51. *Új Látóhatár,* no. 2, 1965: 164-175.

52. *Ibid.,* no. 4, 1965: 357-362.

II. RESPONSIBILITY AND IMPACT

Chapter 6

THE GERMANS AND THE DESTRUCTION
OF HUNGARIAN JEWRY

György Ránki

The tragic history of the destruction of the Hungarian Jews has propelled its students into anguished retrospection. It imposes on them a burden at once hard to accept and impossible to shake off. The crime committed are beyond all doubt those of normal, otherwise rational men, but their historical origin remains mired in continuous, sometimes venomous controversy.

To write the history of 1944 is most frequently to render a verdict, and the verdict of guilty is rarely in doubt. It is not the aim of this study to put the blame for the destruction of Hungarian Jewry on the Germans, not even to try to whitewash the Hungarians involved. There are numerous examples where, as the SS is used as an alibi for the Germans, the Germans are used as an alibi for those Hungarians whose involvement in the crimes is undeniable. But how can one dismiss the major role of the Hungarians? How can one ignore that ultimately Hungary was one of the countries where organized anti-Semitism became a part of government policy, where anti-Semitic laws appeared as a part of legislation, where serious political and military forces—some deeply involved in the violent White Terror—had become a part of the country's ruling elite? In the letter from Prime Minister Gyula Gömbös welcoming the appointment of Hitler as Chancellor of the German Reich, Gömbös referred to himself and Hitler as "fellow racists of long standing who hold a common ideology."[1] Nevertheless, with all due regard to the major Hungarian component, upon examining the events, one must conclude that without the Germans, the Hungarian Holocaust would not have occurred in the same manner.

Three major problems need to be taken into consideration in order to understand the role of Nazi Germany in the destruction of the Hungarian Jews: The stages and elements of the relationship between Germany and Hungary from 1933 to 1945; the emergence of the idea of "the Final Solution" and its role in German foreign policy with regard to the satellite states; and the question of how and to what extent the so-called Jewish problem—the peculiarities of the assimilation process, the particular role of the Jews in the state's economic and cultural life—became either a mere function of foreign policy, or one of the issues in Germany's efforts to keep Hungary in the Axis camp.

Without oversimplifying the issue, the German-Hungarian relationship can be divided into three major periods. In the different periods various issues, but mainly three—economic dependence of Hungary on Germany, the common foreign policy interest related to the revision of the peace treaties, and similarities in the domestic power structure—were dominant in shaping this relationship. None of them was directly connected to the treatment of the Jewish population, although some side effects were present. During the 1930s, a period of economic collaboration, agrarian and industrial interests frequently collided: the majority of the Hungarian industrialists were in clear opposition to German aims, as they had to defend Hungarian industrial interests—and their own positions—against an anti-Semitic economic and domestic policy.

During the next stage, when—with German support—Hungary was able to achieve important successes in the field of foreign policy, a large part of the Jewish population in the territories restored to Hungary between 1938 and 1941 were among those who most heartily welcomed the entering Hungarian troops; at the same time, all of the successes and accomplishments of Hungarian foreign policy were connected with major concessions to Germany, which always included new anti-Jewish measures. Even if there is no direct evidence that the First Anti-Jewish Law, introduced in 1938, was directly connected with any German pressure, it can still be proved that strong domestic forces, including the military leadership, were pressing for those laws. Still, the Hungarian government was not merely yielding to internal pressure and was not simply implementing policy by introducing the First Anti-Jewish Law; rather, it was a well-calculated move to insure German–Hungarian collaboration against Czechoslovakia. Even so, let us suppose for the moment that it was still a voluntary act. It was certainly the last one. The Second Anti-Jewish Law of 1939 and subsequent measures were introduced under direct German pressure or as a payment for German support. Especially in the final stage of the German-Hungarian collaboration—when the basis of common interests had already been seriously eroded the mere fear of German power was what kept this alliance going—the Jewish population of Hungary became an instrument by which the German leadership was able to pressure the Hungarian government to keep them on the desired course.

Although Hungary was willing to introduce a Third Anti-Jewish Law in 1941, and at the same time—with a new decree—the military labor service system was adopted for Jewish males of military age, the Germans were increasingly dissatisfied, and the Jewish question became one of the main issues to be discussed on every occasion, and at every diplomatic level. When the German decision on the Final Solution had been taken, German pressure on Hungary began to increase steadily. Nobody could doubt that the Final Solution was a German invention, even if references concerning the extermination of a part of the Jewish population were frequently present in the anti-Semitic propaganda from the Russian Constantine Pobiedonostsev to some Hungarian rascists or Arrow-Cross pamphleteers. Sporadic—or frequent—killing programs and ideas about a kind of resettlement policy had been present earlier, but by and large a systematic program of anti-Jewish persecutions had never before been implemented.

When in 1942 Hungary's newly appointed Prime Minister, Miklós Kállay, called on Hitler at his headquarters for his introductory visit, Hitler emphasized the necessity of the Final Solution in Hungary. Kállay, defending Hungary's position, referred to the important role of the Jews in Hungary's economic life, implying that any radical measure might be harmful to the German economic interests in Hungary.[2] Hitler was not satisfied with Kállay's response, but felt that future pressure on Hungary might be applied through normal diplomatic channels, as had been done as early as the end of 1941. In a memorandum preparing for the Wannsee Conference, the German Foreign Ministry made the following provisions relating to Hungary: Resettlement of the Jews, overseen by the Hungarian government; Exertion of pressure on Hungary to introduce anti-Jewish laws along the model of the Nuremberg Act.[3]

In the spring of 1942, Hitler intended to demand that the Hungarian government allow Hungarian Jewish nationals to be included in the German resettlement policy, to make the Yellow Star compulsory, and to agree to hand over the Jews of Hungary to Germany in line with the models used by Croatia and Slovakia.[4]

Economic, cultural, and political pressure combined with the strong support given to those political forces inside Hungary who were willing to carry out the German demands to make Hungary's position vis-à-vis Germany more and more difficult.

In September 1942, the pressure was increased even further. Foreign Minister Joachim von Ribbentrop instructed Martin Luther to try to press for the evacuation of the Jews from Hungary since, as everywhere, the Jews were agitating against Germany and were involved in different kinds of sabotage as well. Luther discussed the matter with the Hungarian Minister in Berlin, Döme Sztójay, on October 6[5] and told the Minister "that the time had arrived to extend the general Jewish laws to the Hungarian Jews living in Germany [and German occupied territories] since it is impossible. . . . that the Hungarian Jews alone would be left out." He went on to say that he felt the following measures were desirable. "Progressive laws should be made that would exclude all Jews from the cultural and economic life, [place] distinctive markings on the Jews, and by the evacuation of the Jews to the East, [these laws should] bring about the final solution to the Jewish question in Hungary."

Sztójay well understood these demands, asking only whether they were being presented to the Italians as well. They were. Nevertheless, he felt it necessary to tell Luther that Kállay seemed a little uneasy, since rumors had reached him concerning the fate of the evacuated Jews. Since these concerns were not shared by the Minister, he was willing to accept at face value the reassurances from Luther that "all the evacuated Jews, including the Hungarian Jews, are to be used for road construction in the East, and later transferred to a Jewish reservation."

In the following days the pressure was intensified by a discussion between Ernst von Weizsäcker and Sztójay, through the demands of Dietrich von Jagow, German Minister in Budapest,[6] and through other channels. Partly to relieve the pressure, the Hungarian government was willing to pledge a harsher statement concerning the Jewish question in a talk scheduled for the Hungarian Government Party. However, the speech created just the opposite impression on the Germans, since for political reasons Kállay played down the Jewish question. While the Germans and their strongest supporters in Hungary wanted to present the Jewish question as the single reason for the social ills plaguing the country, the Prime Minister was hastening to "contradict those people who can see no other problem in this country than the Jewish problem. Our country has many problems," he stated, "beside which the Jewish problem pales into insignificance."[7]

During negotiations with the Germans in 1942–1943, Kállay repeated this argument several times. In addition to the economic argument, he referred to the fact that since the Hungarian peasants were not anti-Semitic, if the

Jews were eliminated the Hungarian government would have to force the assimilation of the German i.e., Swabian peasants in Hungary. Although the Germans were receiving support from the Arrow Cross Party, whose deputies had submitted to the Hungarian Parliament several questions concerning the alleged lenient treatment of the Jews in Hungary, Kállay politely yet decisively noted that he was rejecting the German demands concerning the marking and the resettlement of the Hungarian Jews.[8] In a note addressed to the German government, the Hungarian Foreign Ministry referred to the importance of anti-Jewish measures already carried out. The government, however, stressed that the marking of the Jews could make the implementation of previous measures even more difficult, and the "government has neither the opportunity nor the technical capability" for the deportation.

The reassurance, that the Hungarian government would make all efforts to urgently solve the Jewish question sounded all too vague to be taken too seriously by the Germans.

The Kállay government's resistance to German pressure became even stronger after the military debacle at Stalingrad and the fatal defeat of the Hungarian army at Voronezh. From early 1943, Hungary slowly began to disassociate itself from Germany. No more troops were sent to the Russian front.[9] Preparations were made to give more freedom of expression and organization to left-wing opposition parties. Feelers were sent out to all of the capitals of the neutral countries regarding Hungary's departure from the Axis camp. German demands that Hungary send troops as security forces to the Balkans were refused.

The treatment of the Jews in Hungary became one of the main issues discussed at a meeting between Hitler and Horthy on April 17–18, 1943. It is problematic to what extent Hitler used this issue as a pretext for putting more pressure on Hungary and to what extent Hitler's anti-Semitic obsession had become an independent issue. Although Hitler raised the issue as a part of a general attack against Hungary—or against the policy of the Kállay government—a substantial part of the negotiation was nevertheless devoted to the Jewish question. Hitler repeatedly used his well-known argument against the Jews: the Jews had started World War II, had caused leftist revolutions, and even stood behind the bombardment of the civilian population. The Jews were the natural allies of Bolshevism and—as was added by Ribbentrop—they were the agents of the "British Secret Service." It was inconceivable to Ribbentrop how "Hungary can pursue such a pro-Jewish policy." Horthy tried to defend his Prime Minister and his policy. He referred to his own anti-Semitic past and the measures introduced against the

Jewish population up to that point: "He had done everything against the Jews that could have been possible in an honest way, but still he could not kill them, or destroy them in any way."

The question was raised again at the next meeting. In the protocol of the meeting one can find one of the rare statements where the meaning of the Final Solution was clearly expressed in the presence of Hitler. "On the question of Horthy—what he should do with the Jews after they had been deprived of nearly every kind of livelihood, as he cannot kill them—the Foreign Minister declared that Jews are to be either killed or sent to concentration camps. There is no other way." Hitler raised the stakes. "The Jews did not have even the capability to organize. These are mere parasites." Horthy, he insisted, would have to pursue the same policy that was carried out in Poland. "If the Jews were not willing to work, they were shot, and those who could not work died."[10]

Even though Hitler repeatedly warned the Regent that Jews had to be handled like tuberculosis bacilli, and nations that did not eliminate the Jews were doomed to perish, Horthy's answer—sent in written form a couple of weeks later—was a polite but flat refusal.[11]

Josef Goebbels expressed German dissatisfaction with Hungary quite frankly in his diary: "The Jewish question is being solved least satisfactorily by the Hungarians. The Hungarian state is permeated with Jews, and the Führer did not succeed during his talks with Horthy in convincing the latter of the necessity of more stringent measures."[12]

Germany was receiving substantial support from the right-wing pressure groups in Hungary—among them Minister Sztójay, who transmitted to his government a new demand formulated by Ribbentrop "that the Jews should be interned." According to the Minister, since "the German attitude toward the Jewish question had stiffened and had reached the gravest severity," the Jewish question must be solved to avert German intervention.[13]

At this stage, the Jewish population of Hungary was close to one million (including baptized Jews) and was constantly increasing by the growing number of refugees from neighboring countries. Any report prepared by different German agencies on the domestic situation and the foreign policy of Hungary regarded the Hungarian Jews as "Enemy Number 1," a real threat to Germany's interest in Hungary.[14] Hitler's dissatisfaction was increased further by the constant complaints of the leaders of the neighboring satellite countries. There, the deportation of many of the Jews had already taken place, and they referred constantly to the Hungarian situation whenever they were reluctant to carry out any further deportation. On the other hand, as they regarded Hungary as their principal enemy, they used every opportunity to brand Hungary as a "Jewish-influenced" state.

General Ion Antonescu asserted that "he also doesn't have the slightest confidence in Hungary, because there it is not that the Hungarian people determine the country's history but rather that the politics are made by the Jews. It was like this in the past as it is today and it will remain the same in the future as well" *(er zu Ungarn auch nicht das geringste Vertrauen habe, weil dort nicht das ungarische Volk die Geschichte des Landes bestimme, sondern die Politik von den Juden gemacht werde. Das sei früher wie heute so gewesen und würde auch in Zukunft so bleiben).*[15] It was not very difficult to arouse Hitler's anger at the Hungarians, since as early as July 1941, in a conversation with the Croatian General Eugen Kvaternik, he stated: "When there are no Jews left in Europe, there won't be anybody to impede the collaboration of the European states." As he asserted, "I don't care where the Jews would be transported—to Siberia or to Madagascar—but I would put the same demand to every state, i.e., the demand of deportation. The last state where the Jews would be able to maintain themselves would be Hungary."[16]

Hitler's objections to Hungary's Jewish policy became to well-known that Josef Tiso, Ante Pavelic, and Antonescu took every opportunity either to directly blame Hungary, or to make indirect—allusions against that country's policy.

Monsignor Tiso, in April 1943, openly denounced the Hungarians as being lenient to the Jews. He mentioned that "Hungary was slowly becoming the ghetto of Europe, since all the Jews from the different countries are taking refuge there."

In fact, the obsession with the Final Solution had become a force guiding nearly all of Hitler's actions. And yet one must come to the conclusion that its handling had become a well-honed instrument designed to push Hungary and the Southeast European states ever more into the German orbit—and to keep them there, by a special combination of political, economic, and military pressure from outside and by substantial support given to outright anti-Semitic forces within. The most remarkable evidence that Hitler was using the Jewish question as a mere tool is that the issue was never raised in any high-level negotiations with Bulgarian statesmen, to whom the issue could not have had much political meaning. The number of Jews in the country was insignificant. Undoubtedly, German pressure could not have succeeded in Hungary if Germany had not been strong enough to carry out the occupation of the country on March 19, 1944. All evidence shows that after the occupation of the country, the Germans regarded the implementation of the Final Solution as one of their principal objectives.

They sent Adolf Eichmann and his staff to Hungary, and of course a major part of Hungarian Jews met their deaths in concentration camps.

The instructions to Edmund Veesenmayer stated that a Higher SS and Police Leader would be appointed to his staff to carry out the Final Solution.[17] In Veesenmayer's first report he referred to the radical anti-Jewish legislation of the new Hungarian government as one of the most important indications of its reliability.[18] In early April, Ribbentrop gave direct instructions to Veesenmayer to keep strict eyes on Hungarian legislation and not to allow the Hungarians to include too many exemptions.

"The Foreign Minister regards it as necessary that in the Hungarian Ministry of the Interior the Jewish desk should be controlled, or even conducted, by somebody who is either regarded as reliable by Veesenmayer or, eventually, a direct employee of the *Sicherheitsdienst.*" One can go on with evidence to the effect that upon Veesenmayer's demand, Sztójay made a binding commitment on April 13 to transfer 50,000 Jews to Germany as a labor force.[19] The first report signed by Veesenmayer concerning the first 1,800 Jews who had been deported is dated April 29.[20]

It is not necessary to repeat here the story of the deportation. After the brilliant book by Randolph L. Braham, it is absolutely clear that the mass deportation to Auschwitz started on May 15 and ended on July 10 with the deportation of 437,402 Jews from the Hungarian countryside. It is well-known that the actual work was done by the Hungarians, but still the Germans were very much in control. In Eberhard von Thadden's memo of May 26 it is made abundantly clear that even the master plan for the deportation of the Budapest Jews was elaborated by the Germans.[21] In the middle of June 1944, when—due to different foreign and domestic pressures and the successful landing of the Western Allies in France—Horthy finally gave up his passivity and began to reconsider his attitude toward the handling of the Jewish question, he repeatedly had to face strong German resistance. When Sztójay met Hitler in a kind of introductory visit and transmitted Horthy's request to the Führer to restore Hungarian sovereignty, the answer was sharp: not until the Jewish question had been totally solved in Hungary.[22] Meanwhile, Horthy increasingly came to the conclusion that the Jewish question had been handled contrary to the country's interests. In time, Horthy also received a memo from Count István Bethlen, who was in hiding, and who urged Horthy to establish a new government.[23] Bethlen urged Horthy "to put an end to the inhuman, stupid, and cruel persecution of the Jews, which does not behoove the Hungarian character, but with which the current government has besmirched the Hungarian name before the eyes of the world and which has given rise to the most loathsome corruption, robberies, and thieveries, into which, unfortunately, a considerable part of the Hungarian intelligentsia is also drawn. It will hardly be possible to erase this stain from our good reputation, but these barbarities must be put to an end because, otherwise, Hungarian-Christian society itself will become incurably infected."[24]

Since international pressure on Horthy had intensified during the last days of June, he convened a Crown Council meeting on June 26. The result of the two-day meeting—was the dismissal of Laszló Baky and László Endre, the two leading figures of the deportation, from their positions, but Horthy took no decisive stand to end the deportations themselves. Veesenmayer first took notice of Horthy's intervention in his report of June 30, but he was still sure that Horthy's objection could be overcome, and it would mean no more than a slight delay in the timetable of the Final Solution.[25] However, a few days later, on July 6, the Regent finally did put a stop to the deportations. Those few days, of course, meant the deportation of some additional 30,000 to 40,000 Jews from the area surrounding the capital. On July 4, Horthy talked with Veesenmeyer and brought up the question of the atrocities and the deportation of the Jews, but he did not yet express his decision to put a halt to the process and was seemingly willing to accept Veesenmayer's argument that the only reason the Gestapo and the Germans were in Hungary was to help Hungary get rid of the Jews.[26] Accordingly, Veesenmayer, in his report of July 7, proudly stated that the deportation of the Jews from Zone V was ending, but the action against Budapest (Zone I) was only temporarily suspended. During the following days, Sztójay continued to haggle for concessions from the Germans concerning converted and Christian Jews. "I did not leave him any doubt," said Veesenmayer, "that the Reich insists on the unconditional and earliest possible execution of the Budapest action."[27]

On July 6, however, Veesenmayer was summoned to Horthy, who informed him that he was willing to make a stronger stand concerning the further deportation of the Jews. But the overconfident Plenipotentiary did not yet feel the danger, particularly after having spoken with Andor Jaross, the Minister of the Interior, who told him that he was willing to go on with the deportation—if necessary even against the wishes of the Regent. "I don't see any reason for being concerned," reported Veesenmayer on July 9,[28] but actually during the next days when he put these comments in writing he noted that, with the action against the area surrounding the capital, the deportation of the Jews from the countryside, and the removal of 437,404 people, the matter could be regarded as closed, though he was unable to provide any further information concerning Budapest. During the next couple of days he worked hard to impede the formation of a new military government proposed by the Regent. He wrote that, "The composition of this cabinet would mean the final halt to the deportation of the Jews."[29] So on July 17, Veesenmayer, using extremely harsh language, presented a démarche from Hitler, in which the Führer requested again that the Hungarian government finish without any further delay the measures against the Budapest Jews. By mid-July, however, Horthy was willing to yield to the German pressure concerning the eventual formation of the new government, but he was not willing to make any further concessions concerning the deportations. Even if the issue was far from being regarded as closed, the only group which was deported from the country during the summer was the one in the Kistarcsa internment camp, where the Germans with their Hungarian henchmen successfully smuggled out 1,220 more Jewish prisoners.

And still, could it all have been done without Hungarian collaboration, without the active support of the Hungarian gendarmerie, and a large part of the executive system, without deep-rooted traditional anti-Semitism in a large segment of the Hungarian population? After the German occupation of the country, which indicated that one of its main goals was "to solve the Jewish question," all the demands—formerly rejected—were fulfilled. On April 5, the wearing of the Yellow Star had already been introduced, Jews were dismissed from their jobs, and they were entirely eliminated from the country's economic and cultural life; then their wealth was confiscated, they were deprived of all human rights, and they were forced to move to the ghettos. And on May 15 the process of deportation was started. Under the leadership of Eichmann's specialists, a few thousand gendarmes, railwaymen, and civil servants carried out, with record speed, the removal of 437,000 Jews from the Hungarian countryside.

Could the German demands have been rejected or sabotaged?

The discussion concerning the meaning and significance of the German occupation is still going on. Some of the participants in the discussion emphasize that by the acceptance of the occupation as a fact, and by the refusal to launch a process of resistance which might have had little hope for success, Horthy was actually able to avoid the worst—namely, that the Germans would have put the Arrow Cross henchmen into power. By keeping his post, Horthy was able to become instrumental in saving 200,000 Budapest Jews from deportation. Other views stress that without the established and continuing power system (besides the changes of the cabinet, only a few hundred top officials were dismissed, some of them even arrested, by the Germans) the Germans would not have been able to carry out the deportation at all. Those German intelligence agents[30] who finally influenced Hitler not to remove Horthy but to work with him further were entirely right:

the Regent's resignation might have created much more difficulty for the Germans than he was able or courageous enough to do by keeping his post.

Of course, the whole issue is not nearly so simple as presented by Helen Fein, according to whom "Hungary was still a self-governing ally of Germany between March and July, 1944." [31] This study aimed at pointing out to what extent the Hungarian government was under constant German pressure concerning the Final Solution, and how Veesenmayer was able to manipulate the issue by connecting the maintenance of this limited self-government with the fulfillment of Hitler's demands concerning the Final Solution. In that sense, the deportation was an important motive for German intervention, or at least, was presented as such. Noncompliance was certainly more dangerous in March than in July or in October, due to radical changes in the military situation. Nevertheless, with all German pressure and eventual Hungarian risk-taking, the process could not be understood if Hungary's ambiguous stand with regard to its Jewish population were not reviewed, and the relatively strong, vehemently anti-Semitic right wing political forces were not taken into consideration as an important part of the game.

Much has been written about the peculiarity of Hungarian Jewry, and its important, almost dominant, role in the country's economic and cultural life: there was a unique combination of a strong assimilation process and a Western type of Jewish social structure with an East European society. [32]

Up to the First World War the process of assimilation of a large majority of Hungarian Jews was regarded as a successful case. The relatively liberal Hungary—was open enough to accept and welcome this assimilation process. Assimilation was a free choice before 1914, although social motivation played an extremely important role and also allowed the maintenance of some existing commitments and loyalties. The great majority of the Jews became consciously Hungarian, and this new identity gradually became more and more decisive. The old tradition partly survived as far as it belonged to the old community, maintaining mostly religious observances, although even religion slowly became secondary. In fact, in 1910, 77 percent of the Hungarian Jews called themselves Hungarian.

Although on the Trianon frontier of Hungary the Jewish population was to a great extent even more assimilated, even more urban middle class, the contradiction in the socioeconomic processes in Hungary, the shock of the revolutions, and the collapse of historical Hungary—with the loss of two-thirds of its former territory—created the emergence of a strong anti-Semitic movement in the country as early as 1919. [33] The atrocities connected with the white terror were over in 1920, and although one of the first anti-Semitic measures—the *Numerus Clausus*—survived, a large part of the Jews thought—along with the whole world—that they were on the road back to normality. Anti-Semitism, however, remained dominant in the country and the process of assimilation (seemingly so successful before the war) was stopped. But still the great majority of Hungarian Jews—in sharp contrast to their Polish and Romanian counterparts—regarded themselves as Hungarians. The Hungarian Jews identified themselves with the Hungarian nation, even if a significant part of the Hungarian nation no longer wanted this identification. And a part of the Hungarians worked directly against letting the Jews become an organic part of Hungarian society and aimed to deepen the gulf between the Hungarians and the Hungarian Jews. The social and economic motivation was too obvious in this activity, even if sometimes it was wrapped in an ideological parcel. The process of creating anti-Jewish sentiment was successful—but only partly—before Hitler came to power. The particular role of the Germans had been that they were successful in widening the existing fissure until it became a canyon. An image was created, particularly between 1938 and 1941, that the Germans supported the Hungarian national goals, the revision of the Trianon Peace Treaty, the menace of Bolshevism, while at the same time they disliked, hated, and persecuted the Jews. In that sense, Hungarian interest and Jewish interest became increasingly separated. To understand why the Jews became second-class citizens in Hungary long before 1944, this has to be taken into consideration. But with all the discrimination and humiliation for some of the lower middle class Jews, particularly as a result from the rest of the population, as Hannah Arendt pointed out in her book.

It is interesting to speculate about how long it takes someone to overcome his innate repugnance toward crime, and what exactly happens when he does so.[34] Certainly, as the Endres and Bakys and their supporters proved, a significant number of Hungarians reached this point in 1944. Still the argument of Helen Fein, that "almost two-thirds of the processing of Jews toward their destination—definition and stripping—occurred in Hungary before the German occupation in 1944" has to be doubted very strongly. It is true that anti-Semitism is to be regarded as "the mentality of the canaille" (T. Mommsen), but to say that anti-Semitism *automatically* led to the Final Solution is a gross oversimplification. It is well-known that anti-Semitic "infection" occurred in Hungary, as in other countries. Of course, the Jewish–Gentile relationship was also a function of socioeconomic or political situations in the country. Some disliked Jews for their conformity to family tradition, or just for being different. Others discovered reasons in biological speculation; still others—because of the Jewish role in big business in Hungary—found anti-Semitic arguments in social dislocation or economic misery. Radical anti-Semites saw Jews as a bulwark of capitalism. Conservatives saw them as a rootless people, or a leading agent of social turmoil or revolution. The growing animosity toward the Jews in the country greatly facilitated the implementation of Hitler's Final Solution.

Though strong anti-Semitic traditions played into German hands, they were also reinforced by the passivity of a large part of the population, and by some mistakes in the policy of Kállay's government. The Kállay government refused to collaborate in the Final Solution, while it was not willing or courageous enough to stop the strong anti-Semitic propaganda. Even if we accept István Deák's frightening conclusion that Kállay was given the chance to ensure the survival of the Jews, provided he remained loyal to the Germans, the question is wrongly formulated. Had Kállay been more loyal to the Germans, he would have certainly had to comply with the German demands and would have sold out the Jews much earlier, as substantial pressure was put on him from his domestic opposition for this purpose. Kállay was able to protect the Jews insofar as he was not loyal to the Germans and—recognizing his genuine humanistic feeling—he regarded the saving of the Jews as evidence of his own disloyalty; or to look at the issue in reverse, as proof of his loyalty to the Allies. In this sense the survival of the Jews was supposed to serve as an alibi for Hungarian policies. It was a sign that Hungary still preserved a residue of liberal values and was keeping an eye to the future as well, an argument which could have been used during the peace negotiations. Did Kállay risk his achievements by his policy of peace feelers, or by his preparations to pull out of the war? Can we blame him for not remaining "a militarily passive but politically vocal ally of the Third Reich," [35] because in that case "the Jews of Hungary might possibly have survived the war relatively unscathed?"

This author would argue with this assumption from two different perspectives: (1) The role and survival of the Jews might have been an important part of Hungarian politics; nevertheless, there were other considerations in the shaping of Hungarian foreign policy. For the future of the nation, it was not immaterial on which side Hungary would be found at the end of the war. If the Hungarian Jews were to be regarded as a part of the nation, then even the Jews were not indifferent to Hungary's future. If they were merely a special-interest group, then these interests had to come to terms with the country's general interests as well, particularly since—if such was the case—Kállay's defense of the Jews might have been nothing more than a purely humanitarian action. (2) The military situation would have forced Germany to take over Hungary, even without Kállay's attempt to pull out of the war. In that case, the chances of survival might have been so much better that organized deportation might not have been possible. But because of the strategic situation of Hungary, one cannot assume that this military occupation would have occurred for such a short period as in Romania or in Bulgaria. A large amount of persecution or destruction was almost unavoidable under the given circumstances, unless the Jews had been prepared and organized to defend themselves, or unless a well-run Hungarian resistance—organized either from above or from below—had been able to defend and collaborate with the self-defense of the Jewish population. The situation was not present either for the first or for the second option.

Was the peculiar Jewish–Magyar relation then mere illusion? In looking back, one may be very critical. Some might defend the process of assimilation, while others would condemn it, looking at it as having been doomed to failure from the beginning. To come up with the proper, well-founded answer, a large amount of research is still needed. Whether the dilemma of assimilation really existed or was mere hindsight is still open to question. Nevertheless, the whole question cannot be properly answered by the mere study of Hungarian Jewish history, or even Hungarian or Austro-Hungarian history.

The answer—if there is an answer at all which does not transcend human understanding—probably can be found in German history. Since Hitler never made any proper distinction between the Jews who were entirely assimilated or acculturated and those who were still very traditional, does it mean that the destruction was grounded in the German past? Yes and no. Yes, insofar as it was a result of trends of the German past. No, in that we cannot assume that it was the only fruit of the German tree. (Even less was it the only fruit of the Hungarian tree.) The Final Solution was more of a German invention—an invention in an age when politics had become the means not of regulating society for the common good, but of coercing it into submission.[36] How traditional or modern anti-Semitism was changed to a systematic war against the Jews in the Final Solution, how a program of extermination could have been elaborated, completed, and perfected cannot be understood properly except by studying German National-Socialism—by the study of a system and its metaphysical program, envisaging the attainment of Heaven, by bringing Hell to Earth.

Notes

1. *Deutsches Zentralarchiv,* Potsdam. Auswärtiges Amt, Abt. 11 41288.

2. Nicholas (Miklós) Kállay, *Hungarian Premier. A Personal Account of a Nation's Struggle in the Second World War.* New York: Columbia University Press, 1954, p. 70.

3. Randolph L. Braham, *The Destruction of Hungarian Jewry. A Documentary Account.* New York: World Federation of Hungarian Jews, i963, pp. XIV, 230.

4. *A Wilhelmstrasse és Magyarország. Német diplomáciai iratok Magyarországról, 1933-1944* (The Wilhelmstrasse and Hungary. German Diplomatic Papers About Hungary, 1933-1944). Compiled and edited by György Ránki *et al.* Budapest: Kossuth, 1968. p. 660.

5. *Ibid.,* p. 695.

6. *Ibid.,* p. 699.

7. Kállay, *Hungarian Premier,* p. 123.

8. *A Wilhelmstrasse és Magyarország, p. 701.*

9. *C. A. Macartney, October Fifteenth. A History of Modern Hungary, 1929-1945.* Edinburgh: Edinburgh University Press, 1957, 2 vols. See also Gyula Juhász, *Magyarország külpolitikája, 1919-1945* (Hungary's Foreign Policy, 1919-1945). Budapest: Kossuth, 1969, 374 p. Also available in an English translation by Sándor Simon, *Hungarian Foreign Policy, 1919-1945.* Budapest: Akadémiai Kiadó, 1969, 374 p.; Mario Fenyo, *Hitler, Horthy, and Hungary. German-Hungarian Relations, 1941-1944.* New Haven: Yale University Press, 1972, 279 p. For other references consult *The Hungarian Jewish Catastrophe. A Selected and Annotated Bibliography.* Compiled and edited by Randolph L. Braham. New York: Social Science Monographs and the Institute for Holocaust Studies, 1984, 521 p. (Distributed by Columbia University Press.)

10. *Staatsmänner und Diplomaten bei Hitler.* Edited by A. Hillgruber. Frankfurt/Main: Bernard & Graef, 1970, pp. 238-259.

11. *Horthy Miklós titkos iratai* (The Confidential Papers of Miklós Horthy). Edited by Miklós Szinai and László Szücs. Budapest: Kossuth, 1963, pp. 373-386.

12. *The Goebbels Diaries, 1942-1943.* Edited by Louis M. Lochner. Garden City, N.Y.: Doubleday, 1948, p. 357.

13. Randolph L. Braham, *The Politics of Genocide. The Holocaust in Hungary.* New York: Columbia University Press, 1981, p. 243.

14. *A Wilhelmstrasse és Magyarország,* p. 745.

15. György Ránki, "Hitler and the Statesmen of East Central Europe." *In: Society in Change.* Edited by Steven B. Vardy and Ágnes H. Várdy. Boulder, Col.: East European Monographs, 1983, p. 661.

16. *Staatsmänner und Diplomaten bei Hitler, op. cit.*

17. *Magyarország és a második világháború (Hungary and the Second World).* Edited by László Zsigmond *et al.* Budapest: Kossuth, 1961, pp. 443-447.

18. *A Wilhelmstrasse és Magyarország,* p. 818.

19. The Jews were envisioned to become part of a *Jägerstab* Project. See Albert Speer, *Inside the Third Reich.* New York: Macmillan, 1970, p. 395.

20. *A Wilhelmstrasse és Magyarország, p. 837.*

21. Ibid., p. 854.

22. *Horthy Miklós titkos iratai,* pp. 444-449.

23. *Ibid.,* p. 454.

24. *Ibid.*

25. *A Wilhelmstrasse és Magyarország,* p. 872.

26. *Ibid.,* p. 876.

27. *Ibid.,* p. 878.

28. *Ibid.,* p. 880.

29. *Ibid.,* p. 883.

30. *Magyarország és a második világháború,* pp. 443-448.

31. Genocide in Hungary: An Exchange. *New York Review of Books,* May 27, 1982.

32. Péter Hanák, A lezáratlan per (The Unfinished Trial). *Jelenkor* (Contemporary Times), Budapest, May 1983; Viktor Karády and István Kemény, Les juifs dans la structure des classes en Hongrie. *Actes de la Recherche en Sciences Sociales,* Paris, no. 22, June 1978: 25-29; Jacob Katz, The Uniqueness of Hungarian Jewry. *Forum,* Jerusalem, no. 2(27), 1977: 45-53.

33. *Magyarország története, 1918-1945* (History of Hungary, 1918-1945). Vol. 8. Edited by György Ránki. Budapest: Akadémiai Kiadó, 1976.

34. Hannah Arendt, *Eichmann in Jerusalem.* New York: Viking, 1963, p. 87.

35. Braham, *The Politics of Genocide,* p. 226.

36. Peter Gay, *Freud, Jews and Other Germans.* New York: Oxford University Press, 1978, p. 9.

Chapter 7

THE HUNGARIANS AND THE DESTRUCTION
OF THE HUNGARIAN JEWS

Bela Vago

Among the Hungarian Christian clergy who had the honesty and the courage to oppose the Nazis was the Reverend Albert Bereczky. He became a bishop of the Reformed Church after the Liberation and wrote the following words in 1945:

> All that the past Hungarian regime has done against the Jews, and thus also against God's eternal law, must be condemned without any reservation by every true Hungarian and Christian, and they must be penitent for all that was done . . . albeit against their will but in their name and in their presence.[1]

What was in fact done by the Hungarians? What were the deeds so dramatically deplored by Reverend Bereczky? Some thirty years after Bereczky's pamphlet appeared, György Száraz, the eminent Hungarian writer belonging to the second generation of the postwar Hungarian intelligentsia, wrote as follows:

> How should one write about 1944? With passion, which tears up the wounds, or with careful tactfulness? With the passion of the literati, or in objective, dry sentences? With the horror of the contemporary, with the guilt-feeling of the unwilling accomplice, or with the cool calmness of the innocents? In fact, all of us were involved with [the events of 1944]. The onlookers, because they witnessed, the hangmen, because they were hangmen, the victims, because they were victims. All of us were involved in it: the survivors, the eyewitnesses, those who were born

later and those who will be born, because all that happened then is indeed already Hungarian history.[2]

This basic idea is emphasized in an autobiographical novel of a survivor of the Holocaust, Mária Ember, who asserts that the subject of her book is not the *Jewish* fate, but Hungarian history.[3]

These quotations necessarily raise the much-debated question of how the responsibility for the Hungarian Jewish tragedy should be divided between the German Nazis and the Hungarians—not only the different governments during the Second World War, but also the Hungarian society and people as a whole.

During the first two or three postwar decades historical interest was focused on Hitler's Germany, and the blame for the annihilation of Hungarian Jewry was put mainly on the Germans rather than on their Hungarian henchmen. For obvious reasons the Hungarian historiography continues to follow this pattern.

Before proceeding, two assertions are in order:

1. Hungarian public opinion—to use a Pavlovian expression—was conditioned to the humiliation, persecution, segregation, and finally to the physical annihilation of the Jews by systematic indoctrination of extreme anti-Jewish propaganda during a quarter of a century and exacerbated during the Second World War;

2. Although the major catastrophe occurred only after the German occupation of the country, and—in the view of this author, the mass-deportation would not have been realized without the fateful event of March 19, 1944—all that happened in the country after that day was perpetrated not only with Hungarian connivance, but mainly by Hungarians who zealously exploited the new opportunities, and partly took over the initiative for the de-Jewification and the deportation. This policy was supported by the majority of the Hungarian people. Without this willingness, collaboration and local initiatives, the German occupation itself could not have led to the destruction of Hungarian Jewry.

The existence of the Nazi type, racist anti-Semitism in Hungary is well known, requiring no further documentation. However, one must emphasise that the so-called *moderate* anti-Semitic public opinion was poisoned too by anti-Jewish prejudices, characterized by intolerance, arrogance, humiliating disdain, and aimed at the *Entjudung* (dejewification) of the country, short only of physical destruction.

Just a few examples will suffice about the blind and irrational hatred against the Jews by some people considered as moderate. The much respected Count Pál Teleki, Hungary's conservative Prime Minister driven to suicide in the spring of 1941 by the Germans pressuring him to attack Yugoslavia, in his peculiar way had opposed Nazi Germany and mainly the Nazi conquest of Hungary. Yet he was himself the prototypical irrational anti-Semite. In 1939 he conceded that in the struggle against the most dangerous enemy the Hungarians ever had in their history, namely the Jews, one was not entitled to play with rational elements, and he foresaw, that unless a rapid operation was carried out, wrenching out the Jews from the body of the Hungarian people, the life of his people would be at stake.[4]

Admiral Miklós Horthy, the Regent of Hungary, who was not instrumental in the deportation of the Jews from the provinces, and even played a positive role in halting the deportation from the capital early in July 1944, used to label the Jews as *microbes* bent on destroying the Hungarian people. Amazingly enough, his son Miklós, Jr., one of the key figures in the secret preparations for the extrication of Hungary from Hitler's war, and who maintained secret contacts with Jewish personalities for the same aim, confessed in the summer of 1944 to one of the Jewish leaders that he had been an anti-Semite since his birth and even by virtue of his education.[5] And Miklós Kállay, Hungary's Prime Minister in 1942–44, a reasonable man and far from being a rabid anti-Semite, used to promote an unfortunate policy versus the Jews with disastrous consequences; in order to improve his image in Berlin and also to appease his extreme-rightist rivals in the country, he often used to boast of his ultimate goal: to free Hungary of the Jews.

Subjectively Kállay did not contemplate the destruction of the Jews, but objectively he contributed to the anti-Jewish mass hysteria which had reigned in Hungary before the German occupation. Although Kállay managed to oppose the German demands for the deportation, his tactics could not have been understood by the man in the street; on the contrary, his concessions to anti-Semitism and his anti-Jewish statements contributed to the readiness of the Hungarian public opinion to accept and even support the ghettoization and deportation.[6]

When the German troops crossed the Austrian border and Eichmann arrived in Budapest, the Horthy regime had already taken the first steps on the way leading to the Final Solution—at least psychologically, and to a certain extent in fact. The anti-Jewish legislation of the 1941–43 period equalled the Nuremberg laws; the systematic pauperization of the Jewish masses created unsolvable problems, the forced labor system enslaved almost 100,000 men and had claimed tens of thousands of victims. The so-called

Kamenets Podolsk deportations cost at least 15,000 Jewish lives in 1941, and although the Ujvidék massacres in January 1942 were not condoned by the Hungarian government (and were even condemned later by Kallay's administration), the criminals were acting in accord with the prevailing political atmosphere, and with the generally accepted moral standards.[7]

The overwhelming majority of the Hungarian press supported the war on the Eastern front with all its anti-Jewish concomitants. The Hungarian counterpart of the Nazi *Signal* was called *Magyar Futár* (The Hungarian Courier). It was an important vehicle for molding the pro-Axis mood and it serialized a popular anti-Semitic column inciting against the Jews in a *Stürmer*-like tone. It sold half a million copies in a country of 13 million.

No noteworthy resistance movement came into being in Hungary, neither after Mussolini's downfall in the summer of 1943, nor after the German occupation. Although hesitant and amateurish, secret peace feelers were put out during Kállay's premiership, and then again in the months preceding the coup by Ferenc Szálasi on October 15, 1944,[8] public opinion strongly supported Hitler at least until the summer months of 1944. The absence of any noteworthy resistance, and also the utter failure of Horthy's attempt to extricate Hungary from Hitler's war on October 15, only underscore the infatuation of the ruling forces, supported by the masses, with the Nazi policies. The German occupation, in spite of its catastrophic consequences, did not bring about any dramatic political change in public opinion, although the Nazi military presence and the Sztojay rule may have radicalized more people. In fact on March 19, 1944, the psychology of Hungary was well prepared for a smooth and rapid implementation of the *Entjudung*—and as a matter of fact of the *Endlösung* (the Final Solution).

Regarding the devastating share of the Hungarians in all that happened after the German occupation, suffice it to cite a few random examples. From the outset, it should be emphasized that few Hungarians realized the far-reaching significance of the ghettoization and deportation, and of course not every Hungarian applauded the dejewification; thousands of Hungarians risked their freedom by hiding Jewish property, and quite a few of them were ready to hide Jewish persons, or actually rescued them. However, these were mere exceptions; the great majority approved—actively or tacitly—of the measures, although few could have been aware of the ultimate fate of the Jews.

The attitude of the Sztójay administration and then of the Szálasi regime is well known. This study will therefore limit itself to a few examples, proving the dominant role of the Hungarians in carrying out the Nazi deportation plans—a role in which public opinion played a major part.

The first group of Gestapo men, led by Alfred Trenker, who were in charge of silencing the Kállay government were a mere 33. Eichmann arrived with 10 to 12 officers, and Kaltenbrunner's policemen numbered only a few hundred men. The *Wehrmacht* was not directly involved in the Final Solution. Eichmann was not empowered to give direct instructions to any Hungarian authority, and it was agreed from the beginning that the deportation would be carried out by the Hungarian gendarmerie. Although policy after March 19, 1944, was suggested and directed by the Nazis, the methods and details were worked out by the local authorities, and the instructions were sent to the different organs mainly by the Under-Secretaries of State in the Ministry of Internal Affairs, and also by a few other Ministries (e.g., the Ministry of Industry and Commerce, and the Ministry of Finance). Many years after the war, Wilhelm Höttl, the central figure of the Nazi intelligence in Budapest and one of those who were in permanent contact with the leading Germans in Hungary, contended that some of the Hungarians were more fanatical in carrying out the anti-Jewish measures than Eichmann.[9] (He was obviously exaggerating, yet his assertion was characteristic of how the Nazis evaluated the Hungarian readiness to cooperate with them.) Hermann Krumey—a leading figure of the Eichmann-*Sonderkommahdo*—could tell with some satisfaction to János Gábor, one of the members of the Budapest *Judenrat* (Jewish Council), that the Hungarian gendarmes were carrying out their work with genuine "Asian" brutality.[10] During the first years of the German occupation of Holland, 350 denunciations against hidden Jews and Jewish property reached the Nazi rulers; in Budapest, during the first eight days of the occupation, the Nazis were bombarded with some 30,000 denunciations, and this number probably increased to 35,000 by the end of the spring.[11]

One should recall that the highlight of the campaign for the uprooting of what was labeled as the nefarious Jewish cultural influence was the festive destruction of books written by Jews and democratic authors. Symbolically the State Secretary Mihály Kolosváry-Borcsa, the spiritual father of the cultural *Entjudung,* started the destruction by destroying a volume of poems by the eminent romantic Jewish poet József Kiss.[12]

The administration of the ghettoes was a purely Hungarian matter, although one cannot overlook the fact that Eichmann and other SS and Nazi police officers, as well as the staff of the German Legation in Budapest were in constant touch with the Hungarian authorities, overseeing not only the ghettoization but also the deportation process. The sanitary and living conditions in the ghettoes were subhuman. Because of the brutal behavior of the gendarmerie and the sadism of the civilians in charge of the concentration, spoliation and tortures, presumably in most of the ghettoes, the lives of some inmates were spared only by their relatively rapid dispatch to Auschwitz! Thousands of people who had to face, virtually under starvation, the vicissitudes of the rainy, cool spring in the open and overcrowded ghettoes could not have survived for months under those conditions. Many Jews could not bear the humiliation, the spoliation and the tortures; the number of suicides or deaths caused by depression was considerable.

The trauma of the Jewish masses was devastating, and their unpreparedness was total; this occurred in spite of the anti-Jewish legislation started in 1938, and despite the terrible news about the fate of the Jews in Nazi-occupied Europe, because of the loyalty, and the identification of the majority of the Jews with the Hungarian ethos.

In the days after the inauguration of the Sztójay government and before ghettoization, the stigmatized Jews were shunned by their gentile acquaintances. Testimony to this effect was given, among others by Noémi Munkácsi, a noted Jewish writer.[13] Whenever humane gentiles were found trying to help, they were called to task by the authorities and branded as traitors. In some cases pictures were taken of such gentiles as evidence of their disgrace and guilt. Before the deportations from the provinces, and in Budapest during the whole post-March period, the building superintendents were the symbol of denunciation. Regrettably the bulk of the so-called lower classes and even working-class elements joined the traditionally anti-Semitic middle and upper classes in cheering the Nazi-type campaign and measures.

Zoltán Bosnyák, the head of the Nazi-type Hungarian Institute for the Researching of the Jewish Question (A Zsidókérdést Kutató Magyar Intézet), was fully conscious of the significance of his words, when he promised (May 1944) to the soldiers fighting on the Eastern front that they would return home to a clean, Jewless Hungary.[14]

Bosnyák asked the Hungarian society to consider as its duty the silencing of those who sporadically raised their voices against the anti-Jewish measures.[15] In his view the deportation heralded a new, better, and happier future.[16] There is no doubt that he represented the opinion of those in power, and was supported by the majority of the nation. With reference to terms like "majority," "nation," and "public opinion" one must be aware that one cannot measure the weight of these notions by scientific means, and we lack reliable figures expressing public opinion in 1944. Still, one can rely on the testimony of thousands of eyewitnesses and on the personal recollections of scholars belonging to the post-Holocaust generation. One can confidentially affirm that, even to a greater extent than in Germany in the late thirties, the anti-Semitic propaganda had a strong effect in Hungary, and that the society as a whole supported this propaganda—until the final days of the war. As early as ten days after the occupation, Edmund Veesenmayer, Hitler's personal Plenipotentiary in Budapest, praised the new Hungarian government for its "serious approach" to the Nazi solution of the Jewish question, and for the unusual speed with which it had started to carry out this solution.[17]

At the beginning of July 1944, Horthy, ostensibly shocked by the news that reached him about the ghettoization and deportation, wrote a confidential letter to Prime Minister Sztójay, expressing his dismay and consternation at the "brutality" and "inhumanity" of the Hungarians, which he thought surpassed in cruelty even the treatment of the German Jews at the hands of the Nazis themselves. He bluntly put the responsibility for these deeds on the shoulders of the Sztójay government.[18]

The following episode is indicative of the climate that prevailed at the time: When in the first days of the Sztójay regíme a gang robbed and killed two Jewish women, and the judicial authorities, still curtailing such individual criminal acts, sentenced the leader of the gang to death, the criminal addressed the judge with these words: "We were only carrying out the government's intentions, and therefore we deserve recognition and to be decorated." '[19]

About the cynicism of the Sztójay government, one single example: when Gennaro Verolino, the secretary of Angelo Rotta, the Papal Nuncio in Budapest, asked what was the meaning of the expulsion of children, women, and elderly people—if the deportation indeed meant the providing of manpower for the Germans—the answer was that the government realized that the Jews preferred to be sent to "work" accompanied by the members of their families.[20]

Among the many atrocities committed against the forced labor servicemen by the mob in 1944 and even on the eve of the October 15 coup—that is, in a period when there were some chances for the extrication of Hungary from the Nazi war—the following characteristic episode is worthy of special mention: On October 11, a train arrived at Kiskúnhalas carrying forced labor servicemen evacuated from Újvidék. The train was attacked by SS men with hand grenades. When the massacre started, Hungarian *Honvéd* (soldiers) and railway workers joined the few Germans, killed the Jewish labor servicemen, mutilated their corpses, and left the bodies naked in the railway station after chopping off fingers which carried gold rings, and extracting the gold teeth by crushing the victims' faces. No one among the onlookers in the crowded station tried to intervene; as a later report commented, "all the bestial instincts in the human being burst out at the Kiskunhalas railway station."[21]

Perhaps there is no need to dwell on the behavior of the *Nyilas* (Arrow Cross) mob after October 15, but a few examples bearing out the attitude of both the leading personalities (not necessarily *Nvilas*) and the common people would be illuminating. (The wholehearted support of the Nazi trend decreased to some extent after the *Nyilas* ascension to power.)

General Iván Hindy, to whom Professor C. A. Macartney regrettably dedicated his well-known *October Fifteenth,* deplored on October 15 that Horthy was surrounded by a criminal Jew-ridden clique until his downfall.[22] Most of the staff officers followed Szálasi, and political personalities not belonging to the *Nyilas* were ready to serve the puppet regime and the idea of a phantom national unity at a time when the Eastern part of Hungary was already liberated, and when no sane person could doubt the outcome of the war. The Donau-Sender, the Nazi radio, still emitted hysterical anti-Jewish invectives in Hungarian at a time when Nazi Hungary was already nonexistent. (Actually the Hungarians were the last loyal Nazi collaborators, excepting a handful of Croatian Ustashi, and perhaps an insignificant Slovak group.)

One more recollection proving the extent to which the so-called elite of the Hungarian administration was indoctrinated: on November 7, 1944, Hannah Szenes—the Palestinian parachutist—was executed in Budapest; on that day the members of the judicial forum in charge of her trial had already fled from Budapest, and only one young judge had remained behind—a Captain boasting of a Ph.D. degree. He alone was *not* entitled to sentence Senesh; however, he considered it his patriotic duty to send her to death only hours before he too fled from Budapest. Half an hour after the execution he personally informed Senesh's mother about the murder.[23]

Finally, a few remarks about the controversial role of the powerful and influential Christian Churches in the Hungarian-Jewish Holocaust are in order. Some of the leading clergymen excelled in trying to halt the disaster. Above all the name of Baron Vilmos Apor, the Catholic Archbishop of Győr should be remembered. However, the majority of the representatives of the high-ranking clergy of the Catholics and the Protestants, and without doubt the overwhelming majority of the rest of the clergy, were passive onlookers, and quite a few of them cheered the ghettoization and deportation. Thus, for example, clergymen in Szeged, requested by the Jews to lend a helping hand, refused to intercede with the authorities.[24] The two bishops, the Catholic canon, and the lay leader of the local Catholic community in Nyíregyháza argued that they were powerless to do anything for the rescue of Christ's killers.[25] Strangely enough, almost the same argument was brought up by Bishop László Ravasz of the Reformed Church, although he intervened with

Horthy against the anti-Jewish measures in the spring and summer of 1944.[26] Cardinal Jusztinián Serédi of the Catholic Church, who was also worried because of the consequences of the extreme anti-Jewish steps, and had intervened on behalf of the baptized Jews, had conceded some years before that "a number of Jews indeed exerted a destructive influence on Hungary's economic, social, and moral life."'[27] Such assertions were interpreted as the legitimization of all that followed Sztójay's takeover, despite certain moderating warnings of the Church leaders. In Veszprém, a Mass and Te Deum was held in thanksgiving for the liberation of the city from the Jews— although Cardinal József Mindszenty, at that time the Bishop of Veszprém, claimed later that he had forbidden the Guardian of the Franciscans, approached by the *Nyilas,* to say the Mass.[28]

This is not to imply that the Christian Churches condoned the deportation and the physical annihilation of the Jewish population (although some clergymen, as for example the notorious Father András Kun, acted as a common criminal); what must be emphasized is the lack of willingness to help and rescue, the scarcity of courageous protests, and their indisputable contribution to the creation of an anti-Semitic atmosphere propitious for the implementation of the ghettoization and deportation.

Finally, one must react to the two often-voiced apologetic rationalizations of the Hungarian role in the Holocaust: one relates to the impossibility that the Hungarians could have opposed any Nazi *diktat* after March 19; the other is based on the Communist assumption that there are no bad people, only bad leaders—that is, the ruling class and the ruling forces were indeed guilty, but the people itself should be absolved.

As to the first thesis, one may recall the Bulgarian example, and the somehow less unequivocal Romanian attitude. The Bulgarian governments, most of the representatives in the *Sobranie,* the most influential intellectuals, and most leading personalities of the Orthodox Church, jointly succeeded in counteracting the German pressure for the deportation. The Germans, in spite of their military presence in Bulgaria, for pragmatic reasons decided to bow before the Bulgarian determination and to content themselves with the deportation of the "alien" Jews from the Yugoslav and Greek territories occupied by the Bulgarians in the spring of 1941. Romania was under strong Nazi pressure from 1942 to deport its Jews. Although Marshal Ion Antonescu sacrificed the majority of the Jews in Bessarabia and Northern Bukovina, his regime's resolutely courageous rejection of the German demands contributed to the rescue of the overwhelming majority of the Jews in the Old Kingdom and in Southern Transylvania. These two examples prove that irrespective of the character of the political regime in the different countries of Nazi Europe, the fate of the Jews was determined by the willingness of the local population to collaborate with the Nazis or to oppose their *diktat,* and thus salvage part of their independence and honor too. Both examples support the contention that the Nazi plans to annihilate the Jews of the satellite countries were *decisively* influenced by the readiness or refusal of both the local regimes and population to cooperate with the Nazis.

In Hungary, had there been a stalemate and a lack of alternative to Kállay's government, the tragedy would not have occurred. With some reticence one may refer to Veesenmayer, who at the Nuremberg trials testified that in case of a resolute Hungarian refusal the German demand for the Final Solution would not have been implemented at all; on the contrary, Veesenmayer contended, the implementation was made possible only by the wholehearted collaboration of the Hungarian government and the administrative apparatus.[29] Although the objective conditions were indeed unfavorable for a military opposition to the occupation, they were undoubtedly favorable for opposing the German *diktat.* But reality was absolutely different: the extreme Right-wing of the ruling Hungarian Life Party (*Magyar Élet Pártja*—MÉP), the strong *Nyilas* camp, the Imrédy movement, the army, the administrative apparatus, and many other social and political forces were over-zealous to strengthen the Nazi alliance and to implement the Final Solution with lightning speed at the last moment, when the Soviet front had already reached the Carpathians.

Regarding the Communist distinction made between good people and bad leaders, one may recall the words of the late Károly Balla, a Transylvanian writer. Attending a trial of war criminals in 1946 in Cluj (Kolozsvár), where exoneration of the man in the street was the guideline, Balla exclaimed:

> Please tell me where . . . the notion of "Hungarian people" ends, and where the "hordes of Hungarian Fascists" starts. This question torments me because here I fear a terrible mystification and here I suspect that I am going to be misled again, exactly as before, when we were driven into the ghetto by lies, then put into cattlecars and sent to the gas chambers. Let us not allow ourselves to be deceived again, and let us reject the illusions created by the tales we are being fed on. If we swallow these tales once more, we shall again pay a heavy price for doing so.[30]

The line between the elite and the men in the street was nonexistent, or in any case invisible in wartime Hungary. Such a division of responsibility and guilt is impossible.

Finally, one may recall Janusz Korczak's often quoted words: "Those who fled before history, ultimately will be caught up by history." It is clear that people must face their own history—the confrontation is unavoidable. One would wish only that Jewish endeavors to demystify and dissipate myths, and to restore historical truth and accuracy, would be shared by Hungarians today.

Notes

1. Albert Bereczky, A magyar protestantizmus a zsidóüldözés ellen (Hungarian Protestantism Against the Persecution of the Jews). Budapest: Református Traktatus Vállalat, 1945, p. 3.

2. György Száraz, Egy előítélet nyomában (Tracing a Prejudice). Budapest: Magvető, 1976, p. 6.

3. Mária Ember, Hajtűkanyar (Hairpin Bend). Budapest: Szépirodalmi Könyvkiadó, 1974.

4. Béla Vágó, The Shadow of the Swastica. The Rise of Fascism and Anti-Semitism in the Danube Basin, 1936-1939. London: Saxone House—D.C. Heath, 1975, pp. 396-397 (Doc. No. 150).

5. -- --, "Budapest Jewry in the Summer of 1944. OttóKomoly's Diaries." In: Yad Vashem Studies. Vol. 8. Jerusalem: Yad Vashem, 1970, p. 99.

6. -- --, "Germany and the Jewish Policy of the Kállay Government." In: Hungarian-Jewish Studies. Vol. 2 Edited by Randolph L. Braham. New York: World Federation of Hungarian Jews, 1969, pp. 183-210.

7. For details see Randolph L. Braham, The Politics of Genocide. The Holocaust in Hungary. New York: Columbia University Press, 1981, 2 vols.

8. Between late 1943 and March 1944, some officials of the Hungarian Ministry of Foreign Affairs had—with Kállay's consent and presumably with Horthy's knowledge—low level contacts with the British and, to a lesser extent, with the Americans.

9. Péter Bokor, Végjáték a Duna mentén. Interjúk egy filmsorozathoz (Epilogue Alongside the Danube. Interviews to a Film Series). Budapest: RTV Minerva Kossuth, 1982, p. 192. Höttl, who is better known as Walter Hagen, was an SS-Sturmbannführer. Before his assignment to Budapest, Höttl served as Chief of Section VI of the Reich Security Main Office (Reichssicherheitshauptamt) for Southeastern Europe with headquarters in Vienna.

10. Jenő Lévai, Zsidósors Magyarországon (Jewish Fate in Hungary). Budapest: Magyar Téka, 1948, p. 110. János Gábor had served as the Jewish Council's liaison to the Eichmann-Sonderkommando; he was shot by the Nyilas shortly before the liberation of Budapest.

11. *Ibid.,* p. 83. See also Zoltán Moór, *Die ungarischen Juden im Zweiten Weltkrieg, 1944.* Manuscript, Haifa University, Historical Documentation Center, H3d/10, p. 136.

12. *Magyarság* (Magyardom), Budapest, June 16, 1944: 5.

13. Noémi Munkácsi, A nagykanizsai gettó története (History of the Ghetto of Nagykanizsa). *Hatikva,* Buenos Aires, Sept. 15, 1950.

14. Zoltán Bosnyák, A végső harc orájában (In the Last Hour of the Struggle). *Harc* (Battle), Budapest, May 20, 1944: 1. *Harc* was the official organ of the Hungarian Institute for the Researching of the Jewish Question.

15. *Harc,* June 3, 1944: 1.

16. *Ibid.,* June 17, 1944: 2.

17. Edmund Veesenmayer to Ribbentrop, Budapest, March 31, 1944. For the complete text see Document 614 in *A Wilhelmstrasse és Magyarország. Német diplomáciai iratok Magyarországról, 1933-1944* (The Wilhelmstrasse and Hungary. German Diplomatic Papers About Hungary, 1933-1944). Compiled and edited by György Ránki *et al.* (Budapest: Kossuth, 1968, p. 804.

18. *Ibid.,* p. 870. (Document 687). See also Horthy's communication to Sztójay of early June 1944 in *Horthy Miklós titkos iratai* (The Secret Papers of Miklós Horthy). Compiled and edited by Miklós Szinai and László Szücs. Budapest: Kossuth, 1962, pp. 451-452. (Document 85.) György Ránki concedes that some members of the Sztójay government did more harm than the German demands would have justified. See his *1944. március 19* (March 19, 1944). Budapest: Kossuth, 1978, p. 240.

19. Ernő Munkácsi, *Hogyan történt?* (How Did It Happen?) Budapest: Renaissance, 1947, p. 202.

20. Bokor, *op. cit.,* p. 119.

21. *Halasi Hirek* (News From Halas), Oct. 10, 1945: 2.

22. Bokor, *op. cit.,* p. 345.

23. Mrs. Catherine Szenes to the author. Recorded testimony in the Historical Documentation Center of the University of Haifa.

24. Historical Documentation Center, University of Haifa, H3/h91. Dr. Lipót Löw's testimony, Bogota, May 1960.

25. Sándor Gervai, *Nyíregyháza zsidósága élete* (The Life of Nyíregyháza's Jewry). Jerusalem: The Author, 1963, p. 86.

26. For details on Ravasz's intervention with Horthy (April 1944), see Bereczky, *op. cit.,* p. 15. *Cf.* Jenő Lévai, *Fekete könyv a magyar zsidóság szenvedéseiről (Black Book About the Suffering of Hungarian Jewry).* Budapest: Officina, 1946, pp. 113-114.

27. Lévai, *Zsidósors Magyarországon,* pp. 126-127. (In later years, Lévai published an apologetic work, sympathetic to the Catholic Church. See his *Hungarian Jewry and the Papacy.* London: Sands, 1960.

28. *The Destruction of Hungarian Jewry. A Documentary Account.* Compiled and edited by Randolph L. Braham. New York: World Federation of Hungarian Jews, 1963, Vol. 2, p. 625. (Document 289 dated July 20, 1944). For Cardinal Mindszenty's allegations see his *Memoirs. József Cardinal Mindszenty.* London: Weidenfeld and Nicolson, 1974, pp. 17-18.

29. Lévai, *Fekete könyv a magyar zsidóság szenvedéseiről*, pp. 129-130.

30. Personal communication by Miklós Dános, the writer-journalist, to the author.

Chapter 8

DEPORTATION AND ADMINISTRATION IN HUNGARY

Elek Karsai

The system of administration in operation in Hungary on March 19, 1944 was identical to the one set up as far back as 1887, discounting the brief reign of the Republic of Councils (March 1—August 1, 1919). During the first decades of the twentieth century, especially after the liberal and the proletarian revolutions of 1918 and 1919 had been crushed by the counterrevolutionary regime, numerous initiatives had been launched to reform the administration.[1]

When Béla Scitovszky, Minister of the Interior, introduced his bill on July 14, 1928, it became evident that there was no question of a complete reorganization of the administration. Its objective was not to frame a new code of administration, but to affect change in one of its specific areas: in the structure and jurisdiction of municipal and community corporations.

Law No. XXX of 1929 left essentially unchanged the system of administration under which local autonomy continued to assert itself against central government. The daily activity of county administration was supervised by deputy prefects, the only officials in the entire system to be elected for 10 years by the municipal board. Districts were under the control of chief constables who enjoyed virtually unrestricted power. Although prefects had formally been proclaimed leaders of counties and municipal towns, as the government's right-hand men their effective influence over daily matters was much less than that of their subordinates. Decisions brought by the deputy prefects or chief constables could only be changed at the order of the Minister of the Interior and not the prefect.

The mainstays of this system of administration were two forces of coercion: the police and the gendarmerie. The task of the police was to maintain order in the towns and the cities, while the gendarmerie was responsible for order in the larger communities and the villages. The organizational structure of the gendarmerie was modeled on that of the *Honvédség* (the Hungarian Armed Forces), which meant that it did not conform to the county system. Instead district commanders of gendarmerie had jurisdiction over several counties, as was the case with commanders of the army corps. Moreover, gendarmerie district headquarters were subject in all cases to orders by the National Gendarmerie Command and the Minister of the Interior and not the local authorities.

Other branches of the administration to deviate from the county system were the railway and postal services, in so far as the jurisdiction of each railway and postal board extended over several counties.

Having seized power in the autumn of 1919, the Hungarian counterrevolutionary regime drew upon three ideological sources: anti-Communism, ultrachauvinism, which mainfested itself in a pursuit of territorial revision; and anti-Semitism, the alleged justification for which was that many leaders of the 1918 bourgeois-democratic and 1919 proletarian revolutions had been Jewish.

Depending on the given historical situation, the administration gave prominence to either one or the other of these ideologies, but following March 19, 1944, the Hungarian State administration clearly became actuated by anti-Semitism.

In addition, during the counterrevolutionary regime's reign, between 1919 and 1945, there was a marked endeavor at autonomy on county town and community level alike. Corresponding to tradition, the local administrations strove to pursue their own course and aspired to give priority to local interests over those of the nation, whereas the state endeavored to achieve centralization.

With regard to our topic—the deportations and the events preceding them—the starting point is Law No. II. of 1939, the National Defense Law, which invested all governments in office during the war with special powers. Paragraph 141 of the National Defense Law invested the government with special powers, with the responsibility given to all Cabinet members in case of the threat or declaration of war. Since the government of Döme Sztójay took care to observe legality, or at least preserve the semblance of legality following March 19, 1944, it exploited Articles 86, 141, and 212 of the National Defense Law to justify the issuing of prejudicial government decrees or ordinances that discriminated against Hungarian citizens of Jewish descent.[2] Thus the discriminative decrees, which were debated and passed at the March 29, 1944, session of the Council of Ministers, and which enforced the wearing of the Yellow Star, deprived Jewish lawyers from the right to practice, terminated membership of Jews in the chambers of the press, theatre and film, required the registration of Jewish-owned telephones and motor vehicles, prohibited the employment of non-Jews in Jewish households, abound with the stereotypical formula: "The Hungarian Royal Ministry (i.e. the Government) orders the following as empowered by Paragraph 2 of Article 141 of Law No. II. 1939."

All this naturally applied to government decrees published in the official press. Decrees identified as confidential (bearing the symbol *res.*), which were usually not made public, did not refer to Law No. II. of 1939 or any other law. This was the case, for example, with Decree No. 6163/1944. res. of the Minister of the Interior "Concerning the Determination of the Jews' Living Places" passed on April 7, 1944. As it is generally known, this decree determined the implementation of the deportation program.[4]

References to a legal basis served a twofold objective. On the one hand they were designed to convince public opinion that the government was legally empowered to pass the decrees and on the other hand to satisfy the conscience of the administration—insofar as needed—that the implementation of these decrees meant acting in accordance with the spirit of the National Defense Law, i.e., the fatherland being in danger as was suggested on the grounds of Paragraph 141.

After March 19, 1944, following the rapid liquidation of anti-German forces and in the atmosphere of terror that prevailed, neither the paralyzed public opinion nor the administration showed any resistance to the anti-Jewish government decrees. If any local administrations deviated from the national directives, they were aimed at exceeding the target: either by implementing the government decrees ahead of schedule or by taking more severe and harsher measures than required. There are by far less instances of milder measures put in force.

Following Hungary's occupation by the Germans, the resignation of the Kállay government and the installation of the Sztójay government, in compliance with constitutional practice, the prefects of the country resigned and put their posts at the disposal of the government. For some this meant a way out of the new and humilating situation, in the shadow of German bayonets; for others, having been the confidants of Miklós Kállay and Ferenc Keresztes-Fischer, did not meet the approval of the new Minister of the Interior, Andor Jaross, or Secretaries of State László Endre or Laszló Baky. Thus, following March 19, 1944, there were changes in both the prefects and other top positions of the administration,[5] whereas the main body of administration remained in office on the highest government level, as well as in the middle- and lower-ranking bureaucracy. Also to be reckoned with is the fact that practically no changes of personnel had taken place in the armed forces of the Ministry of the Interior—that is, among the officers of the police and the gendarmerie.

However, the role played by the Hungarian administration in the preparation and implementation of the deportations cannot be successfully analyzed without even the briefest review of the attitudes taken by Hungary and the Third Reich on the issue of deportation that came to the fore during fall 1942.

On October 17, 1942 Dietrich von Jagow, the German Minister to Budapest, presented a note to the Ministry of Foreign Affairs, demanding among others, the marking and deportation of 800,000 Hungarian Jews as part of the "Final Solution" of the European Jewish question.

The negative response adopted by the Kállay government was communicated to the *Wilhelmstrasse* by the then Hungarian Minister Sztójay on December 14, 1942. Deputy State Secretary Martin Luther very much regretted to hear this decision but raised another question. Luther urged that some consideration should at least be given to the deportation of Jews who had "infiltrated into Hungary and Carpatho-Ruthenia from Galicia and from Slovakia."[6]

As illustrated by the events of the ensuing months, competent Hungarian government officials did not regard this proposition as a sound basis for negotiations, especially after close to 18,000 "alien" Hungarian Jews were eliminated near Kamenets-Podolsk in August 1941.

The next step to be taken by the Germans was at the meeting of Hitler and Horthy on April 17, 1943, when Hitler called for a radical solution of the Jewish question in Hungary, as was being done in other countries. Horthy turned down this request at their personal meeting. However, in his letter of May 7, 1943 he assured Hitler that the proper measures were under way to gradually segregate the Jews, adding that "as soon as the necessary conditions will have been established, the deportations will commence."[7] At Schloss Klessheim, on March 18, 1944, Horthy consented to the most important of Hitler's demands. He undertook to continue the war at the side of Germany and to approve and participate in the liquidation of anti-German elements and in the radical solution of the Jewish question. Horthy also agreed to the entry of Gestapo and SS units into Hungary with the aim of fulfilling these commitments.[8]

The extent to which the German occupation of March 19, 1944, changed the situation of the Hungarian Jews became obvious on the very day of the occupation itself: since two Gestapo officers appeared at the Sip Street headquarters of the Jewish Community of Pest (*Pesti Izraelita Hitközség-PIH*) and ordered that all leaders of Hungarian Jewry be convened there at 9:30 A.M. the following day. Seeking help, or at least counsel, the leaders of Hungarian Jewry first telephoned the Ministry of Cults and Public Education, then the Ministry of the Interior. They were only able to talk to a minor official on duty at both institutions; finally they succeeded in reaching the Secretary of State in the Prime Minister's office, László Thuránszky, whose reply as to whether or not to negotiate with the Germans would be answered the following morning by the chief commissioner of the police. Early the following morning, March 20, a brief but meaningful reply was forwarded from the office of the police commissioner: "The demands of the Germans must be obeyed."[9]

Ernő Munkácsi, General Secretary of the PIH, in his memoirs published in 1945–46 added: "This attitude determined the policy of the Jewish Council for months and ultimately decided the fate of Hungarian Jewry. The Hungarian government of the time cast off the country's Jewish citizens and delivered them into the hands of the Germans."[10]

While in Budapest the demands raised by the officers of the *Sicherheitsdienst-SD*, at their meeting with the assembled leaders of Jewry, were still rather confined to generalities, which nevertheless clearly indicated that henceforth they aspired for complete authority over Hungarian Jewry; the attitude and actions of the Germans in the country were by far more clearcut as regards the Jewish question. The notary of the community of Sajószentpéter in Borsod County reported on April 6, 1944, that a "few days after their arrival, a German officer brought a poster to my office with the words 'ZSIDÓ-JUDE' and ordered that the poster be printed within twenty-four hours and hung out on all Jewish owned shops. He also brought another poster for printing and posting which directed that Jews—even the exempted ones—immediately start wearing yellow armbands. The following day I was informed that a government decree had been passed concerning the marking of the Jews for purposes of discrimination and at my special request the German Commandant consented to have 'stars' substituted for 'armbands' on the posters and to defer the posting of these until April 4. On the same occasion the German Commandant ordered me to immediately draw up and present an exact list of all the names of the Jews in Sajószentpéter."[11]

In Györ, the largest industrial center of Transdanubia (Dunántul), the "German military command entrusted with the affairs of the Jews" issued a directive on March 23 instructing the Jewish leaders as follows:

"The Jewish Community and all associations within it will be dissolved, their tasks "will be taken over by an *Aeltestenrat* (Council of Elders), to be appointed on the spot and who will bear full personal responsibility for these;

János Biringer, will act as the *Aeltestenrat* of the zone, with local *Aeltestenraete* as his subordinates; he will oversee all the Jews of Zala, Vas, Veszprém, Sopron, Győr, Moson, Pozsony, Komárom, Esztergom, Nyitra, Bars, and Hont counties."

One of the points of the directive orders registers to be drawn up of the leaders and their families, as well as of all the members of each Jewish community. It further stated: "Special emphasis is to be laid on the fact that any change of dwelling place, in fact any kind of travel even over the shortest distance is subject to a special permit . . . Students and commuting workers leave their homes to travel to school or their work place and back, on the condition that they hold school, or factory papers. Students may only travel home, they may no longer travel to school."[12]

The most convincing example of direct German intervention occured in Carpatho-Ruthenia: in Ungvár, at 11 A.M. on April 2, 1944, Gendarmerie-Colonel Győző Tölgyessy personally informed Géza Halász, the Counsellor of the Ministry of the Interior and Deputy Government Commissioner for Carpatho-Ruthenia: "In compliance with the wishes of the German SS commandant of Kassa, all the Jews of Carpatho-Ruthenia are to be evacuated to the towns of Munkács, Ungvár and Beregszász, and moreover, the communities of Huszt and Nagyszőllős may also be used for evacuation purposes. The evacuation operations are to be completed by the evening of April 6."

Halász was afraid to act his own responsibility, not having been before given information from the top government quarters on any such plans, which were barely camouflaged precursors of the deportations. Therefore— as attested by the minutes—he immediately forwarded the request of the SS Commandant to Colonel Király, Head of the Department of Public Security at the Ministry of the Interior, whose "telephone call at 12 o'clock the same day affirmed that the Minister of the Interior ordered the implementation of the request."

The minutes continue: "The operational details were discussed on the spot, the meeting being attended by Brigadier General Zoltán Álgya Papp, Public Safety Commander in Carpatho-Ruthenia, Volant Staff Major Pálffy,

Gendarmerie Lieutenant-Colonel and Záhonyi Gendarmerie Company Commander.

Ministerial Counsellor Géza Halász requested Brigadier General Zoltán Álgya Papp to provide freightcars and rolling stock in the quantity and at the time to be subsequently determined in the telegraphs of the appropriate police chiefs.

The only reason for the postponement of the evacuation of the Carpatho-Ruthenian Jews from the first week of April was that according to the Commander of the First Hungarian Army "the evacuation of the Jews would seriously disrupt the deployment of Army units at present under way."[13]

Further facts of relevance: the Eichmann-*Sonderkommando* had been in direct contact with the Jewish Council it had established with the bypassing of Hungarian authorities since almost the very first day of the occupation. Eichmann himself approved the charter of the Council which continued to provide a framework of its operation until October 15, 1944, and it was he who directed the deportation operations through Under-Secretaries of State Endre and Baky.[14]

There are also numerous instances of direct and official contact with the Hungarian authorities: two of Eichmann's officers attended a meeting on April 7, 1944, at the Ministry of the Interior where a decision was reached on "embarking on the country's dejewification program." In other words a settlement was reached on the deportations, on the operational procedures and the phases of implementation. They also decided to "station a German unit in Munkács to act in conjunction with Gendarmerie Lieutenant Colonel László Ferenczy and Royal Prosecutor Meggyesi, in directing the ghettoization process in the area of Gendarmerie District VIII (Kassa)."[15]

Research to date bears out both the indirect and direct participation of the SS, the SD, and of the German diplomatic corps in effectuating the deportations. German participation partly manifests itself in the passing on of their experience in the implementation of the "Final Solution" in the Nazi-occupied parts of Europe and partly in supervising Hungary's dejewification program. It might seem paradoxical, but the fact remains that the most accurate source of information on the number of Jews evacuated, or rather deported from Hungary, is to be found in the reports forwarded by Edmund Veesenmayer, the Plenipotentiary of the Third Reich.[16]

Apart from the Veesenmayer's reports the other Hungarian or German sources of the time provide incomplete, rather sketchy information on the role played by the German authorities in the Hungarian deportations. This is why special attention should be given to a document which was recently disclosed.

In this document the SS Headquarters advise the headquarters of the Hungarian Gendarmerie of the place and times of deportation trains.

The document was found among the papers of the Mayor's Office of Szeged, since the Commander of the Royal Hungarian Gendarmerie District No. V (Szeged) addressed the following instructions to the Mayor's Office on June 21, 1944:

"With all due respect I herewith forward a true copy of the German SS commandant's memo on the transfer of Jews from entrainment centers for the implementation of appropriate action."

The complete text of the document runs as follows:

Kecskemét: one train each on June 25, 27, a total of two trains;
Szeged: one train each on June 25, 27 and 28, a total of three trains;
Bácsalmás: one train on June 26;
Debrecen: one train each on June 25, 26, 27 and two trains on June 28, a total of five trains;
Nagyvárad: one train on June 26;
Szolnok: one train on June 25 and 27, a total of two trains; and
Békéscsaba: one train to leave on June 26.

On the days prior to the departure, the Jews are to be thoroughly searched in the camps before their transfer to the loading station to make sure no valuables (money, jewelry, securities, savingsbooks) remain in their possession (in keeping with the decree of the Ministry of the Interior), and further to ensure that individuals ordered to be exempted from deportation are not removed.

District gendarmerie headquarters will supervise the search of the Jews.

The persons to be transported are to be supplied with at least five days' food each, and further provisions must be made to ensure the amount of supplies required by the German commander, in case the transportation is of longer duration. Responsible civil service authorities are called to direct special attention to the above tasks."[17]

As regards the implementation of these instructions: on July 1, 1944, the police chief of the Sárvár District reported to the deputy prefect of Vas County to be added that on June 30 "the deputy commander of the German units in charge of the deportation of 6,100 Jews placed in the entrainment center of Sárvár community came to my office to effect the said transport. The Jews will be deported in the two trains to leave on July 4 and 6, but only if we provide the following list of food supplies for the two transports."

According to the reports the German command demanded 37,405 kilograms flour, 900 kilograms margarine, 7,000 kilograms vegetables, 6,100 kilograms bread (half-baked) and four head of cattle.[18]

The police chief requested that these food supplies be issued from the state stores as he could not gather them within the district.

The matter came to a close with the issuing of the food supplies as witnessed by the county notary's memo of July 6. There is no evidence whether the deported Jews of Sárvár benefited from any of these allocations.

Besides the SS, the German Legation in Budapest was also very active in the Hungarian deportations. Its role by far surpassed the mere forwarding statistics as referred to earlier. In the first days of July after the deportation of the Jews had been completed, Regent Horthy halted the deportations from Hungary, thereby withholding his consent to deport the Jews of Budapest. Veesenmayer made numerous efforts in support of Eichmann's repeated demands to have the deportation embargo suspended.[19]

Finally, when on July 6, 1944 Horthy asked Veesenmayer to intercede with the Führer to have the Gestapo units recalled from Hungary as soon as possible—in order to reestablish Hungarian sovereignty—the German Minister replied: "The SS and the SD have limited their activities to joint military operations, exclusively contributed to the restoration of order within Hungary. The same applies to the Jewish program, which is being implemented by Hungary, but in practical terms could never have been solved without our aid."[20]

The Hungarian administration was completely stricken by the German occupation on March 19, 1944. It took days before it could begin to adapt to the new situation. Similarly to the army officers, the top civil service officials—with few exceptions—were ready to continue to serve and discharge the orders of the Regent, the Supreme Commander, and of the government appointed by him.

However with regard to the Jewish question, the situation was by no means clearcut. This was primarily due to the whole series of measures taken by the Gestapo and the SS during the four days of negotiations to form a new government, and to determine the jurisdiction and competence of the Ministry of the Interior. Thus, following March 19, 1944, all Hungarian citizens considered Jewish were subject to measures not only to those issued by the Hungarian administration, but were also compelled—by the approval of the top Hungarian government organs—to act upon the orders of the German authorities entrusted with the Final Solution. This entailed a twofold subordination in practice, which was not and could not be laid down in government decrees or ministerial ordinances, since this would have meant the surrendering of some of the country's sovereignty.

During the first days of the occupation, the Germans demanded priority in dealing with the Jewish question, but they soon became convinced that the Sztójay government desired to—and did—enforce quick and definitive anti-Jewish measures. It might suffice to refer here to the flood of discriminatory decrees passed during their first few weeks in office. The Eichmann *Sonderkommando* for the most part contented itself with simple supervision; but it should be noted that the supervision they exercised was very extensive indeed: it started with the creation of the deportation decree, but there were also instances in which the Germans checked on whether the Jews had been given more than the necessary time to take care of daily shopping.[21]

One must also keep in mind that some of the top officials of the Hungarian administration needed very little prompting to implement measures or pass decrees curbing the civil rights of the Hungarian Jews. One example will suffice: László Endre, Deputy Prefect of Hungary's largest county—Pest-Pilis-Solt-Kiskun—ordered the restriction of Jews' living places on March 21, well before the relevant national decree came out. The alleged justification for this measure was that he "deemed one room sufficient for the needs of a Jewish family."[22] He was unhesitant in instructing the police chiefs of all districts to take steps to disconnect forthwith the telephones of Jewish subscribers and "communist-suspects,"[23] prohibit the use of, and ensure the requisitioning of, radio receivers owned by, the same individuals.[24]

On March 22, Endre ordered that unreliable Jews and Communist-suspects be placed in internment camps or under police surveillance,[25] prohibited Jews from visiting holiday and resort establishments in the county, and forbade them from attending public baths.[26] He also had the police chiefs issue instructions to the gendarmerie commands to check identification papers of the traveling public, and "prevent individuals belonging to the Jewish race from travel."[27]

However, Endre was not the only "hawk" in the administration. It followed from the system of administration itself that many deputy prefects, mayors, and police chiefs were not only able to, but in fact did take more drastic anti-Jewish measures than prescribed by the discriminative decrees or, similar to Endre, adopted these measures before the national laws had been passed.

Let us start with "milder" instances of anti-Jewish action: on May 1, 1944, the president of the Jewish Council of Miskolc informed the Mayor—in writing—of the establishment of the Council, requesting that the Council be permitted to pay him respect, as the senior official of the Miskolc municipal corporation. The mayor refused.[28]

The Mayor of Szeged prohibited Jews compelled to wear marks of discrimination from entering municipal offices; he instructed officials of the Town House *(városháza)* not to admit Jewish clients nor give them any information since "all matters concerning Jews are to be dealt with through the mediation of the Jewish Council."[29]

Especially harsh among the discriminatory decrees was the one passed by the Minister of the Interior that prohibited public relief grants to Jews. Although this measure affected the most wretched, the most afflicted group in society, there was no hesitation on the part of administration organs either in Budapest or elsewhere in the countryside to implement the decree. Let us refer to the Miskolc ruling on the allocation of public relief listing names and monthly grants: one out of thirteen applicants was awarded 12 *Pengős,* the rest were granted 3, 4, 5, 6, 8 *Pengős* by way of monthly relief.[30]

There was no decree in force concerning the cutting off of electric and gas supplies in the ghettos. Nevertheless, on June 10, 1944, the Deputy Mayor of Szeged issued—by telephone!—instructions to the management of the Central Gas and Electricity Corporation of Szeged to cut off electricity and gas supplies, including streetlighting, over the area covering the main ghetto.[31] The Jews in the Szeged ghetto were deported between June 25 and 28, 1944.

It is especially worth studying the orders given by the leaders of the local administration—the mayors and police—for the establishment and the "rules" of the ghettos. The police chief of Edelény District in Borsod County set "the deadline for moving voluntarily into the ghetto of Szendrő as 8 P.M., May 23," pointing out: "Persons refusing compliance will not only be brought forth and sent to internment camps immediately, but in addition members of the Council will be held personally responsible, fined, and punished."

In order to relieve the overburdened village officials he instructed the Jewish Councils to undertake the administrative tasks relating to the notifications of Jews' departure from the villages and registration in the ghetto and he obliged the Jewish Councils of Edelény and Szendrő to take out fire insurance corresponding to the sale value of the Jews' personal property, whether taken into the ghetto or left behind and also to take out insurance on the buildings appointed for the ghetto.

Further: "Inhabitants of the ghetto are strictly forbidden under the pain of punishment to maintain personal contact with individuals outside of the ghetto and permissions to leave the ghetto are not to be sought except in cases of vital importance."[32]

The police chief of Mezőkövesd District (also in Borsod County) obliged the Jewish Council to make a downpayment of 50,000 *Pengős* to cover the cost of the resettlement of the Christian residents and to cover expenses of moving in the Jews. In addition, he ordered the depositing of 1,000 *Pengős* for the renovation of each of the 37 ghetto apartments.[33]

In another Borsod County district, the one around Ózd, the police chief ordered that the ghetto be enclosed by a two-meter-high barbed-wire fence, provided 1,815 square meters of lodging space for 1,008 persons, and also obliged the Jews to take out fire insurance on the furniture taken along or stored; he passed a decree stipulating that "it is prohibited for internees to hold [social] intercourse with persons outside the camp through the fence or the windows."

Further: the Jewish Council was required "to report the disturbers of the peace and punish offenders against camp discipline within their own jurisdiction. Conditions and details of punishment will be regulated by separate instructions."

A completely different situation prevailed in Carpatho-Ruthenia, where the leaders of the administration lost no time regulating the order of life in the ghettos, and employed the most stringest methods in the course of their implementation. At the Ungvár conference of April 15, 1944, attended by *Hauptsturmführer* Dieter Wisliceny, it was generally conceded that "the Jews placed in the Felszabadulás Street brickworks are expected to be held there for 30–45 days."[34]

The almost unbearable daily life in the entrainment camps is amply illustrated by the relevant historical literature, mainly through the valuable recollections of the survivors. The documents of the Carpatho-Ruthenia Government Commissioner reveal further evidence for researchers relating to the history of the Jews of this area and help them draw a more definitive picture of the Holocaust.

Reports by the administration officials of Ungvár—the Mayor, the chief of police, and the commanders of all Jewish entrainment camps—attest to the fact that the Jews rounded up at these camps were considered to be prisoners, and referred to as "internees" *(őrizetesek)*. A report by the commander of the entrainment camp, dated April 19: "The number of Jewish internees transferred up to 9 A.M. this morning is 6,152." Or further on: "The morale of the internees is generally satisfactory and reassuring. The rounding up and the concentration of the internees is taking place smoothly."

The police chief of Ungvár reported in a memo of April 20 that a group of 21 men "carried out the task of removal and confiscation"—a rare instance of plain words to describe how matters really stood.

In a report of April 24 submitted to the Ministry of the Interior the Mayor comments: "The large crowd placed in the brickworks lack even the most fundamental sanitary facilities . . . I respectfully request that the Jews assembled in the entrainment camps of Ungvár be transported as soon as possible."

On May 9, Gyula Gyurics, the head of the administrative board in Ung, authorized the collection of the food supplies that had been left behind after the round up of the Jews—to comply with the request of the Mayor of Ungvár. He had this to add to his appeal: "This cannot be arranged in all cases due, in part, to the great distances, and in part to the fact that the Jews' foodstuffs have already been disposed of and sold in some villages as perishables."

The head of administration in Ung County was of the view that the responsibility of feeding the Jews ought to be undertaken by the Mayor all the more since the assembled Jews were only allowed to take 14 days' food supply with them and the fortnight's term had already expired.

The documents do not make it clear what, if any, arrangements had been made to solve the feeding of the Jews in the entrainment camp of Ungvár, but the exchange of letters sheds some additional light on the situation.

On April 28, 1944, a government decree was published in the official gazette, stating that Jews could be removed from communities with a population of under 10,000 to another community or town. It should be emphasized, parenthetically, that Art. 8 of the decree made this transfer only optional, stipulating that "the top official of the municipality may order" it.[35] About this time, when the Carpatho-Ruthenian Jews had already been languishing in internment camps for eight to ten days, the concentration of the Jews had not yet begun in the greater part of Trianon Hungary, except in the Northeastern and Southwestern areas. By the time this did take place, the Jews in Sopron, Zala, and Békés counties could have had only the slightest foreboding of what was to befall them; they had little, if any, idea of the horror experienced by the Jews in Munkács, Ungvár, and Nyíregyháza. The fact that they only had a presentiment of the future right up to their internment in camps was largely due to the local authorities, or more precisely, the humane attitude of county or district leaders—the prefects or police chiefs. There was, of course, no other choice but to comply with the instructions of the Ministry of the Interior relating to the relocation and ghettoization of the Jews. Life and living conditions in the various ghettos established in May and June, 1944, were far from uniform. This can be illustrated with some of the ghettos in Borsod County already described and with those in Zala and Sopron counties.

The deputy prefect of Zala County ordered the establishment of ghettos on May 4, 1944. The decree stated: "The inhabitants of the enclosed areas must be allowed freedom of worship. Accordingly, Jewish believers may proceed to the synagogue in close order under surveillance; members of other congregations must be granted permits in due time to attend their own churches."

Further: "Maternity homes, old-age homes, hospitals for ordinary patients and for those suffering from infectious diseases must be established to meet the needs within all enclosed areas."

As regards the disposal and selling of foodstuffs left in Jewish apartments the deputy prefect's decree stipulated: "All official functionaries, state or municipal officials, community judges, magistrates, jurors, clergymen, teachers, doctors, pharmacists, in general terms, all so-called professional persons must be excluded from the gains derived from the disposal of the above-mentioned items under the penalty of severe punishment."[36]

The police chief of Keszthely District attended the conference held at the county hall of Zalaegerszeg on May 3, 1944, where the acting deputy prefects passed on verbal instructions to the police chiefs. One of these stipulated:

"All jeering and abuse whatsoever is prohibited in connection with the evacuation of the Jews. All officials involved in the procedure are to carry out their duty with dignified earnestness. The populace must not be allowed to blaspheme and slander."

On the evacuation procedure: "Transport facilities for relocation purposes are to be primarily supplied by Jewish agents, additionally required facilities are to be provided by the public free of charge."[37]

Considering the situation at hand, the attitude shown by Antal Rupprecht, the Prefect of Sopron, was fair—one could state almost humane. On May 26, 1944, he authorized 70 persons to hire agricultural laborers from "among the Jews forced *(sic!)* into the ghetto of Csorna."[38]

Although it might not seem greatly benevolent, the authorization of the Sopron police command to permit Dr. Dezső Kelényi—"an agricultural laborer of Jewish origin"—to use his bicycle between his apartment and work place was in the context of the times quite charitable.[39]

There were very few instances in which the prescribed two hours for shopping by Jews were prolonged in case of an air-raid by so many minutes "as the air-raid had taken up of the two hours."[40]

Since the Ministry of Public Supply had issued a decree on June 22, 1944, regulating "the provisions of food supplies for the Jews interned in camps," it is worth noting that although the majority of the Jews in the countryside had been deported before the publication of the decree, the Deputy Prefect of Sopron County showed noteworthy, commendable speed in that four days later, on June 26, he issued for the Jews concentrated in Sopron sufficient flour, wheat-flour, sugar and lard—for four weeks.[41] The deportation of Jews interned at Sorpon began at dawn on June 29, 1944.

In another corner of the country there were also some officials who could retain their humaneness amidst all the barbarity.

On May 21, 1944, the police chief of Mezőkovácsháza District submitted a report to the Deputy Prefect of Csanád County on the "Jewish camps" in Magyarbánhegyes and Mezőkovácsháza—the two ghettos contained 738 Jews.

A quote from the police chief's report: "Following the lethargy of the first days, the Jews interned at both camps proceeded to settle down, organize sanitation and cooking facilities, and at my instructions the Jews placed in the Magyarbánhegyes ghetto began to cultivate the farm yard and garden lands within the ghetto area. I directed that the youngsters of preschool and school-age be given classes, while Council members appointed by myself are to engage adults in various pursuits to provide activities for all people in the ghetto from morning till evening."

In the conclusion of his report the police chief requested instructions as to the Jews' mail, which for the time being was being handed over to the local boards of the two communities. A note dated July 26, 1944, reads: "Since the Jews have been moved from the county, this report is to be considered null and void."[42]

And what kind of a life did the Jews lead in the ghettos? As the foregoing already illustrated, the middle and lower ranking authorities of administration implemented the directives of the Ministry of the Interior in whatever way they saw fit, and used their own judgment to give them actual content.

The differences were enormous: we come across all shades and degrees of the dejewification program in the intolerable ghettos of Carpatho-Ruthenia, Northeastern Hungary or the environs of Budapest, in comparison to the relatively more humane conditions prevailing in the ghettos of Western Hungary. In the latter area, ghettos even had "regulations" drawn up—as in the case of the ghetto of Vasvár. These "regulations" reflected almost Arcadian conditions. Here are a few of their provisions:

Article 2: "It is prohibited to carry on conversations after bed-time—following the black-out—with special regard to the common rooms."

Article 4: "Rising must be done in due time to finish the tidying or cleaning of all quarters before 8:00 A.M."

Article 6: "All sleeping-quarters are to be scrubbed weekly at hours appointed by the room chief and are otherwise to be kept tidy through sweeping several times a day."[43]

Let there be no misunderstanding: the inhabitants of the ghetto were naturally subject to the general decrees by the Ministry of the Interior, and as such could only leave the ghetto area with special permission. Christians—excepting clergymen—were allowed to enter the ghetto only by special permission, but even the very style of the punitive decrees was different from those issued and enacted in Borsod or Szabolcs counties or in Carpatho-Ruthenia.

As far as the real situation was concerned, the following quote from the report of the Jewish Council of Nyíregyháza dated April 20, 1944, and addressed to the town's chief medical officer is illuminating. The report points out that following the relocation of Jews from the surrounding rural areas into Nyíregyháza "an almost unimaginable extent of crowdedness prevailed in each apartment and with special consideration to the facts that the town has neither a water, nor a drainage-system, the majority of apartments used for quartering purposes has no drinking water well whatsoever, the ones that do exist need repair, there is a shortage of lavatories, the ones that are there are full and unsatisfactory for meeting the needs of a larger contingent; both the Jews quartered there and the entire town are in the danger of an imminent contamination."

The report contained data on 25 apartments. For example: "The building at No. 5 Kossuth Street houses 198 persons, the well needs repair, the water is insufficient, the room is terribly overcrowded, the lavatory is inadequate. No. 7 Kossuth Street houses 153 persons. There is no water at all, food supplies will only be sufficient for one day. The Jews quartered there have no adequate clothing or bedding since they had been forbidden to bring such items with them, they have no or inadequate lavatories; No. 6 Körte Street houses 152 persons. The well is out of order, the lavatory has been filled completely. It has so far been ascertained that two of the inhabitants have lice, their clothes burned, overcrowdedness, lack of sanitation, lack of clothing; No. 6 Nyirfa Street houses 117 persons, the building is dilapidated, terribly overcrowded with a very small yard. Approximately five meters from the entrance there is a lavatory in total disrepair . . ."

Following the description of the quarters, the report continues: "We respectfully call attention to the fact that the inhabitants quartered in these premises have only been provided a supply of three days' food. Prior to their relocation at these premises, they had been concentrated in a camp for two days, where they had had no rest either, the facilities for lying down in these overcrowded premises are minimal which causes them to loose all resistance from the point of view of their health. No elementary articles of personal hygiene, soap, basin, tub, etc, were permitted to be brought and since they have had their money taken away, they have no means to purchase such articles."

This report was accompanied by a six-page memo of the chief medical officer fully backing up the facts stated by the Jewish Council. On the basis of these findings the chief medical officer ordered that "the water of the four public and all private wells be exclusively used for drinking, and that latrines be dug in the yards of the larger houses, and further that the existing lavatories may only be used by children, the old, and the infirm."

The memo of the chief medical officer also included the provisions for the ill: one of the Jewish synagogues and the seven-room school in its courtyard were taken over for use as an emergency hospital, and the incurably ill and Jews suffering from infectious tuberculosis were placed in the synagogue itself. One of its offices served as a ward for the mentally deranged, endangering themselves and the other Jews.

A very objective, dry statement closes the memo: "The necessary typhoid vaccine is not likely to be made available; I will have only the immediately surrounding people vaccinated in cases of disease."[44]

No further facts are available on the sanitary conditions prevailing in the town ghetto of Nyíregyháza and the eleven tobacco-drying sheds on the town's outskirts, but it is obvious from the foregoing that the local sanitation authorities were far from being able—despite any goodwill on their part—to ensure even basic sanitary and health provisions. This must have been known to the persons who issued the orders for the concentration and ghettoization of the Jews of Szabolcs County.

The first trainload of Jews marked for deportation were only sent on their way from Nyíregyháza some four weeks later, on May 17.

When top-level administration authorities issued orders to have Jews removed from the transit camps, they left the task of actually implementing the transportation scheme to local administration authorities. Since orderliness was of paramount importance, all aspects of the procedure were covered. The instructions for the Baja camp include Jews' obligation to hand over their valuables, gold, silver, jewelry, stocks and bonds, savings books, typewriters etc.; house and body search warrants; the limitation of food supplies to 14 days' rations; and the stipulation that in addition the clothes worn only one suit of work-clothes, one spare set of underwear and spare footwear and one overcoat could be taken along by the Jews. Taking along writing utensils such as fountain pens, pencils and writing paper was forbidden.

The order went on:

> When the Jews are ready to leave, they must assemble outside the houses forming a queue.
>
> Following the evacuation of a house or apartment, the policeman on duty is to survey the premises to ensure that no windows or doors are left open, and that all fires and lights are put out . . .
>
> . . . The evacuated house or apartment is to be sealed by the policeman and the keys to the house or apartment marked with a tag . . .
>
> The above having been completed, the policeman is to take the Jews to the railway station and guard them up to the time of the Jews' transfer into the wagons.[45]

Naturally, this procedure could only be carried through in ghettos where orderly conditions prevailed.

Notes

1. During the parliamentary debate on Draft Law No. 1929:XXX, one of the deputies stated: "This draft law proposed by the Minister of the Interior is the 47th attempt at improving the administration and, because I love statistics, for the sake of statistics let me state too that the Minister of the Interior is the 21st Minister of the Interior who appeared with this proposal before the House." *Az 1927–1932. Képviselőházi Napló* (Proceedings of the House of Representatives for 1927–1932). Budapest.

2. *Magyar Törvénytár. 1939. évi törvénycikkek.* (Hungarian Code of Laws. Legislative Acts of 1939). Budapest, 1940, pp. 54-55, 69, 85, 115-116.

3. Ilona Benoschofsky and Elek Karsai, *Vádirat a nácizmus ellen. Dokumentumok a magyarországi zsidóüldözés történetéhez,* (Indictment of Nazism. Documents on the History of Jewish Persecutions in Hungary). Vol. 1. Budapest: Magyar Izraeliták Országos Képviselete, 1958, pp. 51-79. (Cited hereafter as *Vádirat.*)

4. *Ibid.,* pp. 124-127.

5. György Ránki, *1944. március 19. Magyarország német megszállása* (March 19, 1944. Hungary's German Occupation). Budapest: Kossuth, 1978.

6. *Új Magyar Központi Levéltár*—UMKL (New Hungarian Central Archives). Budapest, Küm. Békeelök. oszt. II/2-27/27-32.

7. Elek Karsai, *A budai Vártol a Gyepűig* (From the Fort of Buda to the Borderland). Budapest: Táncsics, 1965, pp. 295, 298.

8. Miklós Szinai and László Szücs, *Horthy Miklós titkos iratai* (The Secret Papers of Miklós Horthy). Budapest: Kossuth, 1965, pp. 430, 467.

9. *Vádirat*, vol. 1, p. 23.

10. *Ibid.*

11. *Miskolci Állami Levéltár. Borsod megye alispáni iratai* (State Archives of Miskolc. Files of the Deputy Prefect of Borsod County). Doc. 1944-7.845.

12. *Győri Állami Levéltár. Pannonhalmi járás főszolgabirói iratai* (State Archives of Győr. Files of the Chief Constable of Pannonhalma District). Doc. 1944-2.005. Among these documents is a report dated March 26, 1944, stating that Kamil Krausz, a resident of Győr and and appointee of the "Jewish leader of Győr," reached an agreement with the communal leaders of Győrszentmiklós about the immediate dissolution of that community and the transfer of leadership to a Jewish Council. The delegate from Győr handed over to Pál Lehner, the head of the Jewish Council, the two-page instruction sheet of the Germans. The end of the report contains the personal data of the community leaders and of their families. In other words, the order of the German command was carried out at least in Győrszentmiklós. Further research is required to determine the extent to which similar measures were put through in other communities.

13. *Országos Levéltár*—OL (National Archives). *Bm. ált. Kárpátaljai kormánybiztos iratai* (Files of the General Government Commissioner of the Ministry of the Interior for Carpatho-Ruthenia). Doc. 3997/1395/162/1.

14. *Vádirat*, vol. 1, pp. 102-105. The question as to why the SD established the Central Jewish Council if it did not enhance its contacts with the provincial Jewish Councils and if its jurisdiction was limited to the capital requires a special investigation.

15. *Ibid.*, pp. 123-124.

16. Randolph L. Braham, *The Destruction of Hungarian Jewry. A Documentary Account.* New York: World Federation of Hungarian Jews, 1963, vol. I, pp. 413, 436. (Cited hereafter as Braham, *Destruction.*)

17. *Szegedi Állami Levéltár* (State Archives of Szeged). Szeged, Doc. Polg.m. 1944-9535.

18. *Szombathelyi Állami Levéltár* (State Archives of Szombathely). *Vas vármegye alisp.* (Deputy Prefect of Vas County). Doc. 1944-2.537.

19. Braham, *Destruction,* vol. I, pp. 461-463, 470-471, 472. See also *Vádirat,* vol. 3, pp. 373-380. When at the July 12, 1944, session of the Council of Ministers Prime Minister Sztójay raised the question of the need for an official communiqué to be issued by the Germans denying foreign reports about the fate of the deported Hungarian Jews it was Veesenmayer himself who drafted the communiqué. *Vádirat,* vol. 3, pp. 207-211.

20. Braham, *Destruction,* vol. I, p. 419.

21. This happened, for example, in the District of Csorna, where the chief constable first determined the shopping hours for Jews between 10:00 a.m. and noon, but then changed it to 11:00 a.m. and 1:00 p.m. as a result of negotiations with a

"German security agent" who appeared in his office. *Soproni Állami Levéltár* (State Archives of Sopron). *Csornai járás főszolg.* (Chief Constable of Csorna District). Doc. 1944-2872.

22. *Pest-Nógrád m. Állami Levéltár* (State Archives of Pest-Nógrád County). *Alsógöd község iratai* (Files of the Village of Alsógöd). Doc. 1944-1.333. The government decree on the expropriation of the apartments of the Jews was issued on April 28, 1944. For text see *Vádirat,* vol. 1, pp. 244-250.

23. *Pest-Nógrád m. Állami Levéltár. Pest Vármegye alisp.* Doc. 1944-18.902. The decree on the registration of Jewish telephone subscribers—not covering the disconnection of the phones owned by the Jews—was issued on March 29, 1944. For text see *Vádirat,* vol. 1, pp. 58-59.

24. *Pest-Nógrád m. Állami Levéltár. Püspökhatvan község iratai.* (Files of the Village of Püspökhatvan). Doc. 1944-566. The decree on the registration of radio permits was issued on April 7, 1944. *Vádirat,* vol. 1, pp. 129-131. The Minister of Defense ordered the confiscation of the radio sets owned by Jews on April 21. *Ibid.,* p. 132.

25. *Pest-Nógrád m. Állami Levéltár. Püspökhatvan község iratai.* Doc. 1944-565. No decree was issued on this matter.

26. *Pest-Nógrád m. Állami Levéltár. Pilisborosjenő.* Doc. 1944-1088. The Minister of the Interior issued a decree prohibiting Jews from using public baths. *Vádirat,* vol. 1, pp. 285-286.

27. *Pest-Nógrád m. Állami Levéltár. Alsógöd.* Doc. 1944-1331. The decree limiting travel by Jews was issued on April 7, 1944.

28. *Miskolci Állami Levéltár. Polgm.* Doc. 1944-19.493. The document contains a note by the town's chief notary: "The request cannot be granted. No action required. June 28, 1944."

29. *Szegedi Állami Levéltár. Polg.* Doc. 1944-7204. The harsh tone of the decision is especially noteworthy. On June 7, 1944, the treasury directorate of Szeged requested that the mayor's decree be changed with an eye on "the extremely important interests of the treasury which has a direct bearing on the prompt payment of public debts." The petition was forwarded to the head of the town's internal revenue office on June 14, 1944, for a recommendation, and on June 24, i.e., one day prior to the deportation of the Jews of Szeged, the following was noted on the document: "The problem of the Szeged Jews has in the meantime been solved."

30. The mayor of Budapest terminated the issuance of welfare payments to Jews on the basis of the decree of the Minister of the Interior. *Vádirat,* vol. 1, p. 269. For the order of the mayor of Miskolc see: *Miskolci Állami Levéltár. Polg.* Doc. 1944-21.945. On May 31, 1944, the town manager was instructed to distribute the decisions among the Jews living in the ghetto through the Jewish Council. On June 22, 1944, the town manager informed the mayor that the decisions could not be distributed to the parties concerned "because the Jews had been removed from the ghetto."

31. *Szegedi Állami Levéltár. Polgm.* Doc. 1944-9090. The head of the firm reported on the same day: "With the shut-off of the main fuses in the buildings within the ghetto, the power supply has been discontinued, and the gas meters have been removed. The electric meters cannot be removed in one day; this task will be carried out next week." *Ibid.*

32. *Miskolci Állami Levéltár. Borsod megye alisp.* (Deputy Prefect of Borsod County). Doc. 1944-9236.

33. *Ibid.*

34. *Országos Levéltár. Bm. ált. Kárpátaljai kormánybiztos iratai.* Doc. lot 3997, 1395. 162/1944. This lot contains other documents pertaining to the Jews of Carpatho-Ruthenia.

35. *Vádirat,* vol. 1, p. 246.

36 *Zalaegerszegi Állami Levéltár. Kaptalantóti körjegyzőség.* (State Archives of Zalaegerszeg. Office of the Notary of Kaptalantó District). Doc. 1944-1047.

37. *Zalaegerszegi Állami Levéltár. Keszthelyi főszolgabiró.* (Chief Constable of Keszthely). Doc. 1944-4489.

38. *Soproni Állami Levéltár. Csornai főszolgabiró.* (Chief Constable of Csorna). Doc. 1944-2988. The employees signed a statement that they were hired at their own request and that they would "refrain from instigation and political activity" and that they would fulfill their work commitments to the best of their abilities or be subject to "the most severe punishment: internment." *Ibid.* The Prefect authorized involvement in agricultural labor in three other cases. *Ibid.,* Doc. 1944-2889, and 1944-3052.

39. *Soproni Állami Levéltár. Sopron polgm.* Doc. 1944-IX-10022.

40. June 6, 1944, decree by the mayor of Sopron. *Ibid.,* Doc. 1944-IX-100/1/ 11.674. The Prefect's decree of May 20, 1944, did not limit the Jews' shopping hours to two, but simply stipulated that Jews could shop in the markets only after 10:00 a.m. *Ibid.,* Doc. 10.491.

41. *Soproni Állami Levéltár. Sopron vármegye alisp.* Doc. 1944-6795.

42. *Szegedi Állami Levéltár. Csanád vm. alisp.* (Deputy Prefect of Csanád County). Doc. 1944-7979/9033.

43. *Szombathelyi Állami Levéltár. Vasvári főszolg.* (State Archives of Szombathely. Chief Constable of Vasvár). Doc. 1944-907.

44. *Nyíregyházi Állami Levéltár. Nyíregyháza város tiszti főorvosa iratai* (State Archives of Nyíregyháza. Files of the Chief Medical Officer of the City of Nyíregyháza). Unnumbered Doc. labeled "Sanitary measures in Jewish camps."

45. *Pécsi Állami Levéltár. Bajai internálótábor iratai* (State Archives of Pécs. Files of the Baja Internment Camp). Doc. 1944-lot II.214.

Chapter 9

THE PALESTINE *YISHUV* AND THE HOLOCAUST IN HUNGARY

Raphael Vago

The last ten years have seen the development of a new direction in Israeli historiography relating to the Palestine Jewish community—the *Yishuv* (Jewish Community), and the Holocaust. If until the beginning of the 1970s the emphasis was more on the diplomatic, political, and military aspects of the Holocaust's impact on the *Yishuv,* the new trend attempts to analyze the concepts, ideas, perceptions, and attitudes of the *Yishuv* leadership, as well as those of the general public.

In commenting on the state of research on the *Yishuv* during the Holocaust, Yehuda Bauer remarked in 1973 that "at present we can only examine the political, diplomatic and military aspects, whereas while we are able to analyze the role of public opinion, this crucial matter has hereto remained unexamined."[1] The new direction in Israeli scholarship relates to the issue by way of an intellectual history of that period. Such an approach should be welcomed, as it offers us new insights into the attitudes of the *Yishuv* to the events in Europe. On the whole, this line of research has been successful, although there are still areas to be covered. The source materials are available and easily accessible: the Palestine press, the minutes of the various public and political organizations, memoirs, and letters.

No attempt is made here to assess the rescue activities of the *Yishuv* during the Holocaust, rather the main lines or thought and attitudes that prevailed among the *Yishuv,* with special emphasis on the Holocaust in Hungary, will be presented.

The *Yishuv,* fragmented into a wide spectrum of political, secular and religious groupings, numbered less than 500,000 people, living under the British Mandate, fighting against it in various forms, lacking adequate financial resources, with insufficient means of communication with occupied Europe. It tried to define its role and place in the face of the unfolding Holocaust. As the news filtered through, the initial response was a sense of hopelessness, the perception that the small *Yishuv* would be unable to help and change the tragic chain of events.

Until November 1942, the *Yishuv* did not have to face the bitter truth, as there was no official announcement that European Jewry was systematically being destroyed, and the *Yishuv* leadership was not convinced that the bits and pieces of information leaking out of Europe were true. There was a peculiar passivity running through the leadership, which had an immediate effect on the wide public—a passivity whose character and manifestations have preoccupied some of the research that has been conducted in the past years.[2] Parallel to the state of mind of wide segments of European Jewry who did not want to know and face the truth, a similar atmosphere prevailed in the *Yishuv.*

The emerging philosophy behind the rescue actions of the *Yishuv* was that steps should be taken, although the leadership did not believe that they could be of any significant impact. For obvious reasons, the general public was not informed about the behind-the-scenes decisions taken by the *Yishuv* leaders nor about their arguments on the various options raised, but the elite's perceptions were well reflected in the daily attitudes of the *Yishuv.* The public's attention was focused on activities to collect funds for aid, but not on a debate deliberating the prospects of saving those Jews who could still be saved. As a consequence, the *Yishuv* leadership had no comprehensive rescue plans ready as the war went on, nor even clear concepts of what to do. This was demonstrated when the *Yishuv* was faced with the rapid developments in Hungary in 1944. As all appeals to the Allies proved to be fruitless—the *Yishuv* concentrated more and more on small-scale rescue attempts, extending material help in particular but at the same time putting into effect such actions as the mission of the paratroopers in the spring of 1944.

One of the topics that still remains to be thoroughly researched is that of the priorities for rescue as perceived by the *Yishuv* and its leadership. The argument was between those calling for total rescue and those advocating priority for persons loyal to the Zionist idea who could be of help in building the national home in Palestine. The latter attitude reflected the almost fanatic belief that the main task of the *Yishuv* was to strengthen itself, to prepare it for statehood, and to serve as a shelter for the remnants of European Jewry.

The most extreme such attitude was expressed by *LEHI*—Freedom Fighters for Israel—which since 1943 had been calling for a "second front." By this it meant that the *Yishuv* should set up a second front not in Europe, where the battle was virtually lost, but in Palestine. LEHI pressed for the concentration of forces where there was still a chance to win—in Palestine, against the British rule. Thus, one of *LEHI's* pamphlets expressed the belief that "We cannot defend European Jewry, and every word of this issue is nonsense or cheating. We can only pray for God's mercy."[3] This, of course, was not the official voice of the *Yishuv,* but of a small, albeit effective splinter group. Yet, in its bizarre rationale it reflected the dilemmas facing the *Yishuv.*

The public mood in the *Yishuv* was influenced by the voices from the elite. The character of that leadership, and the process of decisionmaking is beyond the scope of the present study, but a short outline of the major leading bodies should be made. The *Sochnut*—the Jewish Agency—was the informal government of the *Yishuv,* and it served as the executive arm of the World Zionist Organization in charge of establishing the Jewish National Home. The United Rescue Committee, formed in 1943, was the main body linked to the Jewish Agency which coordinated the rescue activities of the *Yishuv.* Recent research has indicated the almost nonexistent division of labor between the Committee and the Executive of the Jewish Agency.[4] This situation was reflected in the conduct of rescue activities as well as in the psychological and material mobilization of the *Yishuv.* The emerging picture from the various bodies in the *Yishuv* is one of a divided leadership, with political and personal rivalries, working under arduous conditions. But still, this was the "war of the Jews," which unfortunately has been a concomitant of the Jewish nation's history throughout the ages.

In analyzing the *Yishuv's* attitude during the Holocaust in Hungary, two important aspects should be considered. First, the image of Hungarian Jewry in the eyes of the *Yishuv,* and second, the impact of the events in Hungary, which had been predictable beforehand.

It seems that in the eyes of the *Yishuv,* Hungary's Jewry did not engage in "good public relations." Justly, Hungarian Jewry had the reputation of leaning to extremes, a stubborn community, which sought its own peculiar way of life, suspicious of outside interference. The attitudes in the *Yishuv* toward Hungarian Jewry reflected this image. Everything that everybody loved to hate in Jewish history was present among Hungarian Jewry. The religious camp in the *Yishuv* well remembered the assimilationist trend, while the secular, socialist-oriented public expressed its reservation over the presence of ultrareligious, even non-Zionist elements in Hungary. The revisionist movement, which in 1935 had not belonged to the World Zionist Congress and vehemently opposed the MAPAI-led line in the *Yishuv,* criticized those Hungarian Jews who went along with the left-wing movements and participated in the various youth organizations.

In other words, the politically divided *Yishuv* found fault with the similarly divided Hungarian Jewry. This may be true of any analysis made in the *Yishuv* of foreign Jewish communities, but one cannot help feeling that the criticism of Hungarian Jewry was particularly severe. It would be unfair to try to offer solutions for such a difficult problem because for such an attempt one should have recourse to a comparative analysis of the image of various Jewish communities in the eyes of the *Yishuv,* but it should be assumed that the underrepresentations of prominent Hungarian Jews in the *Yishuv's* elite was one of the manifestations of the negative image of that community.

Historians must cope not only with pure facts, but also with imponderable elements and feelings. Assumptions, even if proved to be mistaken, indicate a state of mind which cannot be ignored by historical scholarship. Two cases may illustrate this point. In February 1944, Haim Weisburg, one of the leading activists of the Hungarian immigrant organizations, complained in a letter to Yitshak Grunbaum, Chairman of the United Rescue Committee, that the Committee had been refusing for a long time to take into consideration the views of the representatives of Hungarian Jewry in the *Yishuv.* Weisburg bitterly remarked that "If somebody is from Poland, it does not mean that he knows everything."[5] It should be noted that at the time various immigrant associations were complaining that the Committee leadership was not involving them sufficiently in the assessment of the situation in Europe, and in the decisionmaking process on the activities of the *Yishuv* to rescue European Jewry. Some organizations—for example the Romanian one— complained that the *Yishuv* leadership had an improper list of priorities for rescue activities, a view shared by all bodies representing the immigrants from European countries.[6] This does not necessarily mean that the representatives of Hungarian Jews in the *Yishuv* organs had better sources of information than the leading bodies of the *Yishuv,* but it is incontestable that the Hungarian community felt that they were not treated as partners in the efforts to rescue Hungary's Jewry. From this perception it was not far to the accusation that Polish Jews were running the *Yishuv.*

The second case is an example of the mutual distrust that prevailed between the leaders of Hungarian Jewry in Hungary itself and the leadership of the *Yishuv.* In his *The Politics of Genocide,* Randolph Braham remarks that Joel Brand had a low opinion of the members of the United Rescue

Committee in Jerusalem, and especially of Grunbaum, who according to Brand "had never really understood what had happened in Hungary."[7] Braham considers that this criticism of Grunbaum is somewhat unfair, but from our point of view the issue is not whether Brand was correct in his assessment of the *Yishuv* leaders, but that he felt that way.

Some of the publicists in the *Yishuv* press were of Hungarian origin, and it is quite evident that in their writings they tried to emphasize the great contributions made by Hungarian Jewry to the emergence of the Jewish national movement, both in its secular and religious wings. The name of Theodor Herzl was one that could be favorably evoked in such a campaign to promote the public image of Hungary's Jewry. Yet, the criticism was ever present.

Generally, the Hungarian Zionist movement was presented in the *Yishuv* as having lost its way, and drifting without clear aims—as a movement which could not serve as a guide for the young generation. Such a critical tone was characteristic of all shades of the political spectrum in the *Yishuv*. *Davar* (Word), the daily of the General Federation of Labor, and in fact the organ of *MAPAI* (Workers' Party of Israel) emphasized the generation gap in the Hungarian Zionist movement, and pointed correctly to the lack of firm leadership among Hungary's Jewry.[8] The paper, which certainly reflected the viewpoint of the leading personalities in the *Yishuv,* called for closer contacts between the *Yishuv* in Palestine and Hungary's Jewry. This assessment, made in 1940, reflected the total lack of communication between the leadership of Hungarian Jewry and that of the *Yishuv.* In fact of the divisive fragmentation of political life in the *Yishuv,* one may wonder what kind of example the *Yishuv* could have offered to solve the internal problems of Hungarian Jewry, but the fact is that the lack of contacts between the two sides greatly contributed to the mutual misunderstanding between them.

The *Yishuv,* almost without exception, addressed Hungarian Jewry with the tone of a moralist saying "I have told you so." Even when the catastrophe in Hungary had commenced there were still voices that dealt with the past. In May 1944 *Davar* warned that "this is not the moment to criticize Hungary's Jewry for their assimilation, and to condemn them for having delayed their participation in the general Jewish action for the future."[9] It certainly was not the right moment to remind them of all this, yet the author of the article reiterated a long list of past grievances.

The bitterest critics of Hungarian Jewry in the *Yishuv* were the Revisionists. Their organ, *Hamashkif (The Observer)* wrote in June 1944 that Hungarian Jewry was "shortsighted, and they did not feel the smoke gathering over their heads. They were sitting on a volcano and they did not realize it."[10] The paper further admonished: "they are going to drown, but the *Yishuv* must throw them a lifebelt." The Hungarian Jewish leadership was characterized by the paper as being "without energy and vision," an assessment which seems to have been shared not only by the antiestablishment Revisionists, but by the official leadership as well.

A second aspect to be noted is that of the effect of events in Hungary on the *Yishuv*. Several issues and patterns of reaction must be considered. First, the general public did not have access to information that was known to the leadership. Thus, it would be futile to draw any conclusions as to the reaction in the *Yishuv* to various crucial developments and events such as the so-called Eichmann offer. Second, the tragedy in Hungary struck at a moment when the Allies were on the verge of victory. Certainly the feeling that the war would soon be over provided the *Yishuv* with false feelings of ease. However, at the same time details were pouring in from the liberated areas about the Final Solution in Hungary. Against the background of these tragic events, the *Yishuv* increased its efforts for the establishment of the Jewish State. It seems that in the spring of 1944, when the Holocaust in Hungary began, the *Yishuv* lacked the spiritual resources to cope with continuing catastrophe. Again, as in 1941–42, the leadership and the media hesitated, as if the news were not reliable. From March 1944 on, there was virtually a conspiracy of silence about the fate of Hungarian Jewry and the *Yishuv* was faced with its own helplessness, seeming to cry out, "no, not again." It was a mentality, which cannot be documented by solid evidence, that the *Yishuv* could not face up to the approaching tragedy. Its silence was soon broken by the wave of expectations from Hungary's Jewry. In June 1944, *Davar* published an article under the headline "Why Aren't Hungary's Jews Resisting?"[11] The article, attributed by the paper to a correspondent in Ankara (but, according to recent research,[12] written by Y. Grunbaum), raised the question of resistance and asked why they were not taking up arms as had the Jews in Warsaw. Such resistance, according to the paper, would have made the Germans pay dearly for their designs. In fact, the media in the *Yishuv* as well as the leadership were asking more and more questions without providing answers. Moreover, expectations that there be Warsaw-like resistance from Hungarian Jewry shows the lack of proper analysis of the prevailing conditions in Hungary at that time and failure to appreciate the efficient determination of the Nazi machinery.

Expectations of armed resistance voiced in the *Yishuv* media reflected the views of the highest echelons of the leadership. In June 1944, at one of the meetings of the United Rescue Committee, the question was raised why the Jews were not putting up any resistance in Hungary and why Jerusalem was not giving them directions for defending themselves. Grunbaum replied that the Executive of the Jewish Agency would consider the matter of resistance in Hungary.[13] (It certainly should be noted that the *Yishuv* was taken aback by the events in Hungary and unrealistic expectations served as a substitute for more practical advice.)

The third point in considering the impact of events in Hungary on the *Yishuv* was use of the Holocaust as a topic of internal debate. It is quite evident that nobody in the *Yishuv* had a clear view of what could be done to save Hungarian Jewry or even knew what advice should be given to them. Yet the various political groupings in the *Yishuv* were busy accusing each other as well as Hungary's Jewry for not having foreseen the calamity. Naturally, the loudest voices of criticism were from the antiestablishment groups. The Revisionists accused the *Yishuv* leadership of acting without "energy and imagination" while Hungarian Jewry was being butchered, but were unable to offer any practical advice or help.

The Hungarians in the *Yishuv* had no clear, recognized leadership. Several prominent public personalities, such as Weisburg and the leaders of the HOH (*Hitahdut Olei Hungaria*—Association of Hungarian Immigrants), acted as a "Hungarian lobby," but had limited influence on the higher echelons of the *Yishuv* leadership. If it can be deduced from press coverage, public opinion was not very impressed by the activities of the HOH, which sought, almost in vain, to arouse public response to events in Hungary in the second half of 1944. From April 1944 onward, the HOH's various forums held meetings on the situation in Hungary. These activities were largely ignored by the media in the *Yishuv* except for the Revisionist press, which could make use of the criticism voiced by the HOH against the *Yishuv* leadership. This time the Revisionists were unconcerned that the leading public figures of Hungarian Jews in the *Yishuv* were identified and associated with the various wings of the left and the religious *Mizrachi*. The HOH explicitly accused the *Yishuv* of passivity in face of the tragedy.[14] Such accusations were not even answered by leading members of the establishment. What, in fact, the "Hungarian lobby" demanded was a constant state of "alertness" by the *Yishuv* in reporting and commenting on the events taking place in Hungary.

The atmosphere in the *Yishuv* and the rising voices against the prevailing mood constitute the fourth point to be considered. News on events in Hungary added fuel to the public debate, already started, on how the *Yishuv* was conducting business as usual given the background of events taking place in Hungary. Voices were raised, especially among small groups of intellectuals, complaining that life in the *Yishuv* was going on too smoothly, as if nothing was happening in Europe. These voices were part of a process of soul searching which began when the *Yishuv* first had to face the dimensions of the catastrophe.

This internal protest was expressed by *Al-Domi,* a small group of influential intellectuals, which accused the *Yishuv* leadership for concentrating solely on the building of the national home in Palestine and diverting the *Yishuv's* attention from the tragic events in Europe. The group, which was active between 1943 and 1945, was composed of such prominent intellectuals and men of letters in the *Yishuv* as Martin Buber, Ben-Zion Dinur, and Rabbi Benjamin (Redler-Feldman).[15] They did not belong to the establishment and they had no common political platform beyond the shared goal of creating a deeper awareness of the Holocaust in the *Yishuv.* They pointed out that rescue work organized and coordinated from Palestine required total dedication, which was not necessarily shown by the persons in charge of the rescue efforts in the *Yishuv.* Al-Domi's strongest accusations were aimed at the psychological reactions and daily moral behavior in the *Yishuv.* They called for an emergency atmosphere dedicated to trying to avert the fate of European Jewish communities. They thought the *Yishuv* should live night and day in the shadow of the Holocaust and not treat it as a part-time tragedy while carrying on as usual.

This attitude stood in marked contrast to the pattern of life proferred by the *Yishuv* leaders who tried to oppose the observation of public days of mourning in solidarity with European Jews because such somber manifestations had a depressing effect on public morale. This sobering effect is exactly what *Al-Domi* felt it was necessary to achieve. It is not for us to judge whether student festivities and public songfests should have been discontinued—as *Al-Domi* demanded—but it is important to emphasize that the *Yishuv,* out of utter helplessness, was unable to adopt a widely accepted formula, not only regarding the means of pursuing rescue activities, but also in the functioning of daily life in order to cope emotionally with the tragedy.

Al-Domi's reactions after the March 1944 events in Hungary were not aimed solely at criticizing the *Yishuv's* patterns of behavior. It also accused the establishment of not preparing the *Yishuv* to face the tragedy there—of not providing clear leadership and the means for rescue.[16] It serves no purpose to emphasize that *Al-Domi* itself could offer no practical rescue plan which could have changed the situation and that the group concentrated on the possible "ifs"—*if* the *Yishuv* had been better prepared, better led, etc. However, the character of the criticism made by the influential intellectuals who formed the *Al-Domi* group was different from the other voices in the *Yishuv.* They did not turn against Hungarian Jewry nor remind them of their past mistakes, but turned the criticism inward—the accusations were leveled against the *Yishuv* in general and its establishment in particular.

At its meeting in June 1944 the Writers' Union joined the call for a change in the public attitude to the Holocaust. Its resolutions called for unity in the *Yishuv* and for "tension and awakening."[17] The meeting took place one day before the Day of Mourning for the victims of the Holocaust on June 5, 1944. The Hungarian tragedy figured prominently in the public meeting held on that day. Yet, there was a growing feeling that the prevailing atmosphere in the *Yishuv* was undignified. The religious newspaper *Hatzofe* summed up the dilemma in the behavior of the *Yishuv:* "We woke up just for a moment from our passivity and uttered a passing cry of anguish; we mourned a day or two and then went on with our life as if nothing had happened. . . . And on the day following Mourning Day all emotion evaporated and we queued up at the movies.[18] The Revisionists criticized the pattern of life in the *Yishuv* in the shadow of the Holocaust in a tone similar to that of the religious *Mizrahi.* This criticism was especially strong during the last months of 1944, when the news was concentrating on the fate of Hungarian Jewry. *Hamashkif* bitterly complained in December 1944 that "in the past weeks in the *Yishuv* there has been a weakening in public awareness to the sufferings of our brothers.. . . . Apparently celebrations and festivities have pushed aside all concern for rescue"[19] Actually such accusations were untrue, as the critics' implied "hedonism" of the *Yishuv* did not divert the leadership's attention from the numerous rescue activities. But such criticism pointed justly to the weaknesses of the *Yishuv* during the Holocaust. It was a small, dedicated community with a deep feeling of responsibility for the fate of world Jewry, but was at the same time fragmented and thus unable to form a unified stand toward the chain of events during the Holocaust.

When the Nazi machine of extermination set out to annihilate Hungary's Jews, the weary *Yishuv* only belatedly grasped the magnitude of the catastrophe unfolding before its eyes, against the background of continued silence on the part of the world community.

So the *Yishuv* pursued its internal wars, looking for scapegoats and past errors instead of facing the present realities and searching for viable solutions.

Notes

1. Yehuda Bauer, "The Holocaust and the Struggle of the Yishuv as Factors in the Establishment of the State of Israel." *In: Holocaust and Rebirth—A Symposium.* Jerusalem: Yad Vashem, 1974, pp. 106-67.

2. See, for example, Yoav Gelber, "Zionist Policy and the Fate of European Jewry (1939–1942)." *In: Yad Vashem Studies.* Vol. 13. Jerusalem: Yad Vashem, 1979, pp. 169-210.

3. *Ha'Hazit* (The Front), June–July 1943.

4. Arieh Morgenstern, "Vaad ha'Hatzala ha'Meuhad shel Ha'Sochnut upeulotav b'shanim 1943-1945" (The United Rescue Committee of the Jewish Agency and Its Activity During 1943-1945). *Yalkut Moreshet* (Homeland Anthology), Tel Aviv, vol. 13, June 1971, pp. 60-97; Dinah Porat, *The Role Played By the Jewish Agency in Jerusalem in the Efforts to Rescue the Jews in Europe 1942-1945.* Unpublished Ph.D. Thesis in Hebrew, Tel Aviv: Tel Aviv University, 1983.

5. H. Weisburg to Y. Grunbaum, Jan. 20, 1944, Central Zionist Archive (CZA S 26/1251).

6. Association of Immigrants from Romania to M. Sharett, Jan. 11, 1944 (CZA S 25/5743). See also A. Morgenstern, *op. cit.*

7. Randolph L. Braham, *The Politics of Genocide. The Holocaust in Hungary.* New York: Columbia University Press, 1981, p. 950.

8. *Davar* (Word), Tel Aviv, Oct. 3, 1940. See Also Raphael Vago, "The Destruction of Hungarian Jewry as Reflected in the Palestine Press." *In: Hungarian-Jewish Studies.* Vol. III. Edited by Randolph L. Braham. New York: World Federation of Hungarian Jews, 1973, pp. 291-324.

9. *Davar,* May 17, 1944.

10. *Hamashkif* (The Observer), Tel Aviv, June 2, 1944.

11. *Davar,* June 22, 1945.

12. S. B. Beit-Zvi, *Post Ugandian Zionism in the Crucible of the Holocaust,* Tel Aviv: Bronfman, 1977, p. 371.

13. Minutes of the United Rescue Committee, June 29, 1944 (CZA S 26/1238).

14. *Hamashkif,* May 16, 1944.

15. Dina Porat, Al-Domi: Palestinian Intellectuals and the Holocaust, 1943–1945. *Studies in Zionism,* vol. 5, no. 1, 1984, pp. 97-124.

16. Porat, *op. cit.,* p. 111-125.

17. *Davar,* June 5, 1944.

18. *Hatzofe,* July 18, 1944.

19. *Hamashkif,* Dec. 5, 1944.

Chapter 10

THE *HALUTZ* RESISTANCE AND THE ANTI-NAZI MOVEMENTS IN HUNGARY, 1944

Asher Cohen

This paper requires a short methodological preface. As with all historical research on underground movements, this one too has to face the problem of the scarcity of written sources and has to rely to a great extent on oral ones. But my situation was additionally complicated, since I was unable to consult integral sections of the existing sources on one half of the topic.

On the *Halutz* (Pioneer) Resistance we have important information in the letters written to and from the Zionist delegations in Istanbul and in Geneva and most valuable oral sources which came from interviews of the one-time resisters, most of them living today in Israel.[1] But unfortunately, on the Hungarian anti-Nazi resistance I had no access at all to archives in Hungary and I could only consult the research done and the documents published by Hungarian research institutions. These rely mainly on oral sources and seem to ignore any organized Jewish and, even more, Zionist resistance groups.[2]

A second methodological remark concerns the scope of the paper, which deals only with the cooperation between the Jewish *Halutz* resistance and Hungarian anti-Fascist resistance organizations. It does not deal with the equally important and for the moment unexplored topic of Jewish participation as individuals in the various movements.

The *Halutz* resistance originated in March 1942, the time when waves of refugees were beginning to arrive in Hungary from Slovakia and Poland, escaping deportation to German concentration and extermination camps. These refugees, who came illegally into the country, could not stay unless they were supplied with false Hungarian identity papers—a task that fell to the local Zionist youth movements. Thus, unintentionally, a *Halutz* underground was created even though up to March 1944 only the refugees and not the Hungarian youth led an underground life.[3] But the permanent contact with the refugees who came to Hungary in the second half of 1943, especially the Polish, brought an important twofold change into the very small but still semi-legal Hungarian Zionist movement. They conveyed the technical ability to create an illegal organization and instilled a relative awareness of the German's genocidal policies, which enabled the *Halutz* youth to react quickly and efficiently after March 19, 1944.

The ten-month-long German occupation can be divided for the *Halutz* resistance into three distinct periods: from March 19 to the beginning of May, from May to October 15, and from then to the day of the liberation of Pest.

The first period involved the transformation of the semi-legal (since December 1943) headquarters of the movements in Budapest into an underground organization. During this period, while most of the Jews of Hungary were deported to Auschwitz, the few underground leaflets of Communist origin made no mention of the Jews, nor of saving Jews from deportation. Furthermore, during discussions in the underground Communist Party, members were implicitly instructed not to help Jews. They justified this by their own fragile illicit situation. This directive excluded the Jewish party members.

The second period (from May to October) is characterized by the first rescue attempts, by bringing mainly movement members from smaller towns to Budapest and then smuggling them to Romania, then relatively safe. These activities were later widened and the majority of the rescued were unorganized Jews. By the end of this period, for the first time contacts were made with non-Jewish anti-Nazi elements: one through the adult Zionist organization led by Ottó Komoly and Rezső (Rudolph) Kasztner,[4] and the second through the personal contacts of left-wing Zionist youth *(Hashomer Hatzair)* with members of the Communist underground.

In comparison with the *Halutz* underground of the Zionist youth movements, the Hungarian resistance was organized much later and was much less united. The "Hungarian Front" *(Magyar Front)*, with which Komoly had manifold contacts, was established in May 1944. It was the first overall political organization, although it lacked a popular resistance movement which could be a counterpart to the *Halutz* resistance.

The Communist resistance groups, with which the *Halutz* resistance had some contacts before October 15, were very small and divided between the illegal "Peace Party" *(Béke párt)*—called the "Moscovite Line" (or the "Line" for short) and the groups led by Pál Demény, the "Communists' Party of Hungary" *(Kommunisták Magyarországi Pártja).* This theoretically more leftist party had the most intensive contacts with the Zionist underground.

The main contribution of the *Halutz* resistance at this time was their ability to quickly supply a great variety, and quantity, of false papers. According to the testimonies at our disposal, at the end of the summer of 1944, the non-Jewish organizations were the biggest "clients" of the "laboratory" of false papers.[5] In exchange, the Hungarians helped to hide Jewish activists, especially those who deserted from the labor service companies. Still, the main interest of the Zionists was in the field of political concessions. They believed that if Hungary were liberated by the Red Army, it would be ruled by the Communists, and it seemed to them that it was the right moment to ask for Communist "recognition" of the Zionist movement or at least of its so-called "progressive" left wing. On this subject, according to the *Halutz* resisters' testimonies, the Demény group proved to be more flexible than the "Line," although it seems that no definite and clear agreement was ever reached.

Komoly's diary reveals that at the same time, serious discussions were being held with such men as Zoltán Tildy, Miklós Mester, Albert Bereczky, and perhaps also with Anna Kéthly and Árpád Szakasits and others, on including Komoly in a future liberated Hungarian government stemming from the Hungarian Front. The Jewish role in any future political system was so highly overevaluated during the summer of 1944 that deep concern was expressed on the steps to be taken to prevent furious Jewish revenge after the liberation, and many discussions were devoted to this subject.

Practical and meaningful contacts of the *Halutz* resistance with non-Jewish Resistance belong entirely to the third period, after the Arrow Cross takeover on October 15. This unexpected change required a swift reorganization in all the resistance movements. As far as the *Halutz* resistance was concerned, this was achieved relatively quickly for several reasons:

1. The leadership of the Zionist youth movements already lived underground;

2. The organization was based on a small number of "professionals" (after numerous movement members left Hungary for Romania or with the Kasztner train, or were deported);

3. The capacity of the "laboratory" at its peak to provide a great variety of false papers;

4. The possibility of relatively safe hideouts under cover of the Swiss Legation or the International Red Cross bureaus;

5. A relatively important number of experienced members were liberated, at the end of September and the beginning of October, from labor service companies or from jails.[6]

Quite paradoxically, one of the first groups with which practical contacts were made was an ex-Fascist organization, the "Hungarian Independent Socialist Party" *(Független Magyar Szocialista Párt)* led by Kálmán Rátz. From them, some of the *Halutz* members received Arrow Cross papers, uniforms, and armbands, which were extremely helpful in the first days of *Nyilas* (Arrow Cross) rule.[7].

In the beginning of November, the so-called Liberating Committee of the Hungarian National Uprising *(A Magyar Nemzeti Felkelés Felszabadító Bizottsága)* was founded, headed by Endre Bajcsy-Zsilinsky. It had both political and military arms and included a large range of political affiliates, from the Communists to the Horthysts and Legitimists. But unfortunately, on the 22nd of the same month, most of its leadership was arrested. So it is very difficult to assess to what extent the various Hungarian resistance groups were actually coordinated in their political aims or in practical activities.

From the Hungarian sourced, it seems that a twofold tendency, at least in the resistance groups under Communist influence, can be discerned. According to their view of the political situation, it was advisable to avoid a popular uprising similar to that of Warsaw in August 1944. Nevertheless, a willingness to do something against the *Nyilas* rule was felt, especially among the movement's rank and file. On the internal life and organization of the non-Communist groups (who constituted the majority of the underground organizations), the Hungarian sources tell us practically nothing.[8]

From all sources, it seems that a real growth of the Hungarian resistance can be dated from November 1944. This growth was due to:

1. The overall political organization;

2. The growing disintegration of the administrative structure under the Arrow Cross rule and the beginning of the evacuation of industries to the West;

3. The nearness of the Red Army to Budapest, symbolizing the end of the war, and the increasing number of desertions from the Hungarian Army;

4. The establishment at the end of October of the KISKA, *(Kisegitő Karhatalmi Alakulat;* Auxiliary Law Enforcing Units), meant by the Arrow Cross to serve their regime, but which turned out to be a hideout for deserters and resisters of all colors;[9]

5. The help of the *Halutz* "laboratory"—never the only, but always a very important, source of the false identities vital to underground activity.

Besides the very practical help that one side could offer the other, two main issues acted to bring together all resistance groups. Above all, the deep solidarity between all anti-Nazi and anti-German elements was and remained one of the most important motives for all cooperation. Secondly, the resistance was proof of anti-Fascist activity and was seen as one of the main means in preparing a basis for the future post-liberation regime.

The Jews were the surest anti-Nazi element. In addition, the memory of Béla Kun, as it was presented in the interwar period, seemed to make their role among the future rulers of Hungary inevitable. The position of Communists, unquestionably anti-Fascists, was strengthened by the quick advance of the Red Army. There were many other components of the Hungarian Front, such as the Smallholders' Party *(Kisgazda Párt)* or the Peasant Party *(Paraszt Párt;* previously the Populists) and the Radicals, who could prove their longstanding anti-Fascist attitude and therefore expected political compensation. To these, one has to add some of the Horthysts, who considered themselves "purified" because of the abortive armistice attempt of October 15, and looked forward to participation in the future regime.

Obviously, the fields of practical cooperation initiated previously continued to develop and were strengthened after the Arrow Cross takeover. New fields of cooperation developed resulting from the specific situation after November 1944. Permanent members of the various groups were appointed to the specific tasks of increasing collaboration: Some were one-time Zionist members of the Communist resistance, some were Left-wing Zionists who had had previous contacts with the Communist underground, and some had personal friends in the counterpart organization. Infiltration of any *agent provocateur* was therefore practically eliminated.

These contacts from the *Halutz's* side came mainly from the *Hashomer Hatzair* members. The main figures were Rafi Ben-Shalom (Friedel), Moshe Alpan (Pil), Efra Agmon (Teichmann), who was the main contact for identity papers, and Joseph Meyer (Megyeri), responsible for arms and food supplies. On the Communist side the most important person was Pál Demény, in whom the Jewish resistance had full confidence even though he was suspected by some Communists of the "Line." Others were György Non, who took care mainly of the food and arms supplies; Károly Kiss and Sándor Galambos, responsible for false papers, who supplied the "laboratory" with blank documents to fill up or to duplicate; and Iván Kádár, who also helped in relocating the "laboratory." György Aczél cooperated mainly with Komoly and helped in several lifesaving expeditions.[10]

Thanks to its international contacts, the *Halutz* resistance possessed foreign currency, large food supplies (for which they were able to organize transportation), and some relatively important stocks of arms.[11] The food and arms supply that the *Halutz* resistance had to offer has to be evaluated within the context of a city whose administration was disintegrating and which later was under siege. The money obtained from the Jewish organizations was of great value, but beyond the money at their disposal the very name of the Swiss Legation or the International Red Cross—both widely used, and behind which some recognized the American Joint Distribution Committee—had a nearly unlimited purchasing capacity.

After November 1944 the various resistance groups certainly outnumbered the *Halutz* resistance. This enabled the Hungarians to provide some effective armed protection for important Jewish centers, and for activities such as food transport and, much more important, rescue actions. The support given by the non-Jewish resisters is one of the less explored chapters. Hungarian sources indicate many addresses where the *Halutz* resistance had children's houses. From testimonies of the *Halutz* members we learn that several times trucks were sent to return Jews from the road to Hegyeshalom, provided and partially manned by the Communist resistance under the guidance of György Aczél. His name is often mentioned in Komoly's diary in connection with various rescue attempts. These activities might be much more important and of a larger scale than can be shown from the currently available sources.[12]

The "Glass House" in Vadász Street, and the other allegedly "Swiss House" in Wekerle Sándor Street had over 3000 Jews. Five to six thousand others were in the *Halutz* resistance children homes, others in the "protected houses" outside the ghetto. Official protection had gradually vanished, and the only real forces were the armed Arrow Cross men in the streets. Therefore, only armed protection could be of any efficiency. The human resources of the *Halutz* resistance were limited, and without outside assistance would have been insufficient.

The instinctive but intense willingness for "direct action" among the rank and file in all movements brought on the organization of combined armed groups. These had a few successful skirmishes—often more of moral than military importance—with the Arrow Cross men. Some of these street fights were actually not mere tests of arms but important lifesaving activities, liberating Jews driven to the banks of the Danube by the Arrow Cross gangs to be shot. Our limited sources do not permit a full quantitative evaluation of these activities. But, considering rescue of human life as a central task of resistance in this last stage of *Nyilas* rule, their importance and merit is indisputable.

Concluding the topic, the main points to emphasize are that no effective cooperation between Jewish and other resistance movements in Hungary can be observed before October 15. The cause of this tragic delay is due to the very late appearance of any non-Jewish resistance there. After October, cooperation seems rather harmonious. The lifesaving character of the *Halutz* resistance concorded with the policy of the Hungarian resistance.

During this short but extremely violent period, the cooperation was beneficial to both sides. It stemmed from instinctive anti-Nazi solidarity, from complementary means for mutual help and sustenance, and, last but not least, from mutual political aspirations.

Notes

1. For the representation in Istanbul, which began activities in December, 1942, see the memoirs of Menachem Bader, *Shlihuyot Atzuvot* (Sad Delegations). Merhavia: 1954. See also Dalia Ofer, "The Activities of the Jewish Agency Delegation in Istanbul in 1943."—*Rescue Attempts During the Holocaust,* Jerusalem: Yad Vashem, 1976, pp. 435-450. Parts of the archive of the Istanbul delegation can be found in a number of archives in Israel in the original or in copies. I consulted the Ghetto Fighters' House (Israel) collection, which seems to be the most complete on the subject: Z.1063/H. Many testimonies concerning the *Halutz* resistance in Hungary are preserved in the archive at the Ghetto Fighters' House and in the Center for Historical Documentation at Haifa University (hereafter—"Center").

2. On the Hungarian resistance see Refs. no. 1313-1341 in *The Hungarian Jewish Catastrophe. A Selected and Annotated Bibliography.* Compiled and edited by Randolph L. Braham. New York: Institute for Holocaust Studies of The City University of New York, 1984. (Distributed by Columbia University Press.) I have received fragments of testimonies by members of the Hungarian Communist resistance from David Gur whom I would like to thank for his help. These testimonies largely confirm those collected in Israel, mainly from the *Hashomer Hatzair* members of the *Halutz* resistance (see note 5).

3. Randolph L. Braham, *The Politics of Genocide. The Holocaust in Hungary.* New York: Columbia University Press, 1981, pp. 998-1011; Asher Cohen, *Hamahteret Hahalutzit Be-Hungaria 1942-1945* (The Halutz Resistance in Hungary 1942-1945), Tel Aviv: Hakibbutz Hameuchad, 1984, 342 p.

4. Braham, pp. 932-995; *Der Kastner Bericht.* Edited by Ernest Landau. Munich: Kindler, 1961, 367 p.; "The Diary of Ottó Komoly, August 21–September 16, 1944." *In: Hungarian Jewish Studies.* Vol. 3. Edited by Randolph L. Braham. New York:

World Federation of Hungarian Jews, 1973, pp. 147-250; Unpublished parts consulted from a copy deposited in: "Center" H3C6, and from original photocopies in Professor Bela Vago's personal collection for which I wish to express my gratitude.

5. Important information from the *Halutz* resisters' point of view: Rafi Ben-Shalom, *Neevaknu lemaan hachaim* (We Struggled for Life). Tel Aviv: Moreshet, 1977, 223 p. This book based on testimonies written in Budapest in 1945 also includes those of Joseph Meyer (Megyeri), pp. 149-160, Efra Agmon (Teichmann) pp. 161-175, David Gur (Grosz) pp. 176-205. Other important information in: "Center" H3C59, H3C22/3, H3C1, H3C14/18, H3C22/5, H3C14/19, H3C14/1, H3C3, see note no. 2.

6. See sources in notes 3, 4 and also: Mihály Salamon, *"Keresztény" voltam Európában* (I Was a Christian in Europe). Tel Aviv: Népünk Kiadása, 1956, 220 p.; Central Zionist Archives (Jerusalem), L15/277; Moreshet Archives (Givat Chaviva, Israel), D.1.1147, D.1.1150, A.710; Yad Vashem Archives (Jerusalem), P.10/172, 03-2416-K, 1253/83-W.

7. J. Meyer, pp. 150-151.

8. I. Pintér, *Magyar Front és az ellenállás* (Hungarian Front and the Resistance). Budapest: Kossuth: 1970, pp. 214-329. Another group led by Imre Radó, which included mainly Jews and Social Democrats, were not part of but linked by personal contacts to both the *Halutz* and the Communist resistance. From their center in Visegrádi Street 36, the men of the "Radó group" led an important lifesaving activity by distributing false papers. A detailed diary of one of the members, Shmuel Goren (Tamás Gellért) is deposited in the "Center" H3H73. The group is fleetingly mentioned in *Magyar Szabadságharocosok a fasizmus ellen* (Hungarian Freedom Fighters Against Fascism). Edited by János Harsányi. Budapest: Zrinyi, 1969, p. 542.

9. Éva Teleki, *Nyilas uralom Magyaroszágon* (*Nyilas* Rule in Hungary). Budapest: Kossuth, 1974, pp. 88-217.

10. R. Ben-Shalom, pp. 118-127, 153-160, 190-205; Harsányi, pp. 532-533, 539-543; *Harcok, emlékek* (Battles, Memories). Edited by Katalin Petrák and Ernő Vágó. Budapest: Zrinyi, 1969, pp. 34-36. In these testimonies, published in Hungary, the *Halutz* resistance is never mentioned by name but indications are clear; such as Megyeri's name, "Left wing refugees from Slovakia" supplying false papers, the address of the "Swiss Red Cross" in Vadász Street, etc.

11. Most important were of course the food supplies. In addition to note 5, see the testimony of Alexander (Sanyi) Grossmann, "Center" C3H1. For some of the arms which were received thanks to some Polish members of the *Halutz* resistance, see: "Center" H3C14/1.

12. See note 10, and also the testimony of Moshe Weisskopf, "Center" C3H15/13.

Chapter 11

RAOUL WALLENBERG:
THE RIGHTEOUS GENTILE FROM SWEDEN

Elenore Lester

The story of Raoul Wallenberg, the Swedish diplomat who rescued thousands of Hungarian Jews between July 9, 1944 and January 17, 1945 is unique. There were other righteous gentiles in Hungary, as in other countries, but the fact is that nearly all of the six million Jewish victims of the Holocaust died seeing themselves abandoned by the world. Only in Budapest in the hellish winter of 1944 did the Jews have an official advocate from the civilized world, a representative of a neutral country whose sole purpose in being there was to intercede on their behalf against those intent on destroying them. Wallenberg's diplomatic status gave him a power base from which to attempt to rescue large numbers, but his success in doing so can be attributed only to his personal courage, resourcefulness and dedication.

Wallenberg's work in Budapest cannot be overpraised, but it is important to recognize at the same time that it would not have been possible without the support of the Swedish and the American governments. Wallenberg was sent to Budapest at the request of the American War Refugee Board with $100,000 from the American Jewish Joint Distribution Committee (AJDC). While recognizing the value of what was accomplished with this support, one must recognize that Wallenberg's mission points up the bitter fact that large-scale rescue was possible, even during one of the worst periods of the Holocaust.

It is illuminating to review the events that led up to Wallenberg's mission. The story really starts on January 13, 1944, when a young general counsel in the U.S. Treasury Department, Josiah E. DuBois, Jr., presented his boss,

147

Secretary of the Treasury Henry Morgenthau, a document titled "Report to the Secretary of the Treasury on the Acquiescence of this Government in the Murder of the Jews." It was a searing indictment of the machinations of the American State Department to sabotage all possibilities of rescuing Jews by bringing them into the United States in even the limited number allowed under the quota laws of the period. Morgenthau retitled the document, "A Personal Report to the President" and submitted it to Roosevelt. A struggle within the Administration ensued and Roosevelt resolved it by setting up a special agency to help "rescue the victims of enemy oppression who are in imminent danger of death." The term Jew was not used. Roosevelt, the astute politician, did not want the public to get the idea that he was doing anything special for the Jews. Thus, the agency set up to rescue Jews was called the War Refugee Board (WRB). John Pehle, who had worked with DuBois on the report to Morgenthau, was appointed director and the new agency officially went into business January 22, 1944, eight weeks before the Germans occupied Hungary.

It was through the efforts of Pehle that Raoul Wallenberg was sent to Budapest. However, the idea of sending a representative of neutral Sweden to make a personal effort to intercede on behalf of the Jews did not take root until late in May, when the dejewification of Hungary was well advanced. It was not until June 9, while the cattle cars were rolling toward Auschwitz with 10,000 to 12,000 victims daily, that Iver C. Olsen, representative of the WRB in Stockholm, and incidentally of the Office of Strategic Services (OSS, predecessor of the CIA), made contact with Raoul Wallenberg and recommended him for the job. It was not until June 23, while the crematoria were working round the clock, that the Swedish Foreign Office came through with official approval, giving Wallenberg the status of second secretary to the Swedish Legation in Budapest. It was not until July 9, the day after completion of the deportation program for all of Hungary except Budapest, that Wallenberg arrived. The roundup of the Jews of Budapest had been scheduled for July 10. It was called off by Regent Miklós Horthy, who was at this point trying to extricate himself from the war.

It is interesting to note that during the month in which Wallenberg had been contacted and begun the preparations for his mission, the "Auschwitz Protocols," the document put together by two Auschwitz escapees, giving the map of the camp and full details about what was going on there, was circulating through Washington, London, the Vatican, Geneva, Stockholm, and Istanbul. Nevertheless, a suggestion from Rabbi Michael Dov-Beer Weismandel of Bratislava and others that the rail lines leading to the camp and the crematoria be bombed was turned down by the British and the U.S.

War Department as being "impracticable." We know today that Allied bombers crisscrossed the camp on bombing and reconnaissance missions to the east of Auschwitz throughout the following weeks.[1] During the same period Joel Brand, a leader of the Relief and Rescue Committee of Budapest, brought out the strange message from Hungary that the Nazis were willing to trade one million Jews for winterized trucks to be used exclusively on the Eastern front.[2] This was rejected almost at once although Jewish leaders hoped that at least a pretense at considering it would have brought about a respite in the killings. Finally Regent Horthy's offer in July and August to permit the emigration of between 7,800 and 40,000 Jews to Palestine or other havens was lost in diplomatic wrangling. There is considerable credible evidence that resistance on the part of the British to letting out Jews who might go to Palestine was at the heart of the matter.[3]

From the perspective of the 1980s it would seem that any or all of those possibilities held more promise than sending—without guidelines—a 31-year-old Swedish businessman, who had no diplomatic experience, to Budapest to do something to thwart the death machine. It appears as if Wallenberg was sent to Budapest as a token gesture to show the Jews that something was being attempted. Yet, given the situation that developed, it proved to be an almost miraculously fortunate gesture and Wallenberg was an almost miraculous choice for the job. The fact that he was not a real diplomat, although he knew how to imitate one when necessary, was to his advantage. He was not restricted by a bureaucratic mentality. He was by temperament and training cut out to play a large role in life, but had not yet had the opportunity to fulfill his abilities.

As to Wallenberg's background, it is generally known that he came of a family of bankers and diplomats. The fact is that the Wallenberg family were the Rockefellers of Sweden. His cousins, the late Jacob and Marcus Wallenberg, were tycoons who controlled segments of all of Sweden's major industries. They made the trade agreements for Sweden that preceded World War II. Marcus made the agreements with Great Britain and Jacob made the agreement with Germany, giving the Third Reich the iron ore and ball bearings without which it would have been impossible to fight the war. On his maternal side Wallenberg was the grandson of Sweden's first neurosurgeon and numbered among his ancestors one of the first Jews to come to Sweden in the eighteenth century. This man, Michael Benediks, came to Sweden as a jeweler and became financial adviser to King Johann XIV. He converted to Christianity, married a Christian woman, and raised a large family. Wallenberg was evidently proud of this Jewish ancestor and often spoke of being part Jewish. Hershel Johnson, the American

Ambassador to Stockholm, who interviewed Wallenberg before he left for Budapest, got the impression that he was half Jewish.

Despite his illustrious background Wallenberg was brought up as an upper-middle-class Swedish Lutheran. His father died at the age of 23, three months before Raoul was born, and although he acquired a devoted stepfather at age six, his grandfather, Gustav Wallenberg, supervised his education. Gustav was Swedish Ambassador to Tokyo before World War I, and to Istanbul from the 1920s until his retirement in 1936. Gustav had great dreams for his only grandson. He wanted Raoul to head an international bank. Raoul was interested in finance and business, but his passion was for architecture. His grandfather permitted him to study architecture at the University of Michigan. Raoul graduated in 1935 with the top award given by the American Institute of Architects. Through his grandfather's arrangements, he was sent to work in the Holland Bank in Haifa in 1936. There he discovered he loathed banking and confronted his grandfather with the simple fact that he wasn't cut out for that work. In Haifa, he also discovered German Jewish refugees from Hitlerism and became deeply concerned about what was happening in Germany.

Raoul returned to Stockholm in the fall of 1936 and shortly afterward his grandfather died. He hoped that he would be able to use his architectural training in one of the huge Wallenberg enterprises, but apparently Cousin Jacob put him off. He tried to start a couple of businesses of his own but they failed. Eventually Jacob put him in touch with Kalman Lauer, a Hungarian Jew who reportedly owned the largest food processing and distribution business in East Central Europe. Lauer was living in Sweden and was no longer able to take his customary business trips all over Europe because of the Nazis. He was looking for a partner who knew languages and could travel. At the end of 1941, Raoul became Lauer's partner and made two successful business trips to Vichy France, one to Paris, and one to Budapest and Bucharest, accumulating along the way experience in how the Nazi bureaucracy functioned. Wallenberg became a friend to Mr. Lauer, and when the Germans occupied Hungary he volunteered to go to see what he could do for Mrs. Lauer's family, who lived there. However, Mr. Lauer thought it would be dangerous for him to go. Mrs. Lauer's family was in fact deported and killed.[4]

It was Kalman Lauer who recommended Wallenberg for the mission to Budapest when he learned that someone was being sought for such a job. Wallenberg, with his immense physical energy, was eager for the mission: he spoke German like a native and had some experience in dealing with Nazi bureaucracy. Wallenberg knew enough about the world of diplomacy to know that although it could give him a power base, it could also restrict him. Therefore, before he agreed to accept the job, he made nine stipulations which freed him to do whatever he considered necessary to save lives, including engaging in bribery.

When Raoul Wallenberg arrived in Budapest more than 200,000 Jews were cowering in assigned yellow-star houses. They were allowed out on the streets only two hours a day and forced to wear the humiliating star. They knew that their families and friends in the countryside had been carried off. They did not know what had become of them but had reason to suspect the worse. They awaited their own fate. They were the last Jews in Hungary aside from some 150,000 men in forced labor companies, dying at a rapid rate, and some 18,000 in special labor camps at Strasshof and other areas near Vienna.[5]

At that time some 8,000 Budapest Jews held papers which, by a special agreement with the Hungarian government, were supposed to entitle them to emigration when conditions permitted. The Swiss Consul had sponsored a collective passport for the emigration of more than 7,000 to Palestine, and the Swedes had distributed 300 to 400 papers for emigration to Sweden of Hungarian Jews who had business or family connections in Sweden. These were, in effect, provisional passports, putting the bearer under Swedish protection.

Wallenberg noted that several individuals had used the Swedish papers successfully when they were threatened with deportations. He had the insight to recognize that even in the savage lunatic asylum Europe had become, bureaucracy remained bureaucracy. He decided to increase the psychological impact of the Swedish papers by designing a larger, more impressive document. It was produced on heavy paper and carried the Swedish triple crown emblem in yellow and blue and left space for a picture of the bearer. It was signed by Swedish Minister Carl Ivan Danielsson. This document rapidly became the most prized possession in Budapest. The Swiss document did not carry the bearer's picture and was unsigned. The same was true of a Portuguese "passport" and an International Red Cross document. In the days when Budapest was being flooded with real and forged documents, including baptismal certificates, the Swedish documents carried the most authority.

Wallenberg ostensibly issued some 4,500 documents by a legal agreement with Hungarian authorities. However, he actually issued about three times more than that number, according to his colleagues at the Swedish Legation. In addition, he tacitly approved the forging of the documents by the young Zionists of Budapest.[6]

According to Lars Berg, Wallenberg's colleague at the Swedish Legation, the diplomatic officials there did not approve of what he was doing and argued strenuously against it. They felt that it was inevitable that the powers-that-be would perceive the inflation of documents and they would lose all validity. However, Wallenberg was persistent and persuasive.[7]

The document upon which Wallenberg built his entire rescue operation was actually a fiction with no precedent in international law. However, Wallenberg's determination convinced both German and Hungarian authorities who had not the slightest regard for human rights that this magic piece of paper was to be respected. Just as important, he was able to convince the Jews that it could save them.

Word of Wallenberg's aggressive approach to his task quickly got back to Stockholm, and Iver C. Olsen reported to Pehle at the WRB:

> I get the impression indirectly that the Swedish Foreign Office is somewhat uneasy about Wallenberg's actions in Budapest and perhaps feel that he has jumped in with too big a splash. They would prefer, of course, to approach the Jewish problem in the finest traditions of European diplomacy, which wouldn't help too much.[8]

In one of Wallenberg's first reports to Stockholm, he wrote of the "lack of courage" he found among Budapest Jews. Total despair would have been a more accurate description. However, he recognized their condition as a kind of "apathy" brought on by their perception "that they had been abandoned." He set about trying to relieve them of that feeling. He energetically got to work establishing Section C of the Legation, concerned solely with the activities to help Jews. He accumulated a staff of about 40, mainly Jews, and got permission for them from Hungarian authorities to remove the yellow star badge. This enabled them to move freely about the city at all times. Wallenberg rightly guessed that along with the *Schutzpässe* (protective passports) they distributed, they would bring along hope and courage. He also set about establishing two hospitals and stocking them with medical supplies and he purchased large quantities of food, which were stored in various parts of the city and became a lifeline during the siege of Budapest by the Russians.

On August 4, Wallenberg visited Horthy and explained his purpose in Budapest and urged the Regent to stand by his decision to end the deportations. At this point Adolf Eichmann, the head of the Special Commando *(Sonderkommando),* was pressing hard for a resumption of deportations. He had ordered one for August 5. However, when Horthy learned about it through the Jewish Council *(Zsidó Tanács)* he cancelled it.

Eichmann set another date, August 25. This time Wallenberg performed two important actions—he met with representatives of the neutral legations and of the Papal Nuncio's office to draft and present an appeal to Horthy, and secondly visited Lieutenant Colonel László Ferenczy, the man who had supervised the deportations from the countryside and who was now in charge of Jewish affairs in Budapest. He requested permission to place his Swedish passport holders in protected houses until they could be transported to Sweden. He was able to get three protected houses and at the same time Alexander Kasser, General Secretary of the Swedish Red Cross, secured three houses.[9]

Horthy cancelled the scheduled August 25 deportations the day after Heinrich Himmler himself cancelled all further deportations. Eichmann was recalled from Budapest and received the Iron Cross, second class, for his services in Hungary.

From that time on, up to October 15, the Jews of Budapest breathed easier and Wallenberg was planning to wind up his work, dissolve his staff, and leave Budapest before the Russians arrived. He wrote to Olsen on October 12 that he felt that the mission had been successful and modestly thanked him for his efforts on behalf of the Hungarian Jews.[10]

However, three days later Wallenberg's work in Budapest began again in earnest. Horthy's attempt to surrender to the Allies resulted in a coup staged by pro-Nazi Hungarian elements and the Germans and Ference Szálasi came to power at the head of the Arrow Cross *(Nyilas)* government. Sweden immediately broke off relations with the new government. This made it virtually impossible for the Swedish Legation to function in Budapest. Danielsson requested direction from his Foreign Office as to whether the Legation should stay or go. He was told to use his own judgment. The Legation staff voted to stay. Wallenberg's determination to stay was a strong factor in the decision to remain in Budapest. If the Swedes had left there can be little doubt that the Budapest Jews would have been totally at the mercy of the Arrow Cross and the SS. Wallenberg became the backbone of the rescue operations. At the same time he was endangering his own life and that of the entire Legation. In December the *Nyilas* invaded the Swedish Legation and carried two women employees off to the ghetto, where they threatened their lives.[11]

One of the first acts of the new government was to issue a statement that no foreign papers of any sort would be recognized. At this point, Wallenberg appealed to a woman he knew to be sympathetic to what he was doing— the Baroness Kemény, wife of the *Nyilas* Foreign Minister Gábor Kemény. The Baroness was very young, beautiful, and cultivated and had known nothing of the nature of Nazism when she married her husband. She learned in Budapest. Wallenberg had met her socially and they established a rapport. She was at that time pregnant with her first child. Wallenberg went to her and told her that if the Jews under the protection of the neutrals were harmed, her child would surely be born fatherless. Her husband would be hanged as a war criminal. She must use her influence to get the order revoked. She did exactly that and insisted, on Wallenberg's terms, that an announcement to that effect be made on the radio. She accompanied her husband to the radio station to make sure that he carried out his promise.[12]

Wallenberg did not perceive his role in Budapest as limited to saving only those privileged by contacts, money, or simply the physical and moral strength to stand in line day after day to secure a Swedish document. There are innumerable testimonials to the fact that when Wallenberg learned about a deportation he would go to the train station, set out his folding table and his large official-looking Legation book, and ask those holding Swedish documents to come forward. Then he asked those who had made their applications and been accepted, but had not yet received their documents, to come forward. At this point, anyone with a scrap of paper and enough courage would step up to Wallenberg's improvised desk, and be checked off, very solemnly, in the big book. Then Wallenberg would march his proteges out of the station while the SS looked on.

Early in November, when Eichmann was no longer able to get trains for deportations, he ordered a series of death marches to Hegyeshalom at the Austro-Hungarian border, presumably in order to supply labor to the Germans. The unspeakable conditions of this journey have been described in many reports, but perhaps the best statement on the matter is the fact that *Waffen*-SS General Hans Jüttner was so horrified that he protested to high SS authorities.[13]

At this point Wallenberg, as well as other representatives of neutral countries and of the Red Cross and the Vatican, set up checkpoints along the road and managed to take out some of the marchers who carried documents. They also brought soup and some medical aid, hardly enough to take care of thousands, but it may have strengthened a few who were about to give up. Hundreds committed suicide along the way by giving up and lying in the ditches, where they were eventually shot. On one occasion Wallenberg went to Hegyeshalom, bringing Swedish passports with him. He showed Arrow Cross guards his diplomatic credentials and ordered them to stand aside while he removed Jews with Swedish passports. They pointed their bayonets at him in answer. Wallenberg ran to the other side of the station, clambered to the roof of one of the cars, and shouted through an opening at the top of the car that he had Swedish passes for any who had lost their documents. Hands reached up for the passes. Wallenberg was finally able to convince the officer in charge of the unit to allow him to remove those with documents.[14]

In response to the worsening situation Wallenberg increased his staff to as many as 400, including 40 physicians. He had by this time acquired 32 "protected" buildings. The Swedish flag was not always a protection when a group of Arrow Cross thugs decided to attack. Wallenberg set some of the young men on his staff with a particularly "Aryan" appearance to guard the buildings. At one point he made a deal to exchange some of his food supplies for protection for the buildings. As the Arrow Cross terror raged, many unauthorized persons moved into the buildings, which became so overcrowded that families were actually living on the staircases. Early in December, after the bombings by Allied and Russian planes had disrupted the water supply, Wallenberg had everyone living in the buildings inoculated against paratyphoid typhoid, and cholera.[15] This act alone may have saved countless lives.

In mid-December, when the Russians were fast approaching Budapest, Wallenberg invited Eichmann to dinner to try to persuade him to call off the Jew-killing. The dinner party was held in the apartment of Wallenberg's colleague Lars Berg. Berg has described the meal as elegant, enhanced by fine wines and brandies. From the windows of his apartment in Buda, the diners could see and hear the fire of Russian artillery. Wallenberg discussed Nazism with Eichmann and urged him to give up, warning him he would surely hang as a war criminal. According to Berg, Eichmann said he knew he would die, but vowed, "I will do my job to the end," and clicking his heels as he got up to go said, "As for you Mr. Diplomat, don't think your diplomatic immunity can protect you forever. Even diplomats have accidents." A few days later Wallenberg's car was rammed by a heavy truck and completely demolished, but he was not in it. Wallenberg's colleagues interpreted this "accident" as an attempted assassination.

Wallenberg knew that both the Arrow Cross and Eichmann's men were out to get him and he took to sleeping in different buildings every night. He moved away from the comparative safety of the Swedish Legation in Buda to spend all of his time in Pest, where most of the Jews lived.

Throughout this period, Wallenberg kept up a barrage of diplomatic notes to Interior Minister Gábor Vajna, appealing for some humane treatment of the Jews. He preserved the fiction that he was dealing with a sane government in a rational world and cited diplomatic claims. He managed to get an order for the removal of Jews from some of the Swedish houses to the large ghetto postponed. He played for time, hoping the Russians would come soon. He was also able to buy protection for some of his buildings by giving food to the *Nyilas* from the Swedish stocks when the city was on the brink of famine.[16]

When Eichmann fled Budapest on the night of December 23, he left orders that the large ghetto, which held close to 70,000 Jews, was to be blown up. Between Christmas Eve and the day the Russians entered Pest, the attacks on Jews became increasingly savage. There was the Christmas Day massacre in the orphanage, raids on hospitals, and one into the Swiss-protected "Glass House" at 29 Vadász Street.[17]

During this period Wallenberg learned through his informants that plans for the massacre in the large ghetto were being set up. He undertook to go with his colleague, Per Anger, to see SS Commanding General August Schmidthuber. He came with his usual warning—that if Schmidthuber harmed the Jews he would surely hang as a war criminal. Anger has reported in his book—*With Raoul Wallenberg in Budapest*—that Schmidthuber "was shaken by Wallenberg's words." We know from the postwar testimony of Pál Szalai, the Arrow Cross Party's liaison to the police, that two days before the liberation of the ghetto the mass murder was actually planned, using a force of 500 German soldiers and 200 Hungarian police. Szalai stated that he managed to get to Schmidthuber with his information about plans for the massacre and reminded him of Wallenberg's warning. Schmidthuber immediately cancelled the project.[18]

The number of Jews that Wallenberg is credited with saving is generally given as 100,000. Scholars who are aware that only about 119,000 Budapest Jews survived the war may question the figure. However, since Wallenberg may be considered responsible for saving the ghetto, the figure is realistic. But even this figure does not do justice to the full impact of his presence in Budapest. The following incident, described by a woman who did not have Swedish papers, points up the profound importance of his presence:

In mid-November Susan Tabor and her mother, Margit Brenner, were seized by the *Nyilas* and brought to the brick factory at Óbuda on the outskirts of Buda to spend the night before starting off on the death march. Their husbands were both far from home in forced labor companies. "There was no food, no water, no light, no sanitation facilities," Mrs. Tabor has related.

> There were holes in the floor of the building and some people had fallen in them and hurt themselves in the dark. Some had broken legs. People were in a terrible condition. There was crying and moaning everywhere. Suddenly Wallenberg

appeared among us. He said he would try to bring medical help and asked people who had been hurt to call out. He said he would return with safety passes and would bring food and try to get sanitary facilities. After he left, those broken people managed to rouse themselves and suddenly from all over you could hear they were saying the *Shma—Shma Yisrael Adonai Eloheinu, Adonai Echad (Here O Israel, the Lord is our God. The Lord is One)*. They pulled themselves together, some to face death with dignity, others to find courage to go on. He showed us that we were human beings again because one human being cared about us.[19]

Shortly after Wallenberg appeared, Mrs. Tabor and her mother ripped the yellow stars off their jackets, gave away some of the food they had carried with them and managed to escape and return to Budapest, where they hid out until the end of the war. They emigrated with their husbands to the United States several years later.

Wallenberg was forced to take refuge in the International Red Cross house at 16 Benczur Street during the last days of the Russian siege, but continued to go on rescue missions up to the end. Mrs. János Kondor has testified that on January 16, the day before the Russians liberated Pest, the Swedish-protected house on Jokai Street in which she was living with her husband and two children was invaded by the *Nyilas*. All of the occupants were herded into the courtyard and were faced by a gang pointing machine guns at them and yelling, "You rotten gangsters, you vermin, while we are protecting the country, you are hiding here. Now we will take care of you." Suddenly Wallenberg stormed in with a small group and started shouting at them to get out, this was "an extraterritorial building." Gradually, they lowered their guns and left, leaving behind the food and jewelry they had found when they raided the building.[20]

The following day Wallenberg's work was brought to an end. He had not planned it that way. He had intended to remain in the city until it could be brought out of its crisis. During his last months he had had members of his staff work up an elaborate plan to heal the city's war wounds.[21] Wallenberg wanted to use his large staff of trusted individuals to work on programs for reuniting families, caring for war orphans and the disabled, distributing food, counteracting epidemics, and restoring homes and businesses to the Jews. He eagerly sought contact with higher Russian officers in order to get his plan to Soviet army headquarters as quickly as possible.

Today Wallenberg's notion that he, a representative of the American as well as the Swedish government, would be permitted to run his independent relief agency in a Soviet-controlled area, seems naive. However, Wallenberg had no briefing on Soviet intentions in East Europe and he also could not have realized at that time that the fact that he was in Budapest to aid Jews would not impress the Russians. As a matter of fact when the Russians found Budapest filled with "Swedish" Jews they became highly suspicious. All members of the Swedish Legation were interrogated intensively about Wallenberg's activities, and the thrust of the questioning was: How come a member of Sweden's leading capitalist family was in Budapest solely in order to help Jews? Lars Berg, who was picked up by the Russians separately from other members of the staff, said that he was questioned intensively for many hours and was asked over and over again where Wallenberg and the Swedish Legation had gotten all the money from. (The Russians had blasted open the vault and found the jewelry and securities Budapest Jews had entrusted to them.) They also wanted to know who headed the espionage at the Legation, Berg or Wallenberg.

Wallenberg left Budapest on January 17, 1945 with his own chauffeur, Vilmos Langfelder, accompanied by Russian officers. He told his staff he didn't know whether he was being arrested or going as a "guest." However, he went willingly and apparently cheerfully, looking forward to bringing his plan for the rehabilitation of Budapest to the commander of the Russian forces in Debrecen. The Russians sent the Swedish Foreign Office a note dated January 16, 1945, "We have your Raoul Wallenberg and his effects under our protection." [22]

Neither Wallenberg nor his driver reached Debrecen. After its initial message the Soviet government reported that it did not know what became of him, but assumed that he had been killed by bandits outside of Budapest. However, after Stalin died in 1953, among the tens of thousands of prisoners who were released in the general amnesty were several who had seen Wallenberg in prison in Moscow, or who had communicated with him or Langfelder via code knockings on cell walls. Finally in 1957, after many queries and curiously inept diplomatic efforts on the part of the Swedish Foreign Office, the Soviet government informed the Swedes that a memorandum had been found in their prison files which indicated that "a Walenberg" [sic] had died in his cell in Lubianka Prison on July 17, 1947. Everyone connected with the case was dead, from the medical examiner who had signed the memorandum to the security minister to whom it was addressed, and the minister's chief, Lavrenti Beria, Stalin's hatchet man, who had been shot for "criminal activities" allegedly at Khrushchev's order.[23]

However, by the time the Swedes received the Russian message they already had in their possession a number of reports of sightings of Wallenberg long after July 1947. Since that time and up to the 1980s there have been reports that Wallenberg may still be alive in a Soviet prison.

Can the world really believe such a story? Is it possible that Raoul Wallenberg remains alive in the Soviet Union today? I would put the question in another way. Can the world really believe the Soviet memorandum to Sweden of 1957? The Swedish Foreign Office has a substantial file of carefully screened reports of sightings of Wallenberg in the Soviet Union long after 1947. In view of these reports and the casual nature of the 1957 memorandum, we must confess that we don't know whether or not he is alive. Therefore, we are morally obligated to pursue his case. For the past twenty-eight years the Soviet government has refused repeated appeals from the Swedish government and, in recent years, from the American government to reopen an investigation into Wallenberg's whereabouts. The dissident Andrei Sakharov has urged the Wallenberg Committee to persist in its efforts to get information.[24] Undoubtedly, the Soviet Union assumes that eventually those who concern themselves with his case will give up out of frustration. But if Wallenberg's work in Budapest teaches us anything, it is that we must not give up in the face of evil. Certainly, all who know that in Budapest Wallenberg did not abandon the Jews, even when it seemed hopeless to try to save them, cannot abandon him now.

Notes

1. David Wyman, Why Auschwitz Was Never Bombed. *Commentary,* New York, vol. 65, no. 5, May 1978: 37-46.

2. Yehuda Bauer, *The Holocaust in Historical Perspective.* Seattle: The University of Washington Press, 1978, pp. 94-171.

3. Bela Vago, "The Horthy Offer." *In: Contemporary Views of the Holocaust,* Edited by R. L. Braham. Boston-The Hague: Kluwer-Nijhoff, 1983, pp. 23-45.

4. Material on Wallenberg's life comes mainly from conversations with his half-sister, Mrs. Nina Lagergren in Stockholm Sept. 3-5, 1980, plus letters Mrs. Lagergren turned over to me. Also, conversation with Wallenberg's half-brother, Dr. Guy von Dardel, July 1, 1980 in San Mateo Calif.

5. Randolph L. Braham, *The Politics of Genocide: The Holocaust in Hungary.* New York: Columbia University Press, 1981, pp. 954.

6. Bruce Teicholz, a leader of Zionist underground in Budapest 1943-45. Interview. New York, Jan. 20, 1980.

7. Lars Berg, attache, Swedish Legation in Budapest 1944-45. Interview. New York, Jan. 9, 1979.

8. War Refugee Board File, Box 111, Franklin D. Roosevelt Memorial Library, Hyde Park, N.Y.

9. Alexander and Elizabeth Kasser interview. Dec. 26, 1980. Lech Am Arlberg, Austria.

10. War Refugee Board File, Box 111, Franklin D. Roosevelt Memorial Library, Hyde Park, N.Y.

11. Per Anger, *With Raoul Wallenberg in Budapest*. New York: Holocaust Library, 1981, 187 p.

12. Rudolph Philipp, *Raoul Wallenberg: Diplomat, Kämpe, Samarit*. Stockholm: Fredborgs Förlag, 1946, p. 2.

13. Randolph L. Braham, *Eichmann and the Destruction of Hungarian Jewry*. New York: Twayne Publishers, 1961, p. 35.

14. Sandor W. Ardai, a chauffeur of Wallenberg in Budapest, in Swedish journal "Året Runt," July 7-11, 1957.

15. Raoul, Wallenberg, Report Dec. 8, 1944 to Swedish Foreign Office. In Swedish White Papers.

16. Eugene (Jenö) Lévai, *Black Book on the Martyrdom of Hungarian Jewry*. Zurich: The Central European Times.

17. *Ibid.,* p. 403.

18. *Ibid.,* p. 418.

19. Susan Tabor interview, New York. Jan. 27, 1980.

20. Mrs. Janos Kondor, Letter from Budapest. Dec. 1979.

21. Fredrik Von Dardel, *Raoul Wallenberg*. Stockholm. Proprius Forlag, 1970, 110 p.

22. Swedish Foreign Office. Raoul Wallenberg White Papers.

23. *Ibid.*

24. Communication to Wallenberg Committee, Stockholm. Mar. 21, 1981.

Chapter 12

THE CULTURAL LOSSES OF HUNGARIAN JEWRY

Raphael Patai

A few years ago, after an absence of forty years, I had occasion to revisit Budapest, the city in which I was born and lived during the first twenty-two years of my life. I was invited by the Hungarian Academy of Sciences, which put a pleasant small villa on Rose Hill, overlooking the city, at my disposal for the four weeks' duration of my visit. Since my only duties in exchange for this hospitality were to give a few lectures at the Ethnographic Institute of the Academy, I had ample time not only to revisit the places I remembered from the days of my youth, but also to talk to dozens of people and gather information about the intellectual and cultural life of the Jewish remnant in Budapest, and in Hungary in general.

What I learned can be summarized in one somber statement: while politically they enjoyed equal rights, including full freedom to practice their religion, and while economically they were as well off as, or perhaps even better off than, the average Hungarians, culturally the 80,000 Jews of the country constituted an impoverished community.

I found this conclusion—admittedly based on impressions and not on any systematic study—the more disheartening since cultural life in Hungary as a whole compared favorably with that of the other Communist countries. Moreover, not only did the Jews play a minimal role in Hungarian cultural life, but also Hungarian Jewish culture appeared to have dwindled into insignificance. However, I hasten to add that the same did not seem to have been the case with respect to other aspects of Jewish participation in Hungarian life. The Jews continued to play important roles in the Hungarian economy, in industry, in administration, and in many other activities. In the course of a conversation I had with the head of an important section of the Hungarian Academy of Sciences I asked him why Hungary was so much better off economically than her sister countries in the Russian orbit, and why was the standard of living, including the producton and availability of consumer's goods so much higher. He answered with a smile, "Simple. More Jews have remained here." While this explanation may or may not have been correct, with regard to cultural production the situation I found bore witness to the fact that Hitler's hordes and their Hungarian henchmen had indeed done a thorough job in destroying what was a rich, vibrant, and flourishing Jewish culture.

How can one measure the cultural losses suffered by Hungarian Jewry in the Holocaust? How can one form and convey an idea of the talent, the creativity, the genius that was destroyed? One could, of course, undertake laborious research and assemble long and impressive lists of the names and works of Hungarian Jewish writers and artists, scholars, and scientists who perished in the Holocaust. But would such an enumeration give any idea of the talents of those men and women? Would it enable us to get a feel of the cultural atmosphere of which they were the product and which they created, molded, and nurtured? And would it allow us to make even the vaguest guess as to the amount, kind, and quality of the work they might have produced had they lived?

Such questions, of course, are unanswerable. What is possible, however, is to outline a picture of prewar Hungarian Jewish culture. Such overview should enable us to assess the cultural loss represented by the destruction of Hungarian Jewry, and if not to estimate at least to imagine what could have been.

Let me begin by disposing of a negative side of Hungarian Jewish life. A Zionist leader early in this century termed the Jews of Hungary a dried-out branch on the tree of Jewry. This harsh judgment was correct, but only with reference to the participation of Hungarian Jews in the Zionist movement. For it is a fact that the overwhelming majority of Hungarian Jews, from among whom came Theodor Herzl, and Max Nordau, remained until World War II opposed to Zionism. They considered political Zionism anathema because they were imbued with a shortsighted and narrowminded form of Hungarian patriotism which prompted them to distance themselves not only from Zionism but also from all international Jewish organizations and movements. It was because he so well understood this quirk of the Hungarian Jewish mind that my father organized in 1926 the "Pro Palestine Association of Hungarian Jews," whose program called for the cultural and economic—

that is, strictly nonpolitical—support of the *Yishuv*. This Association succeeded in enlisting the participation of several Hungarian Jewish public figures, from among the elite, and making work for Jewish Palestine "presentable." But its membership remained limited throughout. The support of the movement for the establishment of a Jewish national home in Palestine and of the World Zionist Organization was the task and program of the Hungarian Zionist Organization, which was founded in 1902 by Herzl himself, but which was repeatedly dissolved and outlawed for years by the Hungarian government, and opposed by the Jewish establishment. Thus Vilmos Vázsonyi (born Weiszfeld, 1868–1926), a Hungarian Jewish politician who during World War I served as minister of justice and minister of election rights in two Hungarian governments, roundly condemned Zionism as "un-Magyar,"[1] and Dr. Simon Hevesi, Chief Rabbi of the "Neolog" Jewish community of Pest, stated categorically, "There is no ground for, nor inclination to, Zionism among Hungarian Jews."[2]

The main reason for rejecting rapprochement with international Jewish organizations was the fear that such contact could suggest that Hungarian Jewry had made common cause with Jewries in other countries. Such an action could appear in the eyes of Gentile Hungary as unpatriotic. It was not until November 1918, when defeated Hungary was being dismembered by the victorious Allies, that the Jewish leadership finally decided to address an appeal to the Jews of the *Entente* lands to save their country.[3] By the mid-1920s even Vázsonyi had to admit that Hungarian Jews, like the Russian and Romanian Jews in the past, were sufficiently in danger to require the support of the international Jewish community.[4] One of the results of Jewish support from abroad was that, in 1927, the Hungarian Ministry of the Interior finally approved the bylaws of the Hungarian Zionist Organization, enabling it to function as a legitimate public body. Nevertheless, the appeal of Zionism to the Hungarian Jewish public remained limited, and in such nonpolitical activities as fundraising for the *Keren Kayemeth* (Jewish National Fund) and the *Keren Hayesod* (Palestine Foundation Fund) it had no choice but to join forces with the Pro Palestine Association. Neither the Zionist Organization nor the Pro Palestine Association was able to make more than a small dent in the double wall of solid indifference toward the rebuilding of the Jewish homeland in Palestine and of the vociferous exclusivity of Hungarian patriotism with which Hungarian Jewish plutocracy surrounded itself.

While from the point of view of Zionism Hungarian Jewry was thus indeed a dried-out branch on the tree of Jewry, it produced astoundingly rich fruit on all branches of cultural endeavor. The cultural symbiosis between Christians and Jews in Hungary began in earnest after 1867, when the

Hungarian Parliament emancipated the country's Jews, and it reached a high plateau in 1895 when the "Israelite" religion was granted legal equality with the other denominations (the so-called "reception"). These legal milestones marked the beginning of an era in which the Jews of Hungary threw themselves wholeheartedly and energetically into the cultivation of the arts and sciences.

Assimilation inevitably followed. It took a variety of forms, ranging from the mere adoption of Hungarian surnames to replace the German ones imposed upon the Hungarian Jews by Emperor Joseph II (r. 1780–90), to outright conversion to Christianity. The great majority of Hungarian Jews either sincerely believed in, or paid lip-service to, the tenet that the Jews were as much Hungarian as the Christians, and that the Hungarian nation consisted of several religious groups. The religious difference, they protested, made no difference whatsoever in their total Magyardom. Therefore the Hungarian Jewish leadership concentrated on fighting against anti-Semitism which, as they knew from experience, could not be legislated out of existence. But even in this struggle, the Jews of Hungary considered the fight for rights a strictly internal affair, and as the editor of the 1929 *Hungarian Jewish Lexicon* put it, "they never allowed foreign interference in their interests to impair the sovereignty of the Hungarian nation."[5]

One of the factors which favored the emergence of Jewish talent in Hungary to a greater extent than in other European countries was the late date at which industrialization, urbanization, modernization, and enlightenment reached the nation. Because of its linguistic isolation, its political position as a quasi-colony of Austria, its social dichotomy into a small noble class and a disenfranchised, illiterate, and impoverished majority of peasants, there was a lag of about a century between the onset of modernization in the West and in Hungary. In the West, by the time the Jews were emancipated, modernization was well on its way, so that they were latecomers on the scene; in Hungary, emancipated in 1867, they entered a world in which those great processes of transformation were just about to begin. Consequently, the Jews, with their greater literacy and mobility, found ample opportunity to get in on the ground floor, and to participate in the building of a new Hungary with its rapidly expanding economy, industry, and commerce, with urbanization and all its concomitant cultural activities. It has been pointed out repeatedly that the Jews of Hungary had a far greater share in this movement than their proportion among the population, and that in many areas they were the pioneers and in several had virtual monopoly, especially in the quarter century between their "reception" and the end of World War I. By the turn of the century the number of Jews in the political, financial, economic, industrial, and cultural life of Budapest was so great that the city had earned the anti-Semitic epithet *Judapest.*

A highly visible sign of Jewish successes in industry and commerce was the great number of Jewish families ennobled by Francis Joseph I and Charles IV. Some 340 Jewish families received patents of Hungarian nobility from 1869 to 1918, constituting some 20 percent of the total ennoblements,[6] at a time when only 4 percent of the population was Jewish. One can estimate that by 1918 about one in every 500 Hungarian Jews had a title. Of these Jewish nobles, almost all who were made barons converted to Christianity, and a very high percentage of those entitled to place *von* before their surnames did the same. In addition, there was a very large number of Jews who made fortunes in industry, commerce, finance, and banking, and many of them were rewarded, or managed to acquire, impressive sounding titles such as court councillor or government chief councillor. There was, of course, also a large Jewish middle class of limited means, and needless to say, there were many poor Jews as well. However, there were very few who earned their living with physical labor.

The relevance of these data to our subject is this: Hungarian Jewry comprised a sizable element which, while heir to the traditional Jewish appreciation of learning,[7] was in a position to enable its children to pursue cultural endeavors without having to worry too much about earning a livelihood. They were given the best available education. They were brought up bilingually, in Hungarian and German. For quite a number of them the only remaining real challenge in life was to excel in a field of intellectual or artistic endeavor. In these circumstances, even if the proportion of talented individuals among them was the same as in any other population group, they enjoyed the great advantage of intellectual stimulation in childhood, and of the ability to devote themselves to developing fully whatever talents they possessed.

However, the specific atmosphere in which Hungarian Jews lived in the post-emancipation era was conducive to the development of talent and the achievement of prominence also among children of poor Jews or of Jewish families of limited means. The appreciation of, and aspiration to, learning were common to rich and poor alike. Many children whose mother tongue was Yiddish subsequently learned German and Hungarian. The rapidly expanding economic horizon not only provided opportunities for entrepreneurs, but also brought with it an increasing demand for persons who could serve the developing institutions in administrative, advisory, technical, or scientific capacities. A further direct consequence of these circumstances was the establishment of high schools and universities in which talented

Jewish youths were able first to study and later, often at the price of converting to Christianity, to teach.

Conversion to Christianity was widespread in Hungary in the postemancipation era, especially among those Jews who achieved, or were about to achieve, prominence in one of the many fields which opened up to them. The *Magyar Zsidó Lexikon* (Hungarian Jewish Lexicon), published in 1929, contains numerous examples of this trend. Among the 51 outstanding Hungarian Jewish economists it includes, no less than 25 had converted. Of the 16 Jewish literary critics listed, five were converts. Of the eight Jewish historians who excelled in the historiography of Hungary, two were converts, of the three art historians, two were converts. Of the 13 outstanding Jewish mathematicians listed, seven were converts. The proportion among writers and artists was so high that the editors of the *Lexicon* seem to have been too embarrassed to fill their long lists with the asterisks with which they denote converts. However, the asterisks do appear after the names of converts who merited individual biographies in the *Lexicon.* Since the total number of conversions was not particularly high—in 1919–24 of a total of about 500,000 Hungarian Jews not more than 11,288, (2.26 percent) converted— it is clear that conversion drained away a major part of the economic and intellectual elite of Hungarian Jewry.[8] Nevertheless, the share of the Jews in the economic, intellectual, and cultural life of Hungary until World War II was so great that even this outflow from the community could not diminish it substantially.

Statistics on the Jews' share in Hungarian life are incomplete, but we know that in 1925, after the so-called "White Terror," which claimed several thousands of Jewish victims, had subsided, Hungarian Jewry, which at the time constituted about 5 percent of the population, provided 50.6 percent of all the lawyers, 46.3 percent of the physicians, 41.3 percent of the veterinarians, 34.3 percent of the newspaper editors and journalists, 39.1 percent of the engineers and chemists, 24.5 percent of the singers and musicians, 22.7 percent of the actors, and 16.8 percent of the painters and sculptors. No less than 40.5 percent of all industrial firms were owned by Jews, 19.6 percent of the owners of large estates (over 1,000 *holds* or 1,420 acres) were Jews, as were 26.4 percent of those who owned or rented small estates. As far back as in 1904, an anti-Semitic author demonstrated, on the basis of census figures, that no less than 37.5 percent of Hungary's arable land was owned by Jews.[9] That this intensive participation of the Jews in Hungarian cultural life would have continued is shown by the fact that in the interwar years Jews constituted a disproportionately large percentage of the high school students. In 1925 no less than 25.5 percent of the students who sat for their final examinations were Jews.

In 1920 the Hungarian Parliament passed the so-called *Numerus Clausus* Law which limited the number of students admissible to Hungarian universities to the proportion in the population of the racial or ethnic groups to which they belonged. Only the Jews were forced to reduce their numbers drastically. The Jewish leadership embarked upon an energetic and courageous fight against the new law, but characteristically the thrust of its argument was not that it was unjust and unfair to practice racial discrimination in higher education. Instead, it argued that the Jews in Hungary were not a racial or ethnic group, but a religious denomination, and that therefore the *Numerus Clausus* should not apply to them.

The struggle yielded no legal results, but due to personal connections and string pulling, in 1925 the Jewish students still numbered 7.7 percent in the Faculty of Philosophy of the University of Budapest, 10 percent in its Faculty of Law, and 13.3 percent in its School of Economics. Only in the medical school was their number actually reduced to 5.1%. In the provincial universities the proportion of Jewish students averaged over 10 percent. In the academies of music and schools for theater arts the Jewish students constituted 20 to 25%.[10] As these figures show, despite the *Numerus Clausus,* the Jews continued in the interwar years to gravitate to *academia* and the arts. Also by 1925, a total of more than 1,200 Hungarian Jewish students were enrolled in institutions of higher learning in Austria, Germany, France, Switzerland, Italy, and Czechoslovakia, roughly equaling the total number of Jewish university students in Hungary itself. Thus, despite the hardships it meant for many an individual student, the *Numerus Clausus* in the long run proved a blessing in disguise, since it forced many Hungarian Jewish high school graduates to seek higher education abroad in schools whose academic level was often higher than that of their Hungarian equivalents. Attendance at universities abroad was often the first step in achieving excellence in one of the Western countries.

As for the Hungarian Jewish emigrants, their role in the cultural, scholarly, and scientific life in several Western countries, including the United States, has been so often discussed that it would be redundant to go into it. Enough to say that one often heard it said in the postwar years that the most outstanding mathematicians, atomic scientists, conductors, and film producers were all Hungarian Jews. While in this form the statement is patently untrue, the fact remains that an extraordinarily high percentage of the leaders in the fields mentioned were Hungarian Jews. William O. McCagg, in his book on *Jewish Nobles and Geniuses in Modern Hungary,* quotes the anecdote about a famous physicist who, when asked upon returning from a professional congress in Buenos Aires how men from so many different countries communicated with one another, replied, "Why, of course, we all spoke Hungarian."[11] And then there is the story about the Hollywood film czar who, after interviewing an aspiring director, regretfully tells him, "You know, after all, it is not enough to be Hungarian." What neither of the stories specifies, possibly because it was self-evident, is that in both cases not merely Hungarians, but Hungarian Jews were involved.[12]

Suffice it to note in passing that the available and admittedly insufficient data seem to indicate that Hungarian Jewry as a group comprised proportionately more talented individuals than did the Jewries of other European countries. This is the conclusion which suggests itself not only from a comparison of the numbers of outstanding Jews in or from various European countries, but also from a comparison of the numbers of Jewish authors. I counted the numbers of authors listed in the 1972 *Encyclopaedia Judaica* (which, incidentally, had no Hungarians among its editors) as English, French, German, Hungarian, Polish, Romanian, and Russian, and found that the number of Hungarian Jewish authors listed (90) exceeded by far that of Jewish authors writing in any other language except German (154). However, the German list includes also Austrian, Czech, English, French, Hungarian, and Swiss Jewish authors, so that as a language of Jewish literary activity it is not comparable to Hungarian, in which certainly only Hungarian-born authors wrote. Hence, by this yardstick, Hungarian Jewish literary talent comes out on top, and this despite the much greater number of Jews who spoke English, German, Polish, or Russian.

How can one explain this unique profusion of genius, or, if we prefer a more modest designation, of outstanding talent, among Hungarian Jews in the two generations preceding the Holocaust? A definitive answer is elusive, but a number of factors can be adduced which must have contributed to the emergence of what McCagg called "this galaxy of Hungarian 'geniuses.'" McCagg discusses the social circumstances which favored the development of Hungarian Jewish economic and scientific genius, and attributes it in part to

the fantasia-like atmosphere of turn-of-the-century Budapest, which stimulated the imagination; in part to the great urbanization movement of the nineteenth century, which mobilized both men and minds out of traditional cadres; in part to the peculiar patterns of cultural Westernization in Hungary, which led in the nineteenth century to an extravagant and often rather shallow nationalism among the Magyars, Germans, and Jews, and which ended towards 1900 in a revulsion-

like flight into science among the young; and in part to the triumph of the
economic "take-off" process in Hungary which generated enormous optimism in
Man's capacity for material accomplishment.[13]

Somewhat later McCagg cites Theodor von Kármán and other outstanding
Hungarian Jewish scientists to the effect that among the conditions which
favored the development of prodigiously endowed minds in Hungary was "a
tradition of respect for intellectual work, and perhaps particularly for
scientific work, which pervaded both Magyar and Jewish society there.
Perhaps because in Széchenyi's day Hungary had been so little educated,
culture became after mid-century a matter of the highest prestige there."[14]
While these explanations may be correct, their value is diminished by
McCagg's failure to differentiate between Jews and Gentiles, and the crux
of the matter is precisely that it was Hungarian Jewry, and not the Gentile
population, which produced that "galaxy of geniuses." Only as an aside, and
as an afterthought, does McCagg hint at a difference between Jews and
Gentiles when he says that "particularly in Jewish families, where this
Magyar respect for education mingled with Jewish traditions, at least one son
in every family was usually encouraged to pursue an intellectual career."[15]
This, of course, is a patent and gross exaggeration which, if it were literally
true, would have meant that there were some 150,000 to 200,000 Jewish
intellectuals in Hungary, corresponding to the number of families which
made up the Jewish population in pre-Trianon Hungary.

In trying, then, to come to grips with the issue of this galaxy of Hungarian
Jewish talent, one must answer two separate questions. One is why were
there proportionately more Jewish than Gentile talented individuals in
Hungary? and the second is why were there proportionately more talented
individuals in Hungarian Jewry than in the Jewries of other Western
countries?

The first of these questions has been discussed in some detail, albeit in a
more general context, in my 1977 book *The Jewish Mind*.[16] In it I came to
the conclusion that Jewish intellectual, scholarly, and scientific excellence in
the Western world, as measured by such disparate yardsticks as IQ tests and
the Jewish Nobel Prize record, was due partly to the inquisitiveness and
argumentativeness which have been Jewish mental characteristics for many
centuries, nurtured by a concentration on Talmudic study with its method
of *pilpul;* partly to the exposure of Jewish intellectuals first to Talmudic and
subsequently to secular studies; and partly to such features as urban residence,
concentration on commerce imposed upon the Jews by the Gentiles (which
forced them to use their brain rather than brawn in making a living), the

necessity to understand and justify the dissenting position of their own religion within a Christian majority, group solidarity, devotion to family life, and un undogmatic religion whose tenets and commandments had to be grasped intellectually.[17] Additional factors were the centuries-old valuation of learning expressed in a strong emphasis on education, the harsh and often inimical Gentile social environment, which favored the survival of the more intelligent among the Jews, and the traditional marriage preference which enabled the most intelligent young men to marry the richest girls and thus secure the most favorable circumstances for the survival of their offspring. All these circumstances obtained, of course, in Hungary to the same extent as in other European countries. (Since I mentioned the Jewish Nobel Prize record, let me add that of the total of six Nobel laureates who were born in Hungary three were Jews: George de Hevesy, Eugene Wigner and Dennis Gábor.)

In turning now to the second question, I must first of all modify somewhat what I said in *The Jewish Mind* on the role of marginality in producing or stimulating intellectual preeminence. In that book I expressed doubts about Veblen's famous theory that marginality is a basic factor in the development of intellectual excellence. Today I feel I was too hasty in doing so. Marginality, in the sense of starting one's approach to a culture from the outside, instead of being born and reared in it, *is* an important factor in stimulating the intellect to peak performance, and the Hungarian Jewish story is a case in point. The number of Jews in Hungary grew fivefold in the sixty years between 1850 and 1910 (from 190,000 to 940,000).[19] A large proportion of this increase was due to immigration from Eastern Europe. The mother tongue of the immigrants, as well as of most of those who were born in Hungary up to the late nineteenth century was mainly Yiddish. After their emancipation they acquired first German and then Hungarian. They thus approached the culture of Hungary from the outside—a typical marginal situation—and did this precisely at a time when that culture itself was caught up in a maelstrom of rapid transformation from stagnant traditionalism to dynamic modernism.

The fact that throughout those crucial decades there was anti-Semitism in Hungary, albeit in varying forms and to varying degrees,[20] contributed its share to maintaining a feeling of otherness among the Jews, despite all assertions to the contrary and the ceaselessly reiterated claim of being fatherland-loving Magyars of the Israelite faith. This claim, incidentally, was but the Jewish version of the traditional Hungarian overemphasis on patriotism which was a feature of the Hungarian national character satirized by more than one Hungarian writer or poet. A concomitant of it was the tenet that the Hungarians had nothing to do with, or to seek in, other countries.

As stated in the opening lines of one of the two Hungarian national anthems, the *Szózat,* written by Mihály Vörösmarty in 1836 (in my literal translation):

> Be firmly faithful, O Magyar,
> To this your native land,
> It is your cradle, will be your grave
> Which nurses and covers you.
> In the great world outside this land
> There is no room for you,
> Should the hand of fate bless you or smite you
> Here you must live and die.

The Hungarian Jewish establishment officially and demonstratively identified itself with the sentiments expressed in these lines. Its position was that Hungarian Jewry was morally bound to remain in Hungary. If an outstanding Hungarian Jewish personality emigrated, special circumstances were sought to excuse this step. A typical example is provided by the biography of Professor Michael Guttmann in the *Hungarian Jewish Lexicon,* which was published under the patronage of the foremost Hungarian Jewish leaders with the equivalent of the Catholic *imprimatur.* Guttmann was professor of Talmud at the Rabbinical Seminary of Budapest, and in 1921 accepted the invitation of the Breslau Rabbinical Seminary to serve as head of that school. This fact is presented in the *Lexicon* apologetically as follows: "In 1921 he was invited to serve as professor at the Breslau *Jüdisch-Theologisches Seminar,* which position he accepted, since in the Hungarian circumstances he was anyhow unable to broaden the scope of his large-scale scholarly work."[21]

In contrast to this official attitude, individual Hungarian Jews never lost sight of the *külföld,* the foreign countries, and always kept in mind the possibility of going abroad, either temporarily to visit or study, or permanently to live. One example showing the attraction studying abroad held for Hungarian Jewish intellectuals is this: of the 13 oustanding Hungarian Jewish mathematicians listed in the *Hungarian Jewish Lexicon* no less than 11 studied abroad before becoming professors of mathematics at Hungarian universities.[22] Another, is that most students of the Budapest Rabbinical Seminary spent one year at its sister institution in Breslau, for which they were well prepared, since part of the instruction at the Budapest Seminary was in German. To the best of my knowledge, nothing comparable existed in any Gentile institution of higher learning in Hungary.

As for emigration, just as there was a constant stream of individuals moving out of Jewry into the bosom of Christianity, therewith to put the seal on their complete assimilation to Magyardom, there was another stream of individuals who opted to solve the problem of being Jews in Hungary not by leaving Judaism but by leaving Hungary and settling in the West. Both avenues were followed primarily by persons who belonged either to the economic or to the intellectual Jewish elite of the country. In either case, Hungarian Jewry experienced a "brain drain" long before the term was coined in Great Britain.

The fact that emigration was considered an ever-present possibility contributed to the maintenance of marginality among Hungarian Jews and served as a stimulant to intellectual growth. Practically all middle- and upper-class Hungarian Jews made sure that their children knew German in addition to Hungarian, and thereby acquired the ability to move outside the narrow confines of the Hungarian language area. Many spent their vacations abroad, in most cases in Austria, Germany, or other countries to the west of Hungary. The immanence of the great world beyond the borders of Hungary in the consciousness of the Hungarian Jews meant that, more than their Gentile compatriots, they kept up with cultural and scientific developments in the West. This, in turn, broadened their mental horizon and contributed to their aspiration to, and, frequently, attainment of, excellence.

The last factor one ought to mention among the mental stimulants to which the Hungarian Jewish intellectual elite was exposed is the uniquely ambivalent position the Jews as a group occupied in Hungary. In the countries to the east of Hungary the Jews were considered by the Gentiles, and considered themselves, a national minority. Their minority status was guaranteed by the Versailles Peace Conference of 1919, and whether or not confirmed by the individual countries, they were treated *de facto* as an ethnic group separate and different from the body of the nation. In the countries to the west of Hungary the Jews were considered by the Gentiles, and considered themselves, part and parcel of the nation within which they lived, while claiming, and being accorded, the right to follow their own religion. That is to say, in both East and West, there was an agreement in principle between the Jews and the Gentiles as to the nature of the Jewish community, its identity in relation to the majority, and its position in the country.

In Hungary there was no such consensus. The Jews, as already pointed out, claimed to be Magyars who followed the Israelite faith. The Gentiles, on the other hand, considered the Jews a national and racial group different from the Christian Hungarians. The anti-Semites among them referred to the Jews as "the Syrian race," or, as a ditty expressed it, "In the Jew the disgrace/

is not religion but the race." The liberal Hungarians, although they would admit it only in private, also felt that the Jews were an alien race or element in the country. The *Numerus Clausus* gave legal expression to this feeling. It singled out the Jews as a racial group whose numbers at institutions of higher learning had to be limited; it imposed no such restrictions on members of other minority religions.

Thus there was a permanent tension between the Hungarian Jews and Gentiles. The Jews never tired of claiming that they were as much part of the Hungarian nation as the members of the other minority religions in Hungary, and on this basis fought for equal rights and social acceptance, while the Gentiles resorted to various means of exclusion and restriction in order to limit the Jewish share in and influence on Hungarian life. In this situation of tension and struggle the Jews felt impelled constantly to prove themselves by not only asserting that they were patriotic Hungarians, but also by demonstrating that they were able to make valuable contributions to all aspects of Hungarian life, that they possessed talents which they put at the service of the fatherland, and that therefore they amply deserved to be accepted by Gentile Hungary as equals in every respect. These circumstances placed a premium on ability and performance; they constituted a challenge to achieve excellence, and the Hungarian Jews responded to it by actually rising to preeminence.

On the other hand, once this pattern was established, many of them could not resist the lure of the West with its broader horizons, greater opportunities, and richer economic and intellectual rewards. Both tendencies, to excel and to emigrate, were exemplified by the upbringing of Edward Teller (born in Budapest in 1908), who later recalled that his father "literally 'dinned' into him that because of anti-Semitism he, as a Jew, had to excel just to keep abreast; that because of it he would have one day to emigrate to a country where conditions were more favorable to minorities; and that from anti-Semitism a sure escape was science, an international discipline."[23] Theodor von Kármán reported practically the same experience.[24]

These considerations supply at least a partial explanation of Hungarian Jewish excellence at home, of the large-scale emigration from Hungary of outstanding Jewish intellectuals, scientists, and literati, and of the preeminence of Hungarian Jews in the arts and sciences in the Western world. It is this extraordinary cultural productivity which was destroyed by the Holocaust together with the slaughter of the Jews of Hungary.

Notes

1. William O. McCagg, Jr., *Jewish Nobles and Geniuses in Modern Hungary.* Boulder: East European Quarterly, 1972, 254 p. (Distributed by Columbia University Press).

2. Randolph L. Braham, "Hungary, Zionism in." *In: Encyclopedia of Zionism and Israel.* Vol. I. Edited by Raphael Patai. New York: Herzl Press and McGraw Hill, 1971, p. 524.

3. McCagg, p. 206, quoting *Mult és Jövő* (Past and Future), Budapest, Dec. 1918: 459.

4. McCagg, p. 208, note 44, citing *Egyenlőség* (Equality), Budapest, July 4, 1925: 1.

5. *Magyar Zsidó Lexikon* (Hungarian Jewish Lexicon). Edited by Péter Ujvári. Budapest: A Zsidó Lexikon Kiadása, 1929, p. 50.

6. McCagg, pp. 25, 130.

7. Raphael Patai, *The Jewish Mind.* New York: Scribners, 1977, pp. 272-73, 301, 303, 338.

8. *Magyar Zsidó Lexikon,* pp. 512, 396-97, 910, 581, 554-55.

9. McCagg, pp. 185-88, quoting Géza Petrassevich, *Zsidó földbirtokosok és bérlők Magarországon* (Jewish Landowners and Renters in Hungary). Budapest: Stephaneum, 1904, pp. 26ff.

10. *Magyar Zsidó Lexikon,* pp. 562-63.

11. McCagg, p. 15.

12. *Ibid.,* p. 15.

13. *Ibid.,* p. 209.

14. *Ibid.,* pp. 211-12.

15. *Ibid.,* p. 212.

16. Patai, *The Jewish Mind.*

17. *Ibid.,* pp. 331-34.

18. *Ibid.,* p. 335.

19. *Magyar Zsidó Lexikon,* p. 553.

20. Joseph Patai, "Der Antisemitismus in Ungarn, die 'Galizianer,' und die 'Moral'." *Oesterreichische Wochenschrift,* Vienna, July 12, 1918: 425-27.

21. *Magyar Zsidó Lexikon,* p. 328.

22. *Ibid.,* p. 581.

23. Edward Teller and Alan Brown, *Legacy of Hiroshima,* Garden City, N.Y.: Doubleday, 1962, pp. 160-61; and *Life,* Dec. 13, 1963: 89, as quoted by McCagg, p. 164.

24. McCagg, pp. 210-11.

III. INTERPRETATIONS AND REACTIONS

Chapter 13

THE UNIQUENESS OF THE HOLOCAUST IN HUNGARY

Randolph L. Braham

In recent years we have witnessed the flareup of a considerable debate over whether the Holocaust—the destruction of the six million Jews of Europe— was unique or merely a link in the long historical chain of man's inhumanity to man. The debate has not been restricted to historians; it has involved— and continues to involve—representatives from the other disciplines in the social sciences as well as theologian-metaphysicians and spokesmen for the three major *dramatis personae* of the Nazi era: the perpetrators, the onlookers, and the victims—the latter represented primarily by survivors. The arguments supporting the uniqueness thesis are impressive and do not in any way detract from the Nazis' responsibility for the five million other, non-Jewish victims.

While the Holocaust was indeed unique, one can also demonstrate—and this is obviously my intention—that the tragedy that befell the Jews of Hungary in turn involved unique factors that differentiate it from that of other national Jewish communities of Europe. To some extent the tragedy stemmed from certain aspects of Hungary's historical role in East Central Europe; above all, it can be traced to the uniqueness of the Jews' position in Hungary vis-a-vis all other Jewish communities in Eastern Europe. The disastrous set of circumstances which combined to doom Hungarian Jewry in 1944 may be traced, partially at least, to the unique history of that Jewish community. Let me emphasize at the beginning, however, that nothing in my analysis can detract from the ultimate responsibility of the Nazis and their Hungarian accomplices for the Holocaust in Hungary.

177

The destruction of the Jews of Hungary constitutes one of the most perplexing chapters in the history of the Holocaust. Like the pre-Holocaust history of Hungarian Jewry, it is replete with paradoxes. Let me begin with perhaps the most puzzling one: The catastrophe of Hungarian Jewry in 1944 was partially the consequence of the *very* cordial, almost symbiotic relationship that developed between the Hungarian national and Jewish elites during the "Golden Era" (1867–1918) and the distorted perception of the Nazi and Bolshevik menace they shared during the post-World War I period.

After its emancipation in 1867, the Jewish community of Hungary enjoyed an unparalleled level of multilateral development, taking full advantage of the opportunities offered by the so-called "liberal" regime that ruled the country during the pre-World War I era. The Hungarian ruling classes—the gentry and the conservative-aristocratic leaders—adopted a tolerant position toward the Jews. They were motivated not only by economic considerations, but also by the desire to perpetuate their dominant political role in a multinational empire in which the Hungarians constituted a minority. Because of Hungary's feudal tradition, the ruling classes encouraged the Jews to engage in business and industry, so that in the course of time a friendly, cooperative, and mutually advantageous relationship developed between the conservative-aristocratic leaders and the Jewish industrialists, bankers, and financiers—a relationship that was to play a fatal role during the Holocaust. The Jews also took full advantage of their new educational opportunities and within a short time came to play an influential, if not dominant, role in the professions, literature, and the arts.

As a consequence of the Hungarian policy of tolerance, the Jews of Hungary considered themselves an integral part of the Hungarian nation. They eagerly embraced the process of magyarization, opting not only to change their names but also to serve as economic modernizers and cultural magyarizers in the areas inhabited by the other nationalities in the polyglot Hungarian Kingdom. The Hungarian Jews, who had no territorial ambitions and naturally supported the group that offered them the greatest protection—as did the Jews of the Diaspora practically everywhere during their long and arduous history—were soon looked upon as agents for the preservation of the status quo by the oppressed nationalities clamoring for self-determination and independence.

The Jews were naturally cognizant of the protection the regime provided against the threat of anti-Semitism. The prompt and forceful intervention of the government in dealing with anti-Jewish manifestations, however sporadic and local they were at the time, further enhanced the fidelity of the Jews to the Magyar state.

In the course of time the Jews, especially the acculturated and assimilated ones, became ever more assertively pro-Magyar. In many cases this allegiance was not only because of expediency, or gratitude for the opportunities and the safety afforded by the aristocratic-gentry regime, but also because of fervent patriotism. As Professor Oscar Jászi, a noted sociologist and social-democratic statesman of Jewish origin, correctly observed, "there is no doubt that a large mass of these assimilated elements adopted their new ideology quite spontaneously and enthusiastically out of a sincere love of the new fatherland." Jaszi concluded, however, that the "intolerant Magyar nationalism and chauvinism of the Jews had done a great deal to poison relations between the Hungarians and the other nationalities of the prewar era." Paul Ignotus, a noted publicist also of Jewish origin, echoed these sentiments, arguing that the Jews had become "more fervently Magyar than the Magyars themselves." A similar conclusion was reached by the noted British historian Robert Seton-Watson, whose sympathies clearly lay with the oppressed nationalities. He claimed in 1908 that "the Catholic Church and the Jews form today the two chief bulwarks of Magyar chauvinism."

It was to some extent this political and economic symbiosis between the conservative-aristocratic and Jewish leaderships during the so-called Golden Era that determined their views and attitudes toward both the Third Reich and the USSR during the interwar and wartime periods. While the Hungarian leaders looked upon the Third Reich as a vehicle for the possible satisfaction of their revisionist ambitions, they shared with the Jewish leaders a fear of both German and Russian expansionism and above all a mortal fear of Bolshevism. As we shall see it was partially these attitudes and perceptions that guided both leadership groups during the fateful year of 1944 with almost equally disastrous results.

The signs that the commonality of interests *(Interessengemeinschaft)* between the two groups was in fact limited, fragile, and based primarily on expediency were clearly visible even before the end of World War I: in spite of the eagerness with which the Hungarian Jews embraced the Magyar cause and the enthusiasm with which they acculturated themselves, they failed, with relatively few exceptions, to fully integrate themselves into Hungarian society. Their ultimate assimilationist expectations were frustrated, for they were accepted socially neither by the aristocratic-gentry, which exploited them politically and economically for the perpetuation of their feudal privileges, nor by the disenfranchised and impoverished peasantry, which often viewed them as instrumentalities of an oppressive regime.

Christian-Jewish relations were further strained by the presence in the country of a considerable number of mostly impoverished Yiddish-speaking Jews who resisted acculturation, let alone assimilation. In contrast to the assimilated magyarized Jews, they were pejoratively referred to as "Eastern" or "Galician" and almost by definition unworthy of the government's policy of toleration. During the interwar period these Jews became the target of special abuse, for even the "civilized" anti-Semites regarded them as constituting not only a distinct "biological race" but also an "ideological race" representing a grave threat to Christian Magyars. As we shall see it was this perception that induced Miklós Horthy, the Regent of Hungary, to consent to the transfer of a few hundred thousand Jewish laborers to Germany in March 1944, a consent that sealed the fate of almost all of the Jews of Hungary.

The *Interessengemeinschaft* between the Hungarian ruling classes and the Jews came to an end with the collapse of the Habsburg Empire and the dismemberment of the Hungarian Kingdom in 1918. The shortlived Communist dictatorship that followed soon thereafter had a crucial effect upon the evolution of Hungarian domestic and foreign policy during the interwar period. The brief but harsh period of the Kun regime left a bitter legacy in the nation at large, and had a particularly devastating impact upon the Jews of Hungary. Although the overwhelming majority of Jewry had opposed the proletarian dictatorship and perhaps suffered proportionately more than the rest of the population—they were persecuted both as members of the middle class and as followers of an organized religion—popular opinion tended to attach the blame for the abortive dictatorship to the Jews as a whole. In part, this was due to the high visibility of Communists of Jewish origin in the Kun government and administration; however, it was primarily the consequence of anti-Semitic propaganda and anti-Jewish activities by the counterrevolutionary clericalist-nationalist forces that came to power later in 1919—forces dedicated to the reestablishment of the *status quo ante.*

Driven by the so-called "Szeged Idea" (a nebulous amalgam of political-propagandistic views whose central themes included the struggle against Bolshevism, the fostering of anti-Semitism, chauvinistic nationalism, and revisionism—an idea that antedated both Italian Fascism and German Nazism) the counterrevolutionaries engulfed the country in a wave of terror which dwarfed in ferocity and magnitude the Red Terror that had preceded and allegedly warranted it. While their murder squads killed a large number of leftists, including industrial workers and landless peasants as well as   ·

opposition intellectuals, their fury was directed primarily against the Jews; the violence claimed thousands of victims.

Radicalized by the national humiliation, social upheavals, and catastrophic consequences of the lost war—Hungary lost two-thirds of its historic territory, one-third of its Magyar people, and three-fifths of its total population—the counterrevolutionaries organized themselves in a variety of ultrapatriotic associations devoted primarily to the successful resolution of the two major issues that came to obsess Hungary during the interwar period: revisionism and the Jewish question. In the course of time these two issues became interlocked and formed the foundation not only of Hungary's domestic policies, but also of its relations with the Third Reich.

Following the absorption of historic Hungary's major national minorities into the Successor States, the Jews suddenly emerged as the country's most vulnerable minority group. With the transformation of Trianon Hungary into a basically homogeneous state, the Jews lost their importance as statistical recruits to the cause of Magyardom. In the new truncated state they came to be exploited for another purpose: as in Nazi Germany a little later, they were conveniently used as scapegoats for most of the country's misfortunes, including its socioeconomic dislocations.

In this climate it was no surprise that Hungary—the country in which the Jews had enjoyed a "Golden Era" just a few years earlier—emerged as the first country in post-World War I Europe to adopt, in the wake of the White Terror, an anti-Jewish legislation. The so-called *Numerus Clausus* Act (1920), which was adopted in violation of the Minorities Protection Treaty, restricted admission of Jews into institutions of higher learning to six percent of the total enrollment—the alleged percentage of the Jews in the total population. Although this legislation was allowed to expire a few years later, it sanctified the fundamental principle that was to guide many of the civilized anti-Semites of the 1930s, who were eager to solve the Jewish question in an orderly and legal manner. This principle would be formulated by Gyula Gömbös, one of the foremost representatives of the Hungarian radical Right, who stipulated that "the Jews must not be allowed to succeed in any field beyond the level of their ratio in the population."

At any rate, the Jewish leadership viewed the anti-Jewish measures of the counterrevolutionaries merely as temporary aberrations caused by the unfortunate outcome of the war, and so it retained its patriotic stance. The leadership not only embraced the cause of revisionism, but actually protested and rejected all "foreign" interventions on its behalf—including those by the international Jewish organizations—as violations of Hungarian sovereign rights. And indeed, their optimism was for a while reinforced during the

1920s, when Count István Bethlen, a representative of the conservative-aristocratic group of large landholders and financial magnates that had ruled Hungary before the war, headed the Hungarian government.

However, the appointment of Gömbös as Prime Minister in October 1932, coinciding with the spectacular electoral victories of the Nazi Party in Germany, the Jewish question came to the fore once again. It soon became a national obsession that frequently rivaled revisionism in intensity. Borrowing a page from the Nazis' propaganda book, the Hungarian radicals depicted the Jews as naturally unpatriotic, parasitically sapping the energies of the nation, and prone to internationalist—i.e., Bolshevik—tendencies. The propaganda campaign was soon coupled with demands for a definitive solution of the Jewish question. The suggestions offered by the radical Right at the time ranged from legal restrictions on the Jews' professional and economic activities to their orderly "resettlement" out of the country.

Although expediency and temporary tactical considerations induced Gömbös to "revise" his position on the Jewish question, his policies prepared the ground for the disaster that was later to strike Hungary and its Jews. He tied Hungary's destiny almost irrevocably to that of Nazi Germany. He not only abandoned Bethlen's reliance on the Western democracies and the League of Nations as a means to correct the "injustices" of Trianon, but also brought Hungary's foreign policy into line with that of Nazi Germany and made possible the subsequent penetration and direct involvement of the Reich in practically every aspect of the country's life. This was greatly facilitated by the formidable and potentially collaborationist rightist power base Gömbös established during his tenure. He was able not only to replace the civil and military bureaucracies of the state apparatus with his own proteges, but also—and this was perhaps even more crucial—to pack the upper army hierarchy, including the General Staff, with younger, highly nationalistic Germanophile officers. The stage for the anti-Jewish excesses to come was further set through the radicalization of the press and the flourishing of ultra-rightist political movements and parties.

The spectacular domestic and foreign policy successes of the Third Reich, including the *Anschluss* with Austria by which Germany extended its borders to those of Hungary, were achieved largely because of the shortsighted appeasement policies of the Western democracies. The Nazi victories induced successive Hungarian governments to embrace the Axis ever more tightly. They became increasingly eager to see Hungary involved in the establishment of the "New Order" in Europe and reap the benefits of the Nazi revisionist-révanchist policies as an active member of the Axis Alliance.

While this policy yielded considerable dividends, enabling Hungary to fulfill parts of its revisionist ambitions at the expense of Czechoslovakia, Romania, and Yugoslavia, it was in the long run disastrous for the country. It was, of course, even more disastrous for the country's Jews. In retrospect, the policies of the conservative aristocratic-gentry–dominated governments appear to have been quite quixotic. Having embraced the Third Reich for its opposition to Bolshevism and its chief bulwark, the Soviet Union, and for its support of revisionism, these governments were soon compelled to come to grips with the ever more influential Right radicals at home. While they despised and feared these radicals almost as much as the Jews—the Hungarian Nazis had advocated not only the need to solve the Jewish question, but also the necessity to bring about a social revolution that would put an end to the inherited privileges of the conservative-aristocratic elements—the governmental leaders felt compelled to appease them as well as the Germans. In fact, these leaders looked upon the Right radicals' preoccupation with the Jewish question as a blessing in disguise, for it helped deter attention from the grave social-agrarian problems confronting the nation. They were, consequently, ready to adopt a series of anti-Jewish measures. These became more draconic with each territorial acquisition between 1938 and 1941. In addition to passing three major anti-Jewish laws—the third one incorporated the major provisions of the Nuremberg Laws of Nazi Germany—they adopted a discriminatory system of labor service for Jews of military age, a unique institution in Nazi-dominated Europe.

These anti-Jewish measures of the various governments, endorsed by the leaders of the Christian churches, were based on the illusions that guided the ruling elites until the German occupation. They thought that by passing laws that would curtail the Jews' economic power and "harmful" cultural influence, they could not only appease the ultra-rightists who thrived on the social and economic unrest that plagued the country, but also satisfy the Third Reich and at the same time safeguard the vital interests of the Jews themselves. This rationalization was part of the larger quixotic assumption that Hungary could satisfy its revisionist ambitions by embracing the Third Reich without having to jeopardize its own freedom of action.

The upper strata of Hungarian Jewry, including the official national leadership, shared these illusions, convinced that the Jewish community's long history of loyal service to Magyardom would continue to be recognized and their fundamental interests safeguarded by the ruling elite of the country. They accepted, however reluctantly, many of the anti-Jewish measures as reflecting "the spirit of the times" and as necessary tactical moves to "take the sting out of the anti-Semitic drive" of the ultra-rightists at home and abroad. They tended to concur with the rationalizations of the governmental leaders that the anti-Jewish laws were the "best guarantee against anti-Semitism and intolerance." In consequence, they were convinced that the safety and well-being of the Jews were firmly linked to the preservation of the conservative-reactionary regime. And, indeed, as long as this aristocratic elite remained in power, the vital interests of Hungarian Jewry were preserved relatively intact. This remained so even after Hungary entered the war against the Soviet Union in June 1941. The regime continued not only to provide haven to the many thousands of Polish and other refugees, including about 16,000 Jews, but also consistently to oppose the ever greater pressures by the Germans to bring about the Final Solution of the Jewish question. While the Jews in Nazi-controlled Europe were being systematically annihilated, Hungary continued to protect its close to 800,000 Jews until it practically lost its independence.

The pre-occupation record of Hungary was, of course, not spotless. Around 63,000 Jews lost their lives even before the German invasion: over 42,000 labor servicemen died or were killed in the Ukraine and Serbia; close to 20,000 were killed in the drive against the "alien" Jews, and about 1,000 were slaughtered in the Bácska area. Nevertheless, Hungarian Jewry continued to dwell in comparative personal and physical safety. (There were no restrictions on their freedom of movement and they were treated relatively fairly when food was distributed. Although the anti-Jewish laws had a particularly severe economic impact on the lower strata of the Jewish population, including both skilled salaried workers and the unskilled laborers, the economic position of the Jews as a whole was relatively tolerable, primarily because of the well-developed communal self-help system. Also, those in business and industry, while severely curtailed in their activities, were usually able to circumvent some provisions of the anti-Jewish laws or to take advantage of loopholes.)

Following the destruction of the Hungarian armies along the Don and the subsequent defeat of the Germans around Stalingrad early in 1943, the Hungarians began a desperate search for an honorable way out of the war, a search that was intensified after Italy's extrication from the Axis Alliance later that summer. It ultimately led to disaster, primarily because of the irreconcilably conflicting political and socioeconomic objectives the conservative-aristocratic leaders were pursuing. They were eager not only to safeguard the independence and territorial integrity of the country, including the retention of the areas acquired between 1938–41, but also to preserve the antiquated socioeconomic structure of the gentry-dominated society.

While they were apprehensive about a possible German occupation, they were above all paralyzed by the fear of the Soviet Union and Communism. They viewed the latter as the ultimate evil to which even Nazism, if it proved unavoidable, was preferable. Ignoring the geopolitical realities of the area, they consequently unrealistically tried to "solve" their dilemma by maneuvering secretly for a possible separate peace with the Western Powers. The Germans were, of course, fully informed about the nature and scope of the "secret" negotiations between the Hungarians and the Anglo-Americans. The reports by their many agents in Hungary about the "treacherous and pro-Jewish" activities of the Kállay government were reinforced by two secret memoranda by Edmund Veesenmayer, the German expert on East Central Europe, who later became Hitler's plenipotentiary in Hungary.

Veesenmayer had warned the Führer not only about the untrustworthiness of the government, but also about the "danger" represented by the Jews. He contended that the Jews were "enemy No. 1" and that the "1.1 million Jews amounted to as many saboteurs . . . who would have to be looked upon as Bolshevik vanguards." The Germans, consequently, resolved not to permit Hungary to emulate Italy: the extrication of Hungary when the Soviet forces were already crossing the Dniester would have deprived Germany of the Romanian oil fields and exposed the German forces in the central and southern parts of Europe to encirclement and possibly to an immediate crushing defeat. It was primarily to safeguard their security interests that the Germans decided to invade Hungary.

The destruction of Hungarian Jewry, the last surviving large bloc of European Jewry, was to a large extent a concomitant of this German military decision. Ironically, it appears in retrospect that had Hungary continued to remain a militarily passive but vocally loyal ally of the Third Reich instead of provocatively engaging in essentially fruitless, if not merely alibi-establishing, diplomatic maneuvers, the Jews of Hungary might have survived the war relatively unscathed.

The German forces who invaded Hungary on March 19, 1944, were accompanied by a small but highly efficient special commando unit *(Sonderkommando)* headed by Adolf Eichmann, which had a number of contingency plans ready to take advantage of any opportunities to "solve" the Jewish question that might be provided by the new Hungarian leaders. Two years earlier, Eichmann had been approached by some high-ranking Hungarian ultra-rightists to help in the "resettlement" of thousands of "alien" Jews, but he had refused to mobilize his deportation apparatus for such a small-scale operation, preferring to wait until the Hungarians consented to their total removal. The occupation provided that opportunity. The Nazis had found in Hungary a group of accomplices who outdid even them in their eagerness to eliminate the Jews. And, indeed, it was primarily the concerted and singleminded drive by these two groups that made the effectuation of the Final Solution in Hungary possible: one could not have succeeded without the other. While the Germans were eager to solve the Jewish question, they could not have proceeded without the consent of the newly established Hungarian puppet government and the cooperation of the Hungarian instrumentalities of power. The Hungarian ultra-rightists, in turn, though anxious to emulate their German counterparts, could not have achieved their ideologically defined objectives in the absence of the occupation.

As a consequence of the occupation, the Hungarian Jewish community, which survived the first four and a half years of the war relatively intact, was subjected to the most ruthless and concentrated destruction process of the Nazis' war against the Jews. The drive against the Hungarian Jews took place on the very eve of Allied victory, when the grisly details of the Final Solution were already known to the leaders of the world, including those of Hungarian and world Jewry. Informed about the barbarity and speed with which the Hungarian Jews were liquidated, Churchill concluded that it was "probably the greatest and most horrible crime ever committed in the history of the world."

The liquidation of Hungarian Jewry reminds one of the prophesy of Theodore Herzl. In a letter dated March 10, 1903, when Hungarian Jewry was still in the midst of its "Golden Era," the father of Zionism cautioned his friend Ernő Mezei, a member of the Hungarian Parliament as follows: "The hand of fate shall also seize Hungarian Jewry. And the later this occurs, and the stronger this Jewry becomes, the more cruel and hard shall be the blow, which shall be delivered with greater savagery. There is no escape."

Was there no escape? The evidence clearly indicates that had Horthy and the clique around him *really* wanted to save Hungarian Jewry they could have done so. But they were interested only in protecting the assimilated ones and especially those with whom they had good and mutually profitable business and financial relations. They were almost as eager to rid the country of the "Eastern-Galician" Jews as the Right radicals were. It was partially toward this end that Horthy, who obviously considered the imminent Nazi occupation less of an evil than a possible Soviet invasion, had made certain concessions that proved fatal to Hungarian Jewry. Meeting Hitler at Schloss Klessheim the day before the occupation, he consented to the "delivery of a few hundred thousand Jewish workers to Germany for employment in war-related projects." Apparently Horthy was convinced that by giving his consent he would not only satisfy Germany's "legitimate" needs, but also contribute to the struggle against Bolshevism and at the same time get rid of the "Galician Jews" whom he openly detested. The Eichmann-*Sonderkommando* and their Hungarian accomplices took full advantage of this agreement to implement the Final Solution program throughout the country, claiming that "the Jews would be more productive in Germany if they had all members of their families with them."

Once they were given the green light, the dejewification experts proceeded with lightning speed. Time was of the essence, for the Third Reich was threatened by imminent defeat. And, indeed, in no other country was the Final Solution program—the establishment of the *Judenrat,* the isolation, expropriation, ghettoization, concentration, entrainment, and deportation of the Jews—carried out with as much barbarity and speed as in Hungary. Although the dejewification squads were relatively small, they were successful in the speedy implementation of their sinister designs because of the interplay of many domestic and international factors.

The German and Hungarian agents in charge of the Final Solution had at their disposal the instrumentalities of state power—the police, gendarmerie, and civil service—and could proceed unhindered by any internal or external opposition. The puppet government provided them with their "legal" and administrative coverup. With public opinion having been successfully molded by years of vicious anti-Semitic agitation, the population at large was at best passive, while a considerable number of Hungarians proved eager and willing to collaborate for ideological or materialistic reasons. Postwar Hungarian historiography notwithstanding, there was no meaningful resistance anywhere in the country, let alone organized opposition for the protection of the Jews.

The Allies, though fully aware of the realities of the Final Solution, were reluctant to get involved in the Nazis' war against the Jews. When the Western Powers were asked, shortly after the beginning of the deportations from Hungary on May 15, to bomb Auschwitz and the rail lines leading to the camp they declined, stating, among other things, that they had no aircraft for such "secondary targets." Yet, a few months later they had managed to assemble a large air armada to destroy Dresden, the art-laden city which had no real strategic value. The death camps and the rail lines leading to them were also ignored by the Soviet air force, which was strategically in an even better position to bomb them. The record of the leftist, mostly pro-Soviet, underground and partisan forces in Hungary, Slovakia, and Poland is no better in this regard. There is no evidence they engaged in any act of sabotage or resistance to prevent the deportation of the Jews. The attitude of the neutral states—Portugal, Turkey, Spain, Sweden, and Switzerland—was not fundamentally more positive, at least during the first phase of the deportations from Hungary. Their position, like that of the Vatican and the International Red Cross, changed only after the Swiss press began to publicize the horrors of the Final Solution in Hungary late in June 1944. Their pressure upon Horthy, who was probably more influenced by the rapidly deteriorating military situation—by that time the Soviet forces were already at the borders of Hungary and the Western Allies had successfully established their beachheads in Normandy—yielded the desired result. Horthy halted the deportations on July 7 (though the dejewification squads continued their operations around Budapest up to July 9). However, by that time all of Hungary, with the exception of Budapest, was already *Judenrein.* The success of Horthy's belated action is another piece of evidence clearly demonstrating that the German demands for the Final Solution could have been refused or sabotaged even after the occupation. Had Horthy and the Hungarian authorities really been concerned with all their citizens of the Jewish faith, they could have refused to cooperate. Without the Hungarian instrumentalities of power, the Germans would have been as helpless during the first phase of the occupation as they proved to be after early July 1944.

What about the victims, the Jewish masses and their leaders? Though the German invasion of Hungary took place on the eve of the Allied victory, when the secrets of the Final Solution were already known, the ghettoization and deportation process in Hungary was carried out as smoothly as it was almost everywhere else in Nazi-dominated Europe. Misled and discouraged, the Jews of Hungary, with the notable exception of some young Zionist pioneers in Budapest, displayed little or no opposition throughout the occupation period. In accordance with well-tested Nazi camouflage methods, the Jews were lulled into acquiescence by assurances that the deportations involved merely their relocation within the country to perform agricultural labor. They were further assured that the young and the old were included in the transports only out of "consideration for the close family-life pattern of the Jews."

The apprehension of those awaiting for deportation was further assuaged by the communications mailed by the first group of deportees, who were compelled just before their entry into the gas chamber to write brief messages of well-being that were postmarked with the fictitious place name *Waldsee.* Unsophisticated Jews helped to spread the illusions fostered by those engaged in the anti-Jewish drive. When Jews were placed into ghettos in the northeastern parts of the country, those in the more "assimilated" parts of Hungary—the Great Plains and Transdanubia—viewed it as a necessary measure taken by a belligerent trying to safeguard its security in view of the rapidly approaching Soviet front. The rationalization was reinforced by the rumor that the concentration was directed only against the potentially "dangerous" unassimilated Eastern-Galician Jews. When the ghettoization-deportation process was extended to Northern Transylvania and Trianon Hungary proper, the Jews of Budapest, who had just been ordered into special Yellow-Star buildings, continued *their* rationalizations, arguing that "What happened in the countryside cannot possibly happen in Budapest—in the sophisticated city where there were so many foreign diplomats."

As the deportations proceeded and the widespread illusions about the intentions of the Germans and their Hungarian accomplices receded, the Jews were already too physically debilitated and spiritually broken by weeks of severe maltreatment in the ghettos to offer any resistance. Moreover, many of the men of military age were away in labor service companies stationed mostly in the Ukraine and Serbia. In contrast to their national leaders, the Jewish masses had no idea of the assembly-line mass murder that was taking place in Auschwitz and elsewhere in neighboring Poland. The decision of the national Jewish leaders and of the others privy to the great secret not to share it with the Jewish and non-Jewish masses remains one of the most controversial questions of the Holocaust.

Under the conditions of relative normality that prevailed until the German occupation, the acculturated-assimilationist leaders of Hungarian Jewry were quite effective in serving the community. Firmly committed to the values and principles of the traditional conservative-aristocratic system and convinced that the interests of Jewry were intimately intertwined with those of the Magyars, they never contemplated the use of independent political techniques for the advancement of Jewish interests per se. They took pride in calling themselves "Magyars of the Jewish faith" *(Zsidóvallású magyarok)*. The leadership, consisting primarily of patriotic, rich, and generally conservative elements, tried to maintain the established order by faithfully obeying the commands of the government and fully associating itself with the values, beliefs, and interests of the broader Hungarian society. Consequently, the Jewish national leaders' response to the exacerbating anti-Jewish measures during the interwar period was apologetic and isolated from the general struggle of European Jewry. Their loyalty to the Hungarian nation, and their attachment to the gentry-aristocratic establishment, remained unshaken. To the end, they followed an ostrich-like policy, hoping against hope that the ruling elite would protect them from the fate of the Jewish communities of the neighboring countries. They did not, of course, expect that Germany would invade an ally and that this segment of the anti-Nazi Christian leadership would also be among the first victims after an occupation. Practically until the beginning of the deportations, the national Jewish leadership continued to believe that the Hungarian Jewish community, unlike all other large European Jewish communities, would emerge from the war relativey intact even if economically generally ruined. The belief that they would escape the Holocaust—*megusszuk* (we'll get by), they frequently said in self-assurance—while tragically mistaken, was not irrational. After all, Hungary had in fact been an island of safety in an ocean of destruction for four and a half years of the war.

This sense of optimism was sustained by the victories of the Allies. In the West, following the successful landing in Italy, an Anglo-American invasion was only a matter of time; in the East, the Soviet forces were fast approaching Romania. Consequently—and in retrospect this appears to have been the Jewish leaders' major error in judgment—they failed to take any precautionary measures against the possibility of a catastrophe like that of the other Jewish communities in Nazi Europe. In this attitude too, they were not very different from their Christian counterparts, who, while searching for an honorable way out of the war, failed to take any military contingency measures to forestall or, if necessary, oppose a possible German invasion.

That invasion 40 years ago put an end to the uniqueness of the Hungarian-Jewish experience. The Holocaust was indeed a watershed in the history of Hungarian Jewry as in the history of all other Jewish communities in Europe—and in the rest of the world. It "united them," to quote Professor Jacob Katz, "in the fate of a people singular in its suffering and unique in the mystery of its existence."

Chapter 14

THE HOLOCAUST IN
CONTEMPORARY HUNGARIAN LITERATURE

Ivan Sanders

Any survey of Hungarian literature about the Holocaust must be prefaced by the observation that while the destruction of a large part of Hungarian Jewry may have been the most dramatic, the swiftest, the most brutally effective in all of Europe, the literary treatment of the catastrophe is not that extensive. What is more, much of the literature this essay examines was published in the last ten to fifteen years. The kind of soul-searching we find in postwar German literature, for example, is all but missing in Hungarian works written in that period. It is significant that the book which remains to this day the most thoroughgoing and devastating literary examination of the Holocaust in Hungary—Béla Zsolt's autobiographical novel *Kilenc koffer* (Nine Suitcases), written right after the war and serialized in a Budapest weekly at the time—was not published in book form until just a few years ago.[1] For reasons that were psychological as well as political, most Hungarian writers—both Jews and non-Jews—dealt briefly and tangentially with the Holocaust even before 1948. After the Communist takeover, specifically Jewish themes, characters, and problems disappeared altogether from literature. The whole "Jewish question" was seen as an evil vestige of the prewar order—a question that would be solved once and for all under socialism.

The persecution and annihilation of Jews came under the heading of Fascist atrocities; it was considered unnecessary, inappropriate even, to focus specifically on the Jewish tragedy. There were no Jews, only victims of persecution. (The phraseology, incidentally, persists to this day: In Hungary everyone knows that to say of someone that he had been one of the persecuted is a euphemistic way of alluding to that person's Jewishness.)

191

Indeed, there are still writers in Hungary, including Jewish-born writers, who refer to the Holocaust in the most general terms, who place it among safe ideological categories, who downplay, or ignore, the fact that it was directed specifically against Jews. However, they are the exception rather than the rule. Most of those writing about the Holocaust in Hungary today do tread more carefully; they are less ready to accept pat explanations, less apt to repeat Marxist clichés. Whereas in 1965, in the Hungarian edition of a thoroughly tendentious and biased East German book on the Eichmann Trial, one could still read such introductory lines as "The real breeding ground of Eichmann's crimes was German imperialism,"[2] no self-respecting Hungarian writer would be content today with such meaningless oversimplifications. In the introduction to the recent Hungarian translation of a book about Marek Edelman, a leader of the Warsaw Uprising, who still lives in Poland, we get a very different characterization of the Holocaust: "After reading this book, we realize ... that our notions of life, death, courage, honor, when applied to that time and that place, lose their validity. ... What happened then remains unassimilable for the human mind. And those who survived it carry memories, are loyal to judgments, are responsible for decisions, which are incommensurate with the expectations of posterity."[3]

There was one Hungarian writer who as early as 1948 argued that the events of the Holocaust were unique. By insisting on this point he rendered all previously held views and assumptions about Hungarian-Jewish relations obsolete. This writer was a Protestant political essayist, István Bibó, and his study, "The Jewish Question in Hungary,"[4] written in 1948, remains to this day the most penetrating and sensitive analysis of the subject.

Between 1948 and 1956 the Holocaust could not be discussed in Hungary as a Jewish tragedy; in fact most things connected with the Jewish experience seemed to become taboo in those years. After 1956, however, it became clear to just about everyone—to the Communist internationalists who had tried desperately to make Jewishness irrelevant as well as those who ignored the subject out of tact—that the Jewish question had not disappeared, and never would in a society that persists in glossing over its recent history, one that disregards sociological realities and denigrates cultural contributions.

The conspiracy of silence between those who did not dare to speak out on the subject and those who did not care to was finally broken in the late 1960s and early 1970s. A number of autobiographical and semi-autobiographical works appeared then, written by Hungarians who had themselves been victims of persecution during the war. Some of these works raised the question of collective responsibility and strongly implied that old wounds, if not attended to, can continue to fester. For example, Mária Ember began her novel *Hajtűkanyar* (Hairpin Bend), a chronicle of the ordeal of a group of deported Hungarian Jews in 1944, with the following sentence: "The subject of this book is not the proverbial Jewish fate: what this book relates is Hungarian history."

This rather dramatic summation, implying both reproach and allegiance, was echoed by other Hungarian writers preoccupied with the Holocaust. The much-quoted motto became the point of departure for a non-Jewish Hungarian writer's assessment of Hungarian anti-Semitism. This essay—György Száraz's *Egy előitélet nyomában* (Tracing a Prejudice)—makes it clear that anti-Semitism has been an ubiquitous feature of Hungarian Jewish life. Indeed, the essay is not just a survey of a prejudice but a review of Hungarian Jewish history. Reflecting on Mária Ember's statement, Száraz concludes that the horrors of 1944 concern all Hungarians: "The onlookers because they were onlookers, the executioners because they were executioners, the victims because they were victims. All of us are affected by those horrors—the survivors as well as the witnesses, those born after the event as well as those yet unborn. For what happened then has indeed become part of Hungarian history."[6]

Most of the works published in Hungary about the years of darkness are prose narratives. But perhaps a more significant Hungarian contribution to Holocaust literature is in the area of poetry, traditionally the strong point of Hungarian letters. Two poets whose work merits a closer examination are Miklós Radnóti and János Pilinszky, both of them major figures of twentieth-century Hungarian literature. Pilinszky, a Catholic poet, grew up as the sheltered child of middle-class parents. In late 1944 he was drafted into the Hungarian army, and with the retreating Axis forces taken to Germany, where he witnessed the ravages of war as well as the mental anguish of prisoners and concentration camp inmates. He was the first—and for a long time the only—Hungarian poet who dealt insistently with the implications of the Holocaust, seeing it as a moral disaster, a failure of civilization. Pilinszky's is a Christian response to the horrors, and while his victims are never identified—in his famous "KZ-Oratorio" the speakers announce simply: "I come from Warsaw" or "I'm from Prague"—his stark images evoke powerfully and hauntingly *l'univers concentrationnaire*. In that same "KZ-Oratorio" an old woman says:

We lived here like cattle.
Like pigs we knelt in the dust,
and yet by the time the food reached our tongue
it was gentle, like the body of God.

And a young girl exclaims:

> . . . Only the fraying thread
> of the prisoner's dress remains with me.
> I tear off the thread and put it in my mouth.
> Here I lie, dead on the tip of my tongue.[7]

In a poem entitled "Harbach 1944," Pilinszky describes a group of camp inmates harnessed to a giant cart they are forced to drag across German fields and villages. The following is part of the closing section of the poem, in Ted Hughes's fine translation:

> Already their bodies belong to silence.
> And they thrust their faces towards the height
> as if they strained for a scent
> of the faraway celestial troughs[8]

Pilinszky's was a lonely, distant, self-abnegating voice in an otherwise richly polyphonic literature. For a long time Hungary's cultural leadership had no use for his unwavering, self-tormenting pessimism. Nowadays, however, Pilinszky, who died in 1981, is seen as an exemplary figure—a man of rare literary and moral sensibility.

The life of Miklós Radnóti was more poignant, more tragic, and his fate, for some Hungarian Jews at least, has become a kind of object lesson. Born Miklós Glatter, of Jewish parents, he remained indifferent toward his Jewish roots all his life. Yet he died as a persecuted Jew. In late 1944, during a forced march westward across Hungary, Radnóti and members of his forced labor company were shot dead by their Hungarian guards. After the war his body was removed from a mass grave, and his last poems, his most gripping, written days before he was killed, were discovered in his coat pocket. As a poet Radnóti clung with stoic serenity to the humane values of the Western tradition at the very moment the forces of inhumanity were trying frantically to destroy them. In his greatest poems he combined the moral imperatives of the Judeo-Christian tradition with an evocation of the classical ideals of beauty. But he never particularized, and felt no special kinship with, the people who bore the brunt of Nazi savagery. In one of his celebrated eclogues, written in Lager Heidenau, one of the camps set up along the Bor-Pozarevac highway in what is today Yugoslavia, he mentions a "sad Jew" along with Frenchmen, Poles, Italians, Serbs. Radnóti the poet kept watching and writing even in death's jaws. His final, prophetic "Razglednica," or Postcard, is dated October 31, 1944:

I fell beside him; his body turned over,
already taut as a string about to snap.
Shot in the back of the neck. That's how you too will end,
I whispered to myself: just lie quietly.
Patience now flowers into death.
Der springt noch auf, a voice said above me.
On my ear, blood dried, mixed with filth.[9]

Most commentators agree that this man, as well as the poet himself a few days later, was murdered not by German SS-men but by Hungarian guards assigned to their labor service companies. The German line in the poem may be an attempt by Radnóti to place the blame for the butchery entirely on the Germans, and absolve as it were his own countrymen.

A number of Radnóti's friends and contemporaries have written about the poet's last years and about his attitudes toward his Jewishness. In the literary memoirs of István Vas, a fellow poet, we read the following:

If I try to recall what we talked mostly about, I remember only the Jewish question. . . . My own point of view was this: if you were born a Jew, you had a choice. Either you said, "I want to be a Jew" or you said, "I don't want to be a Jew." Personally, I took the second choice. But it is quite impossible to say "I am not a Jew." Yet that is precisely what Miklós said: let Hitler do as he likes, let the whole world turn upside down, still I am not a Jew. Miklós was right, at least as far as he was concerned, and he showed it with his martyr's death. Although they killed him as a Jew, he died as a non-Jew. His last eclogues, elegies, postcards were written not by a Jew, nor by an ex-Jew trying to free himself of his Jewishness.[10]

Interestingly enough, a Soviet émigré, Simon Markish, the son of the famous Soviet Yiddish writer Peretz Markish, quotes precisely this passage in an article on Soviet Jewish intellectuals. According to Markish, "the Radnóti case is an extreme one, where the mental state borders on the pathological, showing a total lack of sensitivity to the environment."[11] Vas, commenting on Markish's article, indignantly rejects this view, charging that only fanaticism that borders on the pathological could make one adopt it. Vas believes Radnóti was "the sanest of all of us," and contends that if one lives in a madhouse one has to have great inner strength and even a lack of sensitivity, a "total immunity," to the environment.[12]

A different kind of response to Radnóti's martyrdom can be found in an article on the poet written by a Hungarian essayist, Sándor Gervai, who was with Radnóti in Bor, Serbia, and who after the war settled in Israel. Gervai tells us that in Bor Radnóti held impromptu readings and often recited his newest poems to friends and other interested listeners. On one occasion their sergeant major confronted Radnóti with the question: "Why does a Jew, doing labor service, need to write poems?" Radnóti answered respectfully but firmly: "I beg to report to the sergeant major that I am a Hungarian poet." Whereupon the sergeant struck Radnóti in the face so hard, he nearly fell over; then, letting loose a stream of obscenities, the sergeant said exactly what he thought about this Jew's claims of being a Hungarian poet. The real tragedy of Radnóti's life, according to someone like Gervai, is that he was so alienated from his Jewish origins that even after a historical turning point he could not return to it. "He felt that he didn't just assimilate but became, through his works, an integral part of Hungarian culture. But he had to discover that reality decided and judged quite differently; he had to realize that ultimately his life was no different from that of a pious grocer from Sip utca [a street in Budapest's Jewish quarter]. They were both put on the same scale and shared the same fate. . . . At the end Radnóti spoke to those about whose plight he did not sing before, and his swan song, his most beautiful, most perfect poetic creations gave the lie to his previously espoused artistic credo, and raised the tragedy of those very Jews to the level of great art."[13]

We don't know of course how Radnóti would have viewed his experiences had he survived, whether he would have reassessed his attitudes toward his Jewishness, so the question remains: Was his particular response to the madness of those years an act of supreme courage and loyalty, or was it pathetic self-delusion? The answer to this question must be very personal, based on one's own inclinations and life experience. (Radnóti's widow, who is also Jewish-born, to this day actively discourages critics and translators from making a point of Radnóti's Jewishness, insisting that in his case this is a simple biographical fact and nothing more.)

Among a younger generation of Hungarian-Jewish writers there are many who have a greater need to reaffirm their Jewish identity, for whom assimilation has not really been a one-way street. The novelist George Konrád, for example, had this to say about the subject in an interview: "I never wanted not to be a Jew. I never wanted to dissolve, in the universality of a liberal assimilation or in the homogeneity of an internationalist Communist assimilation, the uniqueness of my background: that I was born into a Hungarian Jewish family. The Jews are most certainly a people. How, in what manner, they mingled with the Hungarian people: how the two merged, how they remained apart—these are complex historical questions. One thing I know: I am at once a Hungarian and a Jew."[14] Other Hungarian-Jewish self-definitions are somewhat more ambivalent. For example, the young hero of Pál Bárdos's recent autobiographical novel, *A második évtized* (The Second Decade), sums up his feelings this way: "I will consider myself a Jew while there is a single anti-Semite in the world." (Though he does add: "They are sure to survive me.")[15]

There is no question that, even if belatedly, a number of Hungarian writers and intellectuals do deal with the implications of the Holocaust; they discuss more openly the problem of Hungarian and Jewish identity, and even raise some painful questions about the ultimate wisdom of assimilation. For example, the historian Péter Hanák recently published an essay in a Hungarian literary journal on the remarkably successful integration of Jews in the Austrian-Hungarian Monarchy. But his essay, too, is a conspicuously post-Holocaust reexamination of the process. Hanák beings by reviewing the familiar success stories of some of the better-known Jewish merchant families of Hungary, their rise within a few generations to the pinnacle of economic power, and their subsequent contributions in other areas of Hungarian life. Someone like Lajos Hatvany is seen by him as a paradigm of successful assimilation. The scion of one of the richest Hungarian Jewish families, Hatvany as a man of letters and patron became a significantly figure of twentieth-century Hungarian culture. But Hanák also cites the case of the equally gifted Károly Pap, who rejected the assimilationist model, tried, when it was no longer possible, to remain both a Jew and a Hungarian, became an unappreciated writer, and perished in oen of the death camps. Today it is Károly Pap's example rather than Hatvany's that seems to haunt writers preoccupied with the subject of Jewish assimilation. Hanák himself ends his essay on a somber, even tragic, note:

There will be no doubt those who will consider the Final Solution, the ultimate tragedy, as history's judgment on the entire assimilation experience. And then there will be those who will view the Holocaust as a grave but not inevitable catastrophe. Many will feel that in the light of the massive failure of twentieth-century assimilation, the establishment of an independent nation-state was the only realistic solution. Others will consider any one choice made by Jews to be one-sided, a surrender of values. Whether independent Jewish nationhood is chosen, or Jewish survival in the Diaspora, or total assimilation, the choice itself will be seen by these people as a classical example of the Kierkegaardian notion of the tragic "collision of values." There is no question that the arguments in favor of independence are compelling—they are arguments rooted in the instinct for self-preservation, in the ideals of human freedom and dignity. *Vivere necesse est.*

But there will also be those who will argue: *Navigare necesse est; vivere non est necesse.*[16]

Recent literary works about the Hungarian Holocaust, written by such authors as György Moldova, Mária Ember, Imre Kertész, Ágnes Gergely, Pál Bárdos, and György Gera also grapple with the problems of loyalty, responsibility, and identity, and while these novels, based most often on personal experience, are filled with palliative rationalizations, their authors do not conceal their bitterness, either. In György Moldova's *A Szent Imre induló* (Saint Emeric March) for instance, which recounts the experiences of a young boy in the Budapest ghetto, we meet quite an array of Jewish characters, one of whom says at one point: "I didn't expect Horthy to put on a yellow star, as the King of Denmark did, or the clergy and the cabinet to take up our cause, as in Bulgaria; but the deportation of four hundred thousand Jews from the provinces in a matter of weeks had to be a world record." To be sure, Moldova has another Jew, the inmate of a forced labor camp, express more familiar—and under the circumstances rather absurd—sentiments: "These times will pass and everything will turn out all right. I am proud to be a Hungarian."[17]

Other writers are keenly aware of the inadequacy of literary means to convey the enormity of the tragedy. At least two novels—Mária Ember's *Hajtűkanyar* and György Gera's *Terelőút* (Detour)—intersperse the narrative with documents relating to the persecution and deportation of Hungarian Jews: testimonies, newspaper articles, confidential directives—factual material, in other words, which, it is felt, can tell the story more fully than can any fictionalized account. The hero of Gera's novel, the survivor of an Austrian labor camp, is also cognizant of the general ignorance about, and indifference toward, what happened in his country in 1944. At one point he rebels against this indifference and says: "I don't want to be grateful to them for tolerating me in their midst. I will unearth the dead, put their bones on a velvet cushion, and parade these relics of mine throughout the land. And I will cry out, I will scream, I will rave, until they shut me up. And when they do, I will pin a yellow star over my heart. That's how I will go to the opera, and to football games, to night clubs. I'll wear it to the classroom, too—let them see where I come from, at whose behest."[18]

The author of another autobiographical Holocaust novel, Imre Kertész, doesn't attempt to put his experiences into perspective, doesn't allow hindsight to reshape his vision. Though clearly the work of a mature writer, written years after the Holocaust, this novel, *Sorstalanság* (Without Destiny), maintains throughout the illusion of an adolescent point of view, and this makes the account of a fourteen year-old Hungarian Jewish boy's experiences in German concentration camps that much more compelling—and disturbing. Kertész's young hero assumes nothing; he doesn't anticipate, doesn't judge, doesn't rebel. At first his compliance and passivity in the camps strike us as appalling evidence of the victim's servility and self-denigration, of his identification with the aggressor's view of him. But as we read on, we realize that his readiness to accept and understand actually enables him to retain his sanity and even a modicum of dignity. By imputing human motives to his inhuman torturers, by imposing logic, his logic, the logic of a reasonably bright, sensitive, though in many ways quite ordinary teenager, to things that defy logic, he maintains a precarious semblance of normalcy. What he discovers in the camps is of course the "banality of evil," and his "normal" reaction to the process of dehumanization is at once a confirmation of this banality and an unconscious rejection of it.

We should add that over the years facts about the Holocaust have become more generally known in Hungary; the number of survivors' testimonies, written by nonprofessional writers, has also multiplied. Documents reminiscences, and diaries are still being published in fairly large editions.[19] (Quite a few books on the subject have also appeared in Hungarian in Israel, though these works are virtually unknown in Hungary.[20]) The American critic Terrence Des Pres may be right in saying that there is a "terrible sameness" about survival testimonies.[21] These Hungarian narratives are not, generally speaking, literary masterpieces. Yet, because there was silence for so long, and because there is still so much obfuscation, a reluctance to face certain issues squarely, the mere fact that these books are published, that they exist, is significant in itself. The historian György Ránki quotes the famous lines by George Santayana—"Those who do not remember the past are condemned to relive it"—at the beginning of his book *March 19, 1944.*[22] This reminder, in the Hungarian context, is more pointed, more momentous, than when we read it in, say, William Shirer's well-known *The Rise and Fall of the Third Reich.*

Of course, remembering always implies introspection and self-examination. Books about the Hungarian Jewish experience, including narratives about the Holocaust, are full of critical self-appraisals. It is almost as though many Hungarian Jews felt they can accuse only if at the same time they also incriminate themselves. A book like Béla Zsolt's *Kilenc koffer* rails almost as bitterly against Jewish complacency and self-hatred as it does against the perpetrators of atrocities. Just one example: In the Nagyvárad ghetto hospital Zsolt overhears an obviously bright and spoiled teenage girl insolently attacking her terrified parents: "Why are you Jews? Why? And if you are, how dared you bring me into this world?"[23]

Many Hungarian Jews may still have contradictory feelings about their Jewishness, yet more than one Hungarian Jewish writer's work reflects the awareness that the horrors of forty years ago must be continually confronted. We might cite the example of George Konrád, if only because he is one Hungarian novelist almost all of whose writings are available in English translation. Images and symbols of the Holocaust found their way into Konrád's *The Case Worker,* a novel that offers a shattering picture of the underside of urban life. ("The smell of poverty, that yellow star," says the narrator at one point. "Auschwitz, Auschwitz," mutters a foreign visitor upon seeing carcasses in a slaughterhouse shed.[24]) His second novel, *The City Builder,* which recounts the history of an unnamed East European city, contains passages about the deportation of the town's Jews in 1944. Here, too, as in so much Holocaust literature, trains become fatal conveyances, railroad stations, antechambers to hell.[25] Konrád's latest fiction, just completed, deals at much greater length with family history, and with the fate of the Jewish inhabitants of the narrator's hometown. The novel culminates in a harrowing description of the final journey to Auschwitz—a journey which, but for a stroke of luck, the author himself would have taken. "As a child I decided," says the narrator at the end of his tale, "that everything in the world that militates against Auschwitz is good, and everything that validates it is evil."

Members of the postwar generation of Hungarian writers tend to be less respectful about the Jewish past, and about their own Jewish problems, than some of their elders. The gifted young author Mihály Kornis has written a short story which is a wry, clever and ultimately poignant summary of East European life in the first half of the twentieth century. The story is in the form of a petition: an ordinary—and as yet unborn—Budapest Jew asks "the higher authorities" to grant him exactly the kind of miserable life he winds up having. The petitioner is a familiar figure from Jewish literature: a much-abused, none-too-courageous little guy who is nevertheless tenacious—a born survivor.

Item 3 of the petition reads:

> Next I thought of a Second World War. Nazism, discrimination, persecution I will put up with; yellow star I will put on. My car and my shop I will hand over to the Hungarian Army and the Ministry of Commerce and Industry, Department of de-Judaization, respectively.

(I hereby request that if at all possible my parents not be dispatched to the Mauthausen concentration camp. It looks as though I might be able to work out something for them at the Dohány Street ghetto.)

The petition also contains a supplementary statement in which unconditional loyalty masks indispensable worldly wisdom.

. . . I the undersigned hereby solemnly declare that it is as retail merchant, truck driver, assistant buyer and buyer that I would like to serve the Kingdom of Hungary, Greater Hungary, the Apostolic Regency, and the Hungarian People's Republic.

I will honor and respect the governments of Francis Joseph I, Count Mihály Károlyi, Béla Kun, Miklós Horthy, Mátyás Rákosi, János Kádár, etc., and will obey their laws.

When hearing the Austrian, German, Soviet, Hungarian national anthems (as well as the "Gotterhalte," the "Giovinezza," the "Internationale"), I will stand at attention.

. . .

During the course of my life I will not trouble you with special requests . . . and regardless of whether or not I receive prior notification, I shall accept ı.ıy death with equanimity; and I shall not have strange gods before me, and shall not swear false witness against my neighbor; and neither shall I covet my neighbor's wife, nor his manservant, his ox, his ass, nor anything that shall belong only to my neighbor.[26]

Notes

1. Béla Zsolt, *Kilenc koffer* (Nine Suitcases). Budapest: Magvető, 1980.

2. Friedrich Karl Kaul. *Az Eichmann-ügy* (the Eichmann Case). Budapest: Kossuth, 1965.

3. Hanna Krall, *Egy lépéssel az Úristen előtt* (One Step in Front of God). Budapest: Európa, 1981.

4. István Bibó, "A zsidókérdés Magyarországon" (The Jewish Question in Hungary). *In: A harmadik út* (The Third Way). London: Magyar Könyves Céh, 1960, pp. 227-354.

5. Mária Ember, *Hajtűkanyar* (Hairpin Bend). Budapest: Szépirodalmi Könyvkiadó, 1974.

6. György Száraz, *Egy előítélet nyomában* (Tracing a Prejudice). Budapest: Magvető, 1976.

7. János Pilinszky, "KZ-Oratorio" (Concentration Camp Oratorio). *In: Ocean at the Window. Hungarian Prose and Poetry Since 1945.* Edited by Albert Tezla. Minneapolis: University of Minnesota Press, 1980, pp. 127-133.

8. ——, Harbach 1944. *Lines Review,* no. 59, Sept. 1976: 39.

9. Miklós Radnóti, "Picture Postcards (4)." *In: The Complete Poetry of Miklós Radnóti.* Ann Arbor, Mich.: Ardis, 1980, p. 277.

10. István Vas, *Mért vijjog a saskeselyű?* (Why Does the Vulture Scream?). Budapest: Szépirodalmi Könyvkiadó, 1981, vol. 2, p. 177.

11. Simon Markish, Passers-by: The Soviet Jew as Intellectual. *Commentary,* New York, Dec. 1978: 37.

12. From a private letter written by Vas to the author of this essay.

13. Sándor Gervai, "Radnóti Miklós." *In his: Anat Istennő virágai* (The Flowers of the Goddess Anat). Jerusalem: The Author, 1959, pp. 163-168.

14. Ivan Sanders, The Novelists: George Konrád. *The New Republic,* New York, Jan. 5-12, 1980: 27.

15. Pál Bárdos. *A második évtized* (The Second Decade). Budapest: Szépirodalmi Könyvkiadó, 1981, p. 92.

16. Péter Hanák, A lezáratlan per: A zsidóság asszimilációja a Monarchiában. *Jelenkor* (Present Time), Pécs, vol. 26, May 1983: 460.

17. György Moldova, *A Szent Imre-induló* (The Saint Emeric March). Budapest: Magvető, 1975, p. 91.

18. György Gera, *Terelőút* (Detour). Budapest: Magvető, 1972, p. 96.

19. See, for example, Gáborné Vidor *Háborog a sír* (The Grave is Rising). Budapest: Magvető, 1960; Olga F. Csillag, *Mert megtörtént a XX. században . . .* (Because It Happened in the Twentieth Century. . .). Budapest: Szépirodalmi Könyvkiadó, 1969; László Gerend, *Kiűzettünk városunkból* (We Were Driven From Our City). Budapest: Magvető, 1982; Borbála Szabó, *Budapest napló. 1944 november–1945 január* (Budapest Diary. November 1944–January 1945). Budapest: Magvető, 1983.

20. See, for example, Erzsébet Balla, *József körút 79* (József Boulevard, 79). Tel Aviv: Új Kelet, 1964; Teri Gács, *Mélységből kiáltunk Hozzád* (I'm Crying From the Depth, My Lord). Tel Aviv: Uj Kelet, 1960.

21. Terrence Des Pres, Eros, God and Auschwitz. *The New York Times Book Review,* Jan. 29, 1984: 1.

22. György Ránki, *1944. március 19.* Budapest: Kossuth, 1968.

23. Zsolt, *Kilenc koffer,* p. 75.

24. George Konrad, *The Case Worker.* New York: Harcourt Brace Jovanovich, 1974, pp. 88, 103.

25. ——, *The City Builder.* New York: Harcourt Brace Jovanovich, 1977, p. 63.

26. Mihály Kornis, Petition. *The New Hungarian Quarterly,* Budapest, vol. 23, Winter 1982: 101-104.

IV. THE LINGERING ISSUE

Chapter 15

THE JEWISH QUESTION
IN CONTEMPORARY HUNGARY

András Kovács

In 1945, after Hungary's liberation from the German occupation and the collapse of the old political regime, awakening Hungarian progressives faced a new challenge. Having survived the darkest episode of Hungarian history they confronted the possibility of a completely new start—although this opportunity was not the result of their own doing. It seemed as if everything could be started from scratch in a country whose modern history had been shaped by broken-winged initiatives followed by a series of compromises, and defeats all the way to the worst in 1944. Yet one of the heaviest moral, historical and even political burdens on the awakening historical consciousness was obviously the deportation of about half a million Hungarian citizens of Jewish origin who, having lived with the illusion of assimilation, became victims of the Final Solution. This deportation—apart from the active participation of a minority—was passively accepted by the surrounding majority.

Between 1945 and 1948 the issue of Jews and their persecution was the focus of journalistic debates.[1] Not long after these debates began, however, they came to an abrupt end. For approximately fifteen or twenty years after 1948, the Jewish question became practically a taboo subject. Then, from the mid-1960s on, there again appeared sporadic, mostly literary publications which dealt with the problematic historical relation of Hungarian Jews and the surrounding society.[2] Since the early 1970s, historians have dealt with the subject more frequently. It is striking, however, that works on the subject discuss almost exclusively the history of Hungarian Jews before the war, especially the period of the persecution of Jews. There is hardly anything about what happened after 1945. Even if the Jewish question had survived postwar society merely as a blurred scrap of memory in the depths of social consciousness, the long silence about 1944, the road leading up to it and postwar developments would have been a burden on the historical and political consciousness of present generations. But this is not the case.

What, exactly, is the Jewish question? This has been the subject of lengthy discussions of definition in religious, historical, sociological, and psychological literature. It is not necessary, however, to retrace these debates to define the Jewish question in Hungary today. It is sufficiently defined by an everyday experience: in Hungary Jews and non-Jews differentiate both themselves and each other; they remain aware of their Jewishness or non-Jewishness, and distinguish their "reference groups" accordingly. Though publicly, of course, there is no such thing as a Jewish question and even Jews as such exist at best only in the denominational sense of the word.[3]

According to the popular argument, the Jewish question has remained alive in Hungary, largely due to the absence of a healing discourse.[4] This, however, is not the case: silence in 1950, 1956 and 1980 covered different things in each case. Historians explain the rise of the Jewish question in modern times in terms of the distorted development of Hungarian capitalism. But these historical causes were eliminated, along with capitalism, by the postwar economic and social transformations. Since the Jewish question remains alive to this day, it is reasonable to ask whether new causes have not replaced the original ones.

I

Before 1945, Jews formed a distinct stratificational group in Hungary. As social historical analyses have shown[5], Jews were disproportionately represented in the middle classes in relation to the overall proportion of Jews in society. The level of education and urbanization of Jews differed significantly from other social strata. Jews had different career aspirations, cultural values and the lifestyle of the "genteel middle class." The diverse lifestyle of the "genteel middle class," with an aristocratic-gentry origin and that of the Jewish bourgeois middle class offered alternative integrational patterns through the whole period.

After 1945, with the demolition of the old system, the social status of Jews changed radically. Nationalization, the liquidation of the old political system and later the radical transformation of social structure as a result of rapid industrialization eliminated the special stratificational status of Jews. With the liquidation of the private economic sphere, the system of private employees and free intellectual professions, most Jews lost their means of existence and had to find a new place in society. On the other hand, new fields were opened to them that had been closed before the war, e.g., in the political system, state administration and the army. Jews who had lost their former status during the great social transformations or who tried to exploit new opportunities, may have preferred certain positions in the new occupational structures. This, however, did not lead to a homogenization similar to that of earlier times because their place in the social structure was no longer defined by *coercive* conditions that forced them *as Jews* into certain positions as had been the case under capitalism.

In the decades after 1945, however, not only did the borderlines within the occupational structures become blurred but the contours of different life-styles of Jewish and gentile middle classes increasingly lost their sharpness. In the 1950s, there was a homogenization of consumer and social behavior, habits, and aspirations because of a general levelling through a lack of alternatives—i.e., a "negative" homogenization took place—but from the 1960s on a "positive" homogenization began as life-styles, habits and aspired status symbols became increasingly determined by the norms of a "consumer society." Of course, this did not involve a complete uniformity of life-style or even that of norm regulating everyday life. The new differences, however, though often incorporating elements of the old patterns, were formed within the new value system, and did not follow the sharp outlines of prewar models.

At any rate, those social factors which defined the place of Jews in prewar Hungary partly disappeared, or were significantly weakened. Secondary factors such as intra-group marriages and informal relations may have gained in significance for group identity after the war as a result of the 1944 experiences. But something that had been expected after 1945 did not occur, i.e., Jews, having had their illusions of assimilation brutally frustrated, did not react to persecution with a self-conscious isolation. The Jews who remained in Hungary continued to seek assimilation, the group identity was not reinforced by conscious dissimilatory tendencies.

The sparse Hungarian literature on the subject acknowledges the problem, but can produce only weak arguments to explain it: e.g., "the last generation of Leventes [a paramilitary youth organization functioning between 1928 and 1944] has now only reached its prime of life;" or "there are also retrograde traditions, . . . operating under the surface;" or "young generations even here . . . cannot be immunized against spiritual bacilli;" or "even here, during soccer games there are supporters throwing beer-bottles, alcoholics in pubs and hooligans in side-streets;" or "among Hungarian Jews there can be some who generate stupid or malicious generalizations by their individual behavior," and the like. Even the author of the most honest study published in Hungary on the Jewish question[6] repeats these well-known platitudes about the survival of anti-Semitic traditions and the disreputable elements sustaining them, despite the fact that he probably did not find anti-Semitism and abuse of Jews solely among pro-Fascist ex-youngsters and alcoholics in pubs. Moreover, he seems to know well enough that the Jewish question in Hungary today is largely a problem of the intellectual and middle classes.[7] There are hardly any attempts to attribute the stubborn persistence of the Jewish question to inherent factors of social and political changes after 1945.

Yet, almost four decades after the war, it is increasingly in this direction that the explanation should be sought. According to our hypothesis, the main reason for the re-emergence of the Jewish question is that in the decades after the war, originally separate Jewish and non-Jewish groups reacted to certain social changes and political events in significantly and systematically different ways. In a context unfavorable to the healing of old wounds, these different reactions kept alive a separate Jewish and non-Jewish consciousness despite the disappearance of "hard" group constituting social factors.

II

In postwar Hungary, the confrontation of non-Jews and Jews who had just returned from extermination camps, or were released from the ghettos, could not possibly have been smooth. The unavoidable question was: Were the active participants in the persecution of Jews the only ones responsible for the deaths of approximately half a million Hungarian Jews, or were the passive majority also guilty? Was there national responsibility, given the fact that masses of Hungarian citizens who had considered themselves equal members of the nation were declared outcasts and suffered violent deaths? The debate in postwar Hungary was emotional and influenced by the short-range political considerations extensively analyzed by István Bibó: Hungarians turned out to be incapable of a dispassionate discussion of the questions of responsibility.[8] While the demand for accountability slipped into heated accusations proclaiming the "total responsibility of the fascist nation" and calling for collective repentence, defensive reactions led to declining any responsibility and even to a new anti-Semitic demagogy about "Jewish thirst for revenge" and "lust for power." Ironically, both parties felt justified when, one and a half years after the end of the persecution of Jews, anti-Semitic pogroms occurred again in Miskolc and Kunmadaras.[9]

Moreover, Jews and the surrounding society reacted in different ways to liberation and the end of the war.[10] The appearance of the Soviet army in Hungary liberated the Jews, regardless of their social strata or their attitude toward the Communist regime. The same cannot be said for the rest of society. "I and other surviving Jews had to accept it: we were saved from certain death by Soviet soldiers and no one else. This experience, however, separates rather than unites us with the rest: they probably reacted in different ways to the fact that it was the Russians who brought liberation. They might have felt ashamed that they could not achieve it themselves, but those less ashamed might have pondered whether it might have been better if not the Russians but the British or the Americans had come. We had only one way of reacting to it: we were alive because the Russians *did come.* Maybe the others could have been liberated even under more favorable circumstances."[11]

Of course, the end of the war and the expulsion of the Germans and of the Arrow Cross Party meant liberation not just for Jews. Some of the vast political measures taken during the first year after the war were considered liberating by many other groups: this was demonstrated by the activity of grass-roots peasant organizations regarding the distribution of land, the activity of the spontaneously emerged national committees, the response to the first nationalizations and the relatively high number of votes for left-wing parties during the 1945 elections. Nevertheless, for non-Jews, the experience of liberation was combined with that of losing the war and its consequences: the confrontation with an occupying army, the taking of prisoners of war, and the loss of territories inhabited by Hungarians. For Jews, liberation and the loss of the war cancelled each other out. This immediately implied a conclusion regarding the rest that created an "us" and a "them": "all I want to say is that I was liberated in 1945, and immediately it occurred to me that because of that I could not have anything to do with those who lost the war in '45."[12] Similarly, for non-Jews, anyone who does not consider himself a loser in this war is an "alien" having nothing to do with the cause of Hungarians. This readily explains the frequent emergence of the accusation that Jews wanted to put the whole nation on trial for war crimes. Some Jews on the other hand felt that those who had lost the war would have willingly sacrificed the remaining Jews for a more favorable outcome.

Thus, after the end of the war, the conflicting system of reflections immediately took shape. Although conflicts were sharp and the tone passionate, there seemed to be hope for reconciliation since the reason for confrontation originated in the past and was fueled by the past. This expectation proved to be false, and the past remained continuous with the present. Between 1945 and 1948, and more fully after 1948, a new factor intensified the separation of Jewish and non-Jewish group consciousness: the attitude toward the Communist Party, communist ideology and the new regime.

III

Not only popular reasoning but also a part of the literature explain the new post-1945 version of the Jewish question in terms of the fact that Jews held a disproportionately high number of positions in the new regime.[13] Although probably true, this is difficult to document and, at any rate, it explains very little. As has been pointed out, it is rather the fact that a society is preoccupied with this sort of statistics that needs explanation.[14] The phenomenon itself can be readily explained. First, the new administration badly needed competent people who had not been implicated with the prewar regime. Obviously, large numbers of persecuted Jews fulfilled these conditions. Second, new professions opened up for them for example in the army and in the state administration which even before World War I had mostly been open to the aristocratic middle class and from which people of Jewish origin or religion were even formally excluded in the Horthy regime. These two factors involved favorable career possibilities and a lot of people made use of them. Undoubtedly, in this system of selection the criteria of reliability and earlier persecution might have helped many people into positions for which they would otherwise not have been suitable.[15]

The relation between Jews and communist ideology, however, was not defined primarily by these new openings. This relation was influenced by qualitatively new conditions of the postwar situation. Notwithstanding some demagogic features of Party propaganda such as the declared tolerance for the "little Fascists" meant to win over the masses considered to be anti-Semitic, a significant number of Jews interpreted the message of Party ideology to mean that identification with Communist ideals paved the way for a new promising possibility of assimilation.[16]

Before the war, Hungarian Jews seeking assimilation wanted to become equal members of the nation. Therefore, they sought to incorporate the dominant national ideology of the assimilating community and to be incorporated with in. The craving for assimilation did not end with the collapse in 1944 of the illusion of its having already been achieved. But the nation and national ideology could no longer serve as the basis of assimilation because the Hungarian nation had not defended its Jews.

After 1944, joining the Communist Party and accepting the communist ideology was a way to survive the shock of the failure of assimilation and the resulting rootlessness. As someone wrote in his memoirs, "How could I cope with the idea that my people were hated in this country—or at least that they had still been hated yesterday? How could I cope with the indifference even worse than hatred with which the country had noted their annihilation and forgave me that I survived? I did not cope with it: I was strong enough to face the bare facts. It was better for me to understand: the harm inflicted upon Jews is only a part of the millennial injustice inflicted upon the whole nation. It was better for me to believe that by eliminating social injustice, by liquidating class oppression, anti-Semitism would also disappear. I had no doubt that I had to become a Communist. I knew that a new society . . . would put an end to parasites and exploiters and would terminate poverty and misery . . . all discrimination would come to an end."[17]

Communist Party ideology simply cast the Jewish question and anti-Semitism among the crumbling institutions of a declining world. The Jewish question was a product of the capitalist mode of production and anti-Semitism was the ideology aiming at lessening the tension of capitalist class antagonisms.[18] "Put an end to capitalism and you will have put an end to the Jewish question"—offered this ideology as a new perspective to Jews. In a novel, *Eyeglasses in the Dust,* a communist protagonist of Jewish origin vulgarizes Marx for purposes of agitation as follows: "Marx says that if we do away with bills of exchange, we also do away with Jews."[19] "For a Marxist," according to the same novel, "the Jewis question as such does not exist. Jewry is not the question, but anti-Semitism is. There is an anti-Semite question."[20]

This argument was so attractive for those involved not only because it placed the Jewish question into the past, among the hallmarks of an unjust and declining society, but because its prospects provided important psychological relief for its adherents. In the future society not only Jews would no longer suffer discrimination, but what is more, general human emancipation would eliminate all particular forms of integration, including nations. As the hero of *Eyeglasses in the Dust* states: "I do not believe that the mere fact of belonging to a nation or a people gives dignity to a man. This is a nationalist, Fascist concept . . . I believe, that the concept of man stands above people, nation, race or religion . . . Every people and nation receives dignity from man, from humanity and not the other way round."[21] Thus, as a consequence of unsuccessful attempts of assimilation, the previously accepted mode of integration is placed into a historical perspective. In the process of general emancipation, the nation and its ideology, i.e., nationalism, vanishes together with Jews through the trapdoor of history. These prospects promised not only an end to the threats that all kinds of nationalism have meant for Jews but also offered historical exemption for the failure of assimilation.

The prospect of a classless society was also important in another aspect: it relieved its Jewish followers of guilt over the one-sided class stratification of Jews. "We do not want to be a privileged or a buffer class anymore," declares the leftist Zionist hero of Gyertyán's novel,[22] who argues for emigration to Israel and absorption into the working class there. "Why should an intellectual working in socialism and serving the people belong to privileged strata," his Communist opponent says, citing the doctrines: "socialism . . . eliminates all privileges, even the privileges of intellectuals, by creating equal opportunities for everyone. The children of workers and peasants can become intellectuals. These intellectuals, however, no longer stand above the people. On the contrary, they serve the people. And to become one will depend only on abilities, not origins."[23]

In exchange for creating a society that eliminates the Jewish question, anti-Semitism, national isolation, nationalism and all kinds of class stratification, the Communist Party demanded complete identification with the "movement." To comply with this requirement involved almost total self-abnegation from Jews of bourgeois-intellectual origins: they had to divest themselves of their previous identities—all suspicious "bourgeois remnants." This must have been an enormously difficult task. Yet, Jews who sought relief from past wounds and who hoped to find a new identity in Communist ideals wanted just that: they could achieve their goal—get rid of everything that was "Jewish"—in a way that at the same time involved a new identification and a new community that accepted them: the "movement." "I allowed them to relieve me of the burden of mourning, or rather my right to my own mourning. I wanted to identify with the Communist collective united in the ideal of Communism," recalls Judit Márványi.[24] Though its ideological motives were similar, this identification was not quite the same as that of Jews involved in the illegal Communist Party. It was not the identification of what Max Weber called a "pariah folk" with a political movement that promised salvation but was just as persecuted as they were. There was more to it: this time relief from stigmatization was offered by a dynamic Party and ideology seizing power and holding a dominant position. And this assimilation raised no bad memories, it did not entail the adaptation of an "alien" minority to a ruling majority. Jews and non-Jews, "we are all children of an unjust and deformed society, and one way or another we all bear its marks upon ourselves. So we all have to assimilate to a new human ideal, if you like. We all have to transform into socialist men," or so proclaims the Communist hero in Gyertyán's novel.[25]

Of course, there were significant differences in thinking, attitudes, culture and temperament among those who hoped for this new possibility of assimilation. They looked for the new identity in many different ways. The alternative chosen by the young Communist militant who visited villages organizing cultural evenings and thus hoping for liberation from the rule of "evil madness" was only one of them. The other extreme was the Party secretary, personnel man or security official who could only think in terms of fire and sword to realize the newly found ideals in the midst of a "Fascist people." Typical of this is the Communist headmaster in György Moldova's novel, a former Jewish resistance fighter who wants "to drink Fascist blood" after the war and who is a little disappointed because he feels that his true place would really be with the police or with the state security forces and who considers it the duty of every Jew not merely to be a silent sympathizer but a relentless militant in the new regime since, as he explains to his reluctant protegé, "if this regime is overthrown, they will not take it into consideration that you only wanted to be a meek scholar. Murderers are not in the habit of deliberating too much; you get the same rope as if you had lead a courageous and resolute life . . ."[26] Various motives could have driven this type of functionary who would have employed any means for the sake of achieving his ends. There were some who joined the repressive forces simply out of revenge after the war and were carried away to more and horrible deeds. Some were driven by a fanatic identification with ideals believed to be absolute and superior to anything else, to accept or commit unbelievable absurdities and inhumanities. If, by chance, doubts arose, they cast them aside by the increasingly ruthless performance of superiors' orders that imperceivably but increasingly replaced great ideals. Only through total acceptance of the most absurd tasks, accusations and ruthless measures were such Jews able to disperse their own recurring doubts concerning their origin, careers, and "bourgeois remnants," i.e., the still incomplete identification with the "new." Though this attitude was not only typical of functionaries of Jewish origin and not even of the majority of Jewish Communists, it is still this image of a personality, highly functional in the period of "sharpening class struggle" that even today defines the image of the Jewish Communist of the 1950s in the common consciousness of prejudiced non-Jews and guilt-ridden Jews.

More attention should be paid to another phenomenon, however, which though less spectacular than the participation of Jews in the Party leadership or in the repressive forces, was at least as important in influencing the relation of Jews with their environment in the 1950s. This was a detachment from reality typical of people who suddenly converted to Communist ideals after the months of persecution. The acquisition of ideals that promised relief from the heavy historical burden of the Jewish question was so intense that only very few had enough energy left to examine their reality. The day-to-day experience of melting into the collective gave credence to the goals proclaimed for the far future and hid the reality of the present. As Judit Márványi recalls in her memoirs: "I did not notice that the village was not so happy when we invaded it on Sundays. . . . I did not notice because I did not want to notice: I thought it was temporary, the effect of hostile demoralization. . . . Behind the applauders, did I not see the bitter, hostile face of the working class? I watched those who were as enthusiastic as I was. . . . With our eyes fastened on truth, we admitted into reality only what justified us."[27]

Thus a new vicious circle developed. Jews and non-Jews confronted each other in a context that reinforced the old split. For Jews, or, at least, for a part of them, the new political regime meant something that it could not have meant for others and the intensity of this experience easily blinded them to the latter's problems. Non-Jews, or, at least, part of them now started to talk about the "Jewish thirst for revenge" and "Jewish power": In prejudiced generalizations they declared that they considered the ruling political regime alien and rejected it.

The specific Jewish attitude toward the Communist Party or the political regime after 1948 did not take the form of an articulated Jewish consciousness, for its source was the conviction that this new identification would immediately and forever eliminate all oppressive isolation. If it became conscious at all, then it was only as a peculiarity of personal history on the road leading to the Party. According to the protagonist of Gyertyán's novel: ". . . I could not hide even from myself that my denigration as a Jew also played a part in my social radicalization and social sympathies."[28] In retrospect, however, the content of this peculiar identification is partly cleared up by well-known cases during the 1960s and 1970s where, after disappointment in great ideals, the disillusioned were left with nothing but a re-discovered, reluctantly accepted, completely empty yet nostalgic Jewish consciousness as the somewhat narrow basis of self-identification. The headmaster from the previously quoted novel who thirsted for Fascist blood later comments: "I sacrificed a life to get to where I started from. . . . For thirty years, the world hammered in my head that I was *only* a Jew and I resisted with all my might and now, when the pressure has ended, should I accept it voluntarily? I am glad that I remember some sentences and old festivals from childhood, . . . when I find myself imitating gestures of my poor father."[29]

Yet, Jews who sought a new kind of assimilation or simply new career possibilities in the postwar political regime were only a small part of Hungarian Jewry. The fact that, unlike other social groups, this group established a specific relation to the political regime does not make the generalization valid for all Jews. To see whether the early "fifties"—the era of Stalinism—had really a different meaning *in general* for both Jews and non-Jews, one has to examine the group of Jews too for whom the post-1945 political changes resulted in the loss of livelihood, new threats and fears, i.e., the ones whose objective situation was not different from that of other social groups of similar stratification.

In some quarters and, of course, in right-wing political literature, a stereotype recurs that considers the years up to 1956 a period of Jewish political rule.[30] Yet, as Bibó already pointed out in 1948, the fact that Jews came into important positions of power after the war implies no special advantages for Jews. Indeed "some Jews, persons who suffered from the persecution of Jews, Jewish organizations or Jewish concerns have the occasionally bitter experience regarding their minor and fair or obvious demands that power holders of Jewish origin show no readiness whatsoever to take up these causes as Jewish ones even when these causes have no relation to political tendencies or state policies or they are not contrary to them."[31] Far from being an advantage, being Jewish exempted none from "disadvantages": in the course of the nationalizations the evaluation of Jewish enterprises was no different from others; bourgeois Jews lost their livelihoods just as non-Jews, and their offsprings were deprived of the opportunity of higher education exactly like other members of their class. And just to show how dubious was the argument about various "proportions," according to available sources 30 percent of all deportees in the Stalinist period—20,000 people—were Jewish.[32] Even if these data are exaggerated, this probably represented about 10 percent of Hungarian Jewry at the time.

This, of course, had nothing to do with any political tactic seeking to avoid the accusation of "Jewish solidarity." Jewishness could not serve as a basis for solidarity between Jews inside and outside power: admission to the new elite meant breaking with a Jewish consciousness which was as forbidden as any other deviation from the Marxism-Leninist paradigms. This was particularly bitter for left-wing Zionists who considered all labor parties, and the Communist Party in particular as political allies after liberation.[33] It has even been reported that membership in the Zionist movement, which was summarily liquidated after the war, was filed under the same heading as former fascist party membership in the records of personnel departments.[34] Although with less significance than in the Slansky trial, the charge of Zionism also appeared in transcripts of the Rajk trial,[35] and the arrest of the president of the Jewish community as well as of the head consultant at the Jewish hospital in 1953 indicated that waves of the Soviet anti-Zionist doctors' plot trial (terminated after Stalin's death) reached Hungary as well.[36]

It seems necessary to put the question: If the majority of Jews suffered the same ordeals in the 1950s as the rest of the population, could the hypothesis still be justified according to which even this group of Jews related to the political regime of the 1950s in a different way from the non-Jewish population?

Most Jews were not any better off during these years than other people. From the viewpoint of their reactions, however, their recent memories of 1944, and not their subsequent privations were decisive. The terror they faced under Stalinism did not threaten them with systematic extermination and they were affected by it not as Jews but as class enemies—as bourgeois elements. Moreover, many of them might have felt that even though the world they lived in was horrible, it was still the "lesser evil" and that it might perhaps be just an iron-handed Soviet-controlled dictatorship which could guarantee that the era of pogroms could never return. Many might have thought that in a "fascist country" this was the only chance of survival. All this did not turn them into active supporters of the regime. Yet, they feared any political crisis, they immediately recalled memories of 1944. This became most clear in 1956.

As with all violent historical events that have resulted in radical changes, 1956 has a real history as well as one that lives in people's imagination. The sharpest difference between these two histories may belie just how much anti-Semitism was involved in the 1956 events. Countless unverifiable stories about anti-Semitic manifestations, anti-Jewish actions, threats, beatings and lootings circulated in Jewish circles and even found their way into literature. The hero of Agnes Gergely's novel, *The Interpreter,* actually considers 1956 the final proof of the impossibility of assimilation: "most people behaved like ostriches: they thought that if they did not know themselves who they were, the outside world would not know either. A greengrocer became an engine fitter; on Sundays he drank beer with his pals in the park and for ten years he had the perfect, unclouded feeling of equality. Then, in 1956, they wrote on the wall of his house: 'Ikey kike! You will not escape Auschwitz this time!' Then, he fled the country."[37]

It may have been this kind of fear of anti-Semitic outbursts that chased 20,000 Jews[38] over the border in 1956. But first and foremost, it was the fear, not the experience. There were surprisingly few anti-Semitic manifestations during the 1956 uprising. According to the few available documents, among the unfolding political aspirations there were no anti-Semitic ones—not even within the most conservative groups. In this respect, the most reliable information is in official Hungarian records which use all available data to prove the extreme right-wing character of events. These sources list 21 anti-Semitic manifestations between October 23 and December 31, 1956, primarily in the country's most backward areas.[39] Probably, further "abuse" and "everyday anti-Semitism" appeared on the streets of Budapest and in country towns. At the same time, however, it was often the street itself that intervened against such manifestations.[40]

It is an interesting question as to why anti-Semitism played a much smaller role in 1956 than it could have been expected on the basis of bad traditions, the role of Jews in the Party and in the repressive apparatus, and the previously mentioned attitudes. Many Jews anticipated the worst, though these anticipations turned out to be unjustified. Still, they influenced and distinguished the reactions of the majority of Jews to what happened in 1956 from those of other groups.[41]

Given the stereotypes formed in the 1950s, it does not follow that while non-Jews unanimously opposed Stalinism as a terroristic regime forced onto the country by an alien power, Jews became Stalinism's active or passive supporters. An analysis of collective reflections does not provide an adequate basis to draw conclusions about political behavior. The latter is basically influenced by other factors as well. Besides, such conjecture is also contradicted by facts.[42] The issue under discussion is narrower by definition than the analysis of the political behavior of specific social groups. Our question is whether systematic and group-specific reactions did exist concerning the communist regime. Analyzing the postwar period the answer to this question must be positive. The difference in Jews' and non-Jews' reactions arose immediately after 1945 in connection with the implications of liberation and the question of responsibility, and it persisted even after the final establishment of the Communist Party state. Joining the Communist Party and accepting the Marxist ideology promised something to Jews that it did not promise to others—a personal solution to the torturing problems of identity. A minority took advantage of this promise while the majority, who were affected by the Stalinist regime just like any other group had, on the basis of their historical experiences, ample reasons to fear the loosening of the status quo. Non-Jews obviously had no reason to fear this.

Developments during the 1950s, therefore, resulted in different and differentiating reactions that kept the Jewish question alive.

IV

In the 1960s, the context in which social issues such as the Jewish question arose had fundamentally changed. The consolidating post-1956 regime no longer exerted power by means of campaigns that ruined everyday life and created permanent insecurity but by means of a more or less predictable, institutional logic. This relative stability enabled people to plan their lives and work out longer-term strategies. The tension that Jews had experienced during the 1950s also eased, regardless of their position in the social hierarchy. The composition of the ruling elite had changed radically: most of the compromised functionaries of the pre-1956 regime had to leave and the new political leadership saw to it in a direct way that the number of Jews in leading positions did not exceed certain proportions. First and foremost, however, the selection mechanisms were reformed. The composition of the elite was determined by different interests which were realized through different institutional means than had been the case under Stalinism.

On the other hand, the aspirations of the Jews who remained in Hungary after 1956 also changed. What had led them to join the regime no longer attracted them, partly because the promise that by overturning the world the roots of the Jewish question would forever be eliminated had not been fulfilled. Also, by the mid 1960s, the new generation confronted the Jewish question in a way different from that of their parents. They knew of fascism only from stories, they had been children in the 1950s. In the 1960s, Jews generally realized their expectations in intellectual professions and middle-class positions in Hungarian society. Yet, the mechanism of segregating reactions remained even after 1956. One of the reasons for this did not change: Jews and non-Jews reacted differently to certain political changes.

The present Hungarian political system cannot be accused of political anti-Semitism. Jews are not afflicted by systematic disadvantages compared to other social groups. But nevertheless, the Jewish group consciousness was reinforced by the political anti-Semitism, from time to time reactivated in other East European countries, above all in the form of "anti-cosmopolitan" and anti-Zionist campaigns in Poland and the Soviet Union. Hungarian Jews reacted to this not with an active solidarity but, as so many times before, out of fear. They were afraid that if in a country with a similar system anti-Semitism could become official policy and this policy encouraged underlying anti-Semitic sentiments, then no institutional and ideological guarantees can prevent this from also happening in Hungary. This fear was only strengthened by the East European countries' support of the Arabs in the Middle East conflict. They feared that this foreign policy might also encourage a Hungarian "anti-Zionist" policy. That such forces existed was proved by their unsuccessful public appearance in early 1973.[43]

Other reasons for the reappearance of the Jewish question bear no similarity to the ones discussed. Heretofore the point was that Jews and non-Jews responded differently to some "external" challenges: the changes in political environment. These two systems of reactions can be considered as factors that formed corresponding group consciousness. Nevertheless, the "encounters" of the two groups also permanently reinforced their consciousness, thus, it played a significant role in the reproduction of the Jewish question.

Jewish consciousness is characterized by how it reacts to the existence of the Jewish question. In the decades after 1956, just as in the 1950s, most Jews sought relief from the burden of the Jewish question by silence. This silence, however, was different from that of the 1950s: it brought not even a temporary relief. It was accompanied by the permanent awareness of being silent, some vague tension, uneasiness about the fact that there is *something* to be silent about. Interesting data about this are provided in a series of interviews conducted unofficially in Budapest a few years ago, in the course of which fifty Jewish intellectuals were asked about the present meaning of the Jewish question. Although most of those interviewed (most of them between the ages of 20 and 40) had grown up in the belief that the Jewish question was "obsolete," 44 of them had been uneasy about being Jewish until they reached adulthood. Only 20 percent of the participants were willing to speak unreservedly about the subject. This was not only the consequence of an aversion to giving interviews on the subject. The participants did not talk about the Jewish question at all at their workplace; in their private life at best they talked about it only with other Jews; only seven of them had ever raised the subject with non-Jews. A typical error shows, however, how serious they considered the subject: only three of those interviewed knew how many Jews lived in Hungary at present; 43 of them greatly overestimated the number.

This silence indicates that Hungarian Jews do not want to develop a separate, articulated group self-consciousness and, consequently, it is almost impossible to characterize Jewish consciousness in Hungary. Undoubtedly, this consciousness prevails in a wider stratum than the group of religious Jews. However, it cannot be considered as some sort of consciousness of a nationality or a certain other minority. To the extent that such consciousness exists at all, it contains hardly any active elements of its own history, culture or national identity. Among those interviewed, persecution was the only vivid factor of Jewish history they could identify, and only 16 of them felt some vague, obscure nostalgia for a lost culture of which, however, they had no knowledge. None of them felt any special loyalty towards the state of Israel, at best only an emotionally motivated sympathy; none of them wanted to live there and several were critical of Israeli domestic and foreign policy.

If the sample of those interviewed had been more representative, probably the results would not have been so unanimous. The ideological vacuum of the 1970s, which stimulated several religious and minority "rebirth" movements, may have had some effect on Hungarian Jews, especially among the younger ones. Yet this would not have fundamentally changed the picture: Jewish consciousness in today's Hungary is basically empty: it is simply the consciousness of being different. This difference is perceived by most Jews as discrimination, stigmatization by the environment or as pressure. One of those interviewed characterized the awareness of this dissimilarity as follows: "This is spontaneous, it probably comes from the fact that society compartmentalizes us anyway, so we would rather compartmentalize ourselves." A majority of those interviewed had a Jewish spouse[44] and most of their friends were Jewish. Most of them regarded this as a coincidence, or unconcious, defensive behavior at best. "In Jewish families there is a belief that one should pick a Jewish spouse because otherwise they throw your Jewishness in your face at the first row," says one of them. If it turns out that an acquaintance is a Jew, that "primarily means some relief, some security, the feeling that in this case I do not have to fear any 'attacks,' spiteful remarks." These statements are typical: Hungarian Jewish consciousness today consists mostly of this kind of reactive self-identification, interspersed with obscure fears.

The most difficult question is obviously: What does "stigmatization by the environment" exactly mean, what image do non-Jews have of Jews in present-day Hungary? What is the point of reference for reactive self-identification? It is almost impossible to answer these questions, because there is even less material available than exists for the reconstruction of Jewish consciousness. Behind these questions, however, an underlying theoretical problem is being debated to this day.

According to one important trend in the literature on Jewish question and anti-Semitism, the image of Jews fostered by anti-Semites is not based on experience but is pure projection.[45] With the development of modern society and dissolution of traditional communities, the borderlines that enclosed Jews as an "alien body" have disappeared so that generalizations about Jews as a whole can no longer be made. The image of Jew in modern anti-Semitism is not even a distorted generalization of experiences collected in the course of social interaction but an experienceless projection. The anti-Semite reacts to social conflicts harassing the individual by personalizing the causes of conflicts. He seeks ideological salvation from his anguish to bring about his psychological relief by "scapegoating," by creating the enemy figure of the "evil Jew" who is the cause of his troubles. The "Jew experience" of the anti-Semite is determined by this projection and not the other way around: the generalization by the experience.

From the previous discussion it is clear that the present analysis is more inclined to accept István Bibó's view on this issue. According to Bibó, even modern societies can develop features that separate Jews and non-Jews. This has no racist implications.[46] Bibó's views can perhaps be best interpreted in the framework of a sociological role theory in the broad sense. According to Bibó, in the case of a certain type of social development encounters of Jews and non-Jews take place in a context where both parties appear in determined roles and face each other as role-players. What non-Jews perceive as identifiable "Jewish behavior" is the role Jews are forced into in the course of interaction with non-Jews by a distorted social organization. The same holds for the attitudes Jews identify as the general behavior of non-Jews toward Jews. "One cannot seriously hope to create authentic formulas about the constitution, natural endowment, and original qualities of a community or a group of people, but it can have traits, characteristics, forms of behavior, and conditioning that in a given environment, in a given moment, characterize them, make them distinguishable, recognizable and elicit simplified generalizations from the environment. However, these misleading experiences gain a collective, social significance not in their incidental, isolated occurrence but when at some point of social organization . . . , due to some organizational contradiction, hidden falseness or prejudice, people enter into social intercourse in such a way that they repeatedly and permanently acquire these misleading experiences about each other."[47] This is the experience which serves as a basis for prejudiced generalizations.

Bibó describes three broad generalizations about Jews widespread in prewar times.[48] The first is a traditional sense of ethnic difference typical of peasant societes that consider Jews an alien ethnic group—often without hostility. The second view is burdened with anti-Jewish prejudices that can range from anti-Jewish resentment through prejudiced generalizations about "Jewish characteristics" to the ideology of anti-Semitism that "attributes completely fantastic collective actions, an ability for collective actions, collaboration and behind all these a world-wide conspiracy to Jews."[49] And the third is that of Dezső Szabó and László Németh, according to which a large-scale Jewish and German assimilation is a harmful process endangering the survival of the Hungarian nation insofar as it destroys the substance of the nation.

Although the content of the image of Jews has fundamentally changed in postwar Hungary, the types of generalizations in which this image is expressed are quite similar to the ones described by Bibó.

As sociological surveys conducted in the mid-1960s in villages and in the early 1970s among urban youth have shown, Jews are still seen as a separate group. Anti-Jewish prejudices are strongest in the lowest occupational strata and among those with little education; they diminish as one moves up in social level.[50] Unfortunately, these surveys do not detail the nature of this discrimination. As sporadic sources indicate, the core of the Jewish image is constituted by two types of traditional prejudices. The first type is the prejudiced rationalization of social tensions. Its direction is mostly vertical: its targets are mostly people in a higher level in the social hierarchy. Angry feelings against people in power and beneficiaries of privileges take an anthropomorphic form in the persisting hostile picture of the lazy, slick Jew who lives comfortably without working and attains high positions by means of obscure contacts. "Here anti-Semitic remarks are somehow used in a political sense, anti-Jewish manifestations are intended as anti-communist ones," says a Jewish manual worker in one of the interviews.[51]

The second type of prejudice is mostly horizontal; it is basically a result of rivalry and the focus is on "Jewish solidarity." In Hungary today this is the result of the fact that after 1956 the difference between Jews and non-Jews had a special function: it became a selective mechanism for the distribution of positions. In modern societies a professional career is legitimated by a competence formally certified by educational institutions and distributed among competing candidates according to formal criteria. Of course, the decisions of bureaucratic institutions are also influenced informally by career lobbies.[52] Thus, in spite of formal equality, in France the degrees of the *grandes écoles* are valued more highly than those from other universities. Similarly, in England, going to Oxford or Cambridge provides better career possibilities than degrees from other universities. These lobbies can also be organized on the basis of national or religious loyalties.

In Soviet-type regimes the formal criteria governing professional careers are not homogeneous. Institutionally acquired expertise is only one criterion and not even the most important. Social origins, reliability, and membership in political or other organizations can also play a role of criteria, sometimes even in a formally codified way.[53] Under these circumstances, personal associations play a greater part in professional success than in the theoretically purely bureaucratic systems, since the content of some of the criteria—such as "reliability"—is formally undefinable anyway. Moreover, the range of criteria and the emphasis of individual aspects vary, so that personal guarantees, recommendations, and contacts necessarily play an important role in evaluations. In the case of scientific and cultural careers and institutions this tendency—the formation of career lobbies—is enhanced by the limited possibilities to the institutional foundation of scientific schools and cultural trends, and thus spontaneous groups organize themselves in a lobby-like way.

There are two general prerequisites for the formation of career lobbies: a relative stability that allows for planning longer-range strategies and the existence of groups with some sense of collectivity. In Hungary after 1956, both conditions existed. A wide variety of factors underlying group identity served as an organizational basis for developing territorial or institutional career lobbies and in certain cases the fact that Jews and non-Jews are differentiating themselves and each other. The two kinds of group consciousness that have been sustained and reproduced since 1945 by divergent reactions to political situations could thus become a basis for the formation of career lobbies during the period of consolidation. These lobbies function as a part of the mechanism of selection in distribution of career possibilities among rival candidates. To be Jewish or non-Jewish can imply both advantages and disadvantages in certain situations depending on whether in a given field, if these lobbies have emerged at all, one or the other is dominant. When such is the case, the mechanisms of lobbying continually reproduce negative confrontations between Jews and non-Jews. As Miklós Szabó put it, a career lobby needs an enemy for its cohesion.[54] The reason for this is that it has to justify its nonlegitimate existence and possible failures even to itself. The existence of a rival group serves this purpose best. Career lobbies always consider themselves defensive in character: for non-Jews it is the answer to "Jewish cohesion," for Jews it is self-defense against anti-Semites. Thus a vicious circle develops, a considerable amount of projection settles on the "experience," inducing through a feedback mechanism new "experiences." This phenomenon is important in the reproduction of the Jewish question in Hungary.

V

A concept of the Jewish question that Bibó called "characteristically Hungarian"[55] has also reappeared in the present-day Hungary, although in a different form. This concept, a sort of cultural anti-Semitism was primarily directed against the "alien element" which, in its desire to assimilate, corrupts the "nation" from within. This kind of anti-Semitism is a direct consequence of the characteristically East European nationalism: cultural nationalism.[56]

Cultural nationalism is the outgrowth of a national development where the criteria of belonging to a nation are not primarily institutional and formal (e.g., citizenship), but the nation is defined mainly by criteria such as language, historical and cultural traditions and often expressed by the concept of "national character."[57] Evolving usually in multinational states such as the Hapsburg monarchy, or created by movements attempting to unite an ethnic group divided by state frontiers into a nation (e.g., the Italian Risorgimento in the middle of the nineteenth century), this national consciousness is typical of a "threatened community." "There is a permanent threat that an alien influence can divest the nation of its original character and shape it in another way. In these communities the sense of national identity is cramped. An image of the enemy, compared to which the community feels its identity strengthened belongs organically to the ideological composition of national character. The image of the enemy of the nation-state is provided by alien nations organized into other states. In the case of the development of nations whose identity is not based on a nation-state, but on national culture, however, the alien ethnic groups, which disintegrate national character, is sought inside its own community. According to the visions of spasmodic fear, some . . . infiltrating alien ethnic group pretending assimilation is the enemy that disintegrates the national character to shape it in its own disguised image."[58] The cultural anti-Semitism of Dezső Szabó and László Németh is obviously the consequence of this nationalism, and the reason for the existence of this anti-Semitism up to now is that the cultural nationalist tradition is still alive in Hungary.

The transformation of Hungarian nationalism after 1945 is beyond the scope of the present analysis. Yet, regarding its present state, two elements are relevant: first, problems of independent national existence are still legitimate in East Europe and, second, there are still significant Hungarian minorities living within the territory of states with other ethnic majorities. Thus, no special justification is necessary if national consciousness concentrated on what kind of autonomous political institutions are necessary to define collective national interests and what kind of institutional and legal guarantees are needed for the preservation of the national identity of Hungarian minorities living in neighboring states and what the duty of the Hungarian government would be in this respect. But these questions are not raised or, at least, not in this fashion. Discussions of the national question in institutional-political terms are rare in Hungary since it cannot be discussed meaningfully without dealing with the relationship with the Soviet Union. Similarly, prying into the absence of institutions which guaranteed minority rights would lead directly to the question of the absence of an institutional system that generally guaranteed the expression of all particular interests, and not only that of the national minorities. Thus, for reasons of censorship and deeply internalized self-censorship, the national question in Hungary today is mostly formulated not in political-institutional but in cultural terms, maintaining continuity with cultural nationalism.

Cultural nationalism is not necessarily a negative thing, and it has often expressed progressive endeavors. Problems start when existential questions of national culture are *directly* identified with questions of national existence. For example, when low birth-rates or the deterioration of the language are directly related to the vision of the death of a nation, i.e., when the relation between the cultural and economic-political presuppositions of national existence are left out of consideration. In this case, the concept of nationhood cannot be separated from irrational interpretations. The kind of nationalism that ignores institutional aspects of national existence and cannot formulate threats to the nation in this context can easily resort to the notion of a "nation-destroying alien." In this way one can easily arrive to the image of the prolific gypsy gradually outnumbering the dwindling Hungarians or that of the Jew "forcing" abstract thinking, frivolous life-styles or wanton political radicalism on them and destroying their language. Present cultural nationalism regarding its logical implications, can thus coincide with prewar cultural anti-Semitism.

This does not mean, of course, that today's advocates of cultural nationalism are all anti-Semites. One cannot even say that anti-Semitism is a direct consequence of cultural nationalism. It is only that the ideology of cultural nationalism is conceptually open to these conclusions since it has no inherent safeguards against such consequences. Therefore no one can wonder that those of Jewish origin sensitive to all kinds of nationalism on the basis of their historical experiences are afraid that it can be interpreted this way.

Historical encounters of Hungarian nationalism and Jews after World War I were generally negative. Jews immediately suspected anti-Semitism behind any kind of nationalism and were often insensitive to those issues of independent national existence always so important in East Europe. On the other hand, these suspicions were not always unfounded, as it was unfortunately proved by the often not only theoretical consequences of East European nationalisms. This vicious circle is still occurring in Hungary.

Does the existence of the Jewish question also imply anti-Semitism in Hungary? Generally, the undeniably vivid prejudices against Jews do not necessarily involve anti-Semitism. A prejudice, on the level of the individual, becomes anti-Semitism if it is formulated in generalizations and if it demands sanctions. Anti-Semitism becomes political when being Jewish entails disadvantages systematically sanctioned by rules, written regulations or institutions, or if political forces take steps to institute such sanctions. In present-day Hungary, there is no political anti-Semitism and there is no way of telling how many of the people with prejudices against Jews are anti-Semitic. Nevertheless, these prejudices are the first step on the road to anti-Semitism and can be easily mobilized in political crises as anti-Semitism. This is well known by Jews from their historical experiences, so no one can blame them if their fears, even if they are unclear, are completely unfounded.

VI

The evil logic in which the Jewish question was formulated in Hungary has not been broken after 1945. Modern developments in Hungarian history, and its product—the peculiar Hungarian nationalism—left Jews with a choice: if they chose to be Hungarians, their Jewishness could only be religious. Hungarian Jews accepted this alternative and followed a course of mass assimilation. This assimilation, however, remained superficial and its failure resulted in a deep Jewish identity crisis.[59] After 1944, Jews could not close their eyes to the fact that they had been only seemingly accepted in society but there was no way back to a Jewishness in a wider sense than religious. The Jewry after 1945 got stuck in this interminable position.[60] The situation is awkward: while politics, society, and Jews alike insist on the barely reformulated thesis of assimilation originating from the era of liberal nationalism, the historical background has shifted and all parties are aware of the fact that the old recipe is inadequate. In the literature discussing the Jewish question, with the intention to find remedy for the insane situation two alternatives are elaborated. The most widespread one before and after the war is rooted in the spirit of assimilation.[61] The other, more recent view, however, searches for a solution that would relieve tension caused by the Jewish question by making it possible for Jews to acknowledge a Jewishness more substantial than in the religious sense without, however, risking being labelled "cosmopolitan" or "alien."[62]

It is difficult to tell which of these alternatives will be followed, and it is even more risky to determine which of them is the more desirable. First of all because primarily the social groups concerned should decide what they prefer. These, however, hardly acknowledge even the question. Jews and non-Jews still distinguish themselves from each other, but they do so with a guilty conscience, burdened with repressed complexes. Two traumatized consciousnesses face each other and inflict new wounds on one another: a whole construction of old and new prejudices, suspicions, and fears towers over a foundation that has been suppressed into the social subconscious by spontaneous defense mechanisms. Silence, however, does not resolve problems. Indeed, as Miklós G. Tamás writes,[63] this silence reigns over a soon almost unclarifiable confusion. This silence refuses to acknowledge not only the past, but also the present, thus engendering uncertainty and fear of the future. It does not make too much sense to advise Jews to become more Jewish or less Jewish, or to advise the others not to be upset if Jews want to remain Jews or if they want assimilation. The problem is that no one is able to formulate goals and effectively pursue them. In this situation, what is needed is not a change in position, but finding them in the first place. Not only is the Jewish identity problematic but so is the non-Jewish one. In other words, all social groups in society lack self-consciousness. Public discussion may help, but talk alone does not solve anything—not even the Jewish question. But it could at least clear up what there is to be solved.

Notes

1. For a comprehensive bibliography on the persecution of the Jews in Hungary see Randolph L. Braham, *The Hungarian Jewish Catastrophe. A Selected* and *Annotated Bibliography*. New York: Institute for Holocaust Studies of The City University of New York, 1984, 501 p. See also Arthúr Geyer, *A magyarországi fasizmus zsidóüldözésének bibliográfiája, 1945–1958* (The Bibliography of Jewish Persecutions by Hungarian Fascism, 1945–1958). Budapest: Magyar Izraeliták Országos Képviselete, 1958, 167 p. After the war, spokesmen for practically all political parties were involved in the debate on the Holocaust, the Jewish question, and on the issue of responsibility. On the Communist view, see Erik Molnár, "Zsidókérdés Magyarországon" (Jewish Question in Hungary). *Társadalmi Szemle* (Social Review), Budapest, vol. 1, no. 5, May 1946: 326-334, and Márton Horváth, "Zsidóság és asszimiláció" (Jewry and Assimilation). *Társadalmi Szemle,* July 1946: 495-501. On the Social Democratic view, see Zoltán Horváth, *Hogy vizsgázott a magyarság?* (How Did the Hungarians Pass the Test?). Budapest: Népszava, 1945,

62 p. With respect to the view of the Peasant Party, see József Darvas, "Öszinte szót a zsidókérdésben" (An Honest Word on the Jewish Question). *Szabad Nép* (Free People), Budapest, Mar. 25, 1945. Probably directed by short-range political objectives, Darvas defends the workers and peasants against the Jewish survivors of the Holocaust. He purports that the Jews were trying to enrich themselves without working and by making unjustified demands on account of their suffering. Contrary opinions were advanced in an almost equally passionate tone by *Haladás* (Progress), a periodical edited by Béla Zsolt, the noted Jewish writer, who sympathized with the position of the bourgeois radicals. The fact that the Jewish question could be discussed without political bias and a full moral and historical sense of responsibility was proven by the classic study of István Bibó, "Zsidókérdés Magyarországon 1944 után" (Jewish Question in Hungary After 1944). *Válasz* (Response), Budapest, vol. 8, Oct.–Nov. 1948: 778-877. This essay has been republished in a number of sources, including *A harmadik út* (The Third Road). Edited by Zoltán Szabó. London: Könyves Céh, 1960, pp. 227-354. All further references will be to this edition. For a perceptive analysis of these issues, see also Péter Várdy, "Befejezetlen mult. Mai magyar zsidó valóság." *In: Belső tilalomfák. Tanulmányok a társadalmi öncenzuráról* (Inner Prohibitory Signs. Studies on Social Self-Censorship). Edited by Endre Karátson and Ninon Neményi. The Netherlands: Hollandiai Mikes Kelemen Kör, 1982, pp. 81-146.

2. On the literature about the Jewish question after 1948, see *Encyclopaedia Judaica.* Jerusalem: Keter Publishing, 1972, vol. 8, pp. 1088-1110, and Iván Sanders, "Tétova vonzalmak. Zsidó témák a kortársi magyar irodalomban" (Faltering Affections. Jewish Themes in Contemporary Hungarian Literature). *Új Látóhatár* (New Horizon), Munich, vol. 26, Dec. 15, 1975: 427-443.

3. As many have pointed out, the notion of "Jew" can define various social groups depending on the issue in question. See, for example, Bibó, *op. cit.,* p. 258. Since in the present study we deal with the relation of Jews and their environment, all those who are considered Jewish by their environment or by themselves belong to the category. See also Victor Karády and István Kemény, Les juifs dans la structure des classes en Hongrie: Essai sur les antécédents historiques de crises d'antisémitisme du XXe siècle." *Actes de la Recherche en Sciences Sociales,* Paris, no. 22, June 1978: 25-59. See especially, p. 38.

4. György Száraz, *Egy előítélet nyomában* (In the Footsteps of a Prejudice). Budapest: Magvető, 1976, 287 p. See especially, p. 277.

5. Karády and Kemény, *op. cit.* See especially, charts 5, 6, and 7 in their study.

6. Száraz, p. 271.

7. *Ibid.,* p. 276.

8. Bibó, *op. cit.,* pp. 330ff. On the debates, see Száraz, pp. 249 and 257ff., and Várdy, *op. cit.*

9. The anti-Jewish acts of 1946, which resulted in five deaths, were also reported in the contemporary press. Cf. *Encyclopaedia Judaica, op. cit.,* pp. 1105-1106.

10. Bibó, *op. cit.*, p. 344. See also László Márton, "Zsidó sors, zsidókérdés a háború utáni Magyarországon" (Jewish Fate, Jewish Question in Postwar Hungary). *In: Eszmék nyomában* (In the Path of Ideas). Edited by Sándor Németh. The Netherlands: Hollandiai Mikes Kelemen Kör, 1965, p. 130, François Fejtő, *Judentum und Kommunismus.* Vienna, 1967, p. 83, and Ágnes Erdélyi, "Eltorzult kozmopolita alkat" (Distorted Cosmopolitan Structure). *In: Bibó-Emlékkönyv* (Bibó Memorial Volume). Compiled by Ferenc Donáth *et al.* Budapest: Szamizdat, 1980, pp. 257-266.

11. Erdélyi, *op. cit.*

12. *Ibid.*

13. This argument appears in almost all writings on the subject, regardless of their tendency. See, e.g., Ervin Gyertyán, *Szemüveg a porban* (Eyeglasses in the Dust). Budapest: Magvető, 1975, 593 pp; Fejtő, *op. cit.,* pp. 74ff and pp. 83ff; and Várdy, *op. cit,* p. 97.

14. See Bibó, *op. cit.*

15. *Ibid.,* p. 344. This phenomenon is also discussed by Várdy, *op. cit,* p. 112.

16. On the working class movement as a context of assimilation, see Bibó, *op. cit.,* p. 323. On the relation between Jews and the Communist Party, see Várdy, *op. cit.*

17. Judit Márványi, *Köszönet helyett* (Instead of Thanks). *In: Bibó-Emlékkönyv* (Bibo Memorial Volume), *op. cit.,* pp. 278-291.

18. See Molnár, *op. cit.*

19. Gyertyán, *op. cit.,* p. 139.

20. *Ibid.,* p. 373.

21. *Ibid.,* p. 377.

22. *Ibid.,* p. 386.

23. *Ibid.,* p. 387.

24. Márványi, *op. cit.*

25. Gyertyán, *op. cit.*

26. György Moldova, "Elhuzódó szüzesség" (Prolonged Virginity). *Kortárs* (The Contemporary), Budapest, no. 11, 1980: 1750.

27. Márványi, *op. cit.*

28. Gyertyán, *op. cit.,* p. 140.

29. Moldova in *Kortárs,* no. 1, 1981, p. 265.

30. See David Irving, *Uprising!* London, 1981.

31. Bibó, *op. cit.,* p. 349.

32. Eugene Duschinsky, "Hungary." *In: The Jews in the Soviet Satellites.* Syracuse, N.Y.: Syracuse University Press, 1953, pp. 471-478; Fejtő, *op. cit.,* p. 84; *Encyclopaedia Judaica, op. cit.,* vol. 8, pp. 1106-1107.

33. On the dissolution of the Hungarian Zionist organization and the trial of its leaders see Duschinsky, *op. cit.,* pp. 458-464, 483-485; *Encyclopaedia Judaica, op. cit.,* vol. 8, p. 1106; Márton, *op. cit.,* p. 141.

34. Márton, *op. cit.,* pp. 147ff.

35. *Rajk László és társai a népbiróság előtt* (László Rajk and His Accomplices Before the People's Court). Budapest, 1949, p. 137.

230   THE HOLOCAUST IN HUNGARY — FORTY YEARS LATER

36. Duschinsky, *op. cit.,* pp. 483-485; Márton, *op. cit.,* p. 147 ff.

37. Ágnes Gergely, *A tolmács* (The Interpreter). Budapest: Szépirodalmi Kiadó, 1973, pp. 51-52.

38. *Encyclopaedia Judaica, op. cit.,* vol. 8, p. 1107.

39. See *Ellenforradalmi erők a magyar októberi eseményekben* (Counterrevolutionary Forces in the October Events in Hungary), *Magyar Népköztársaság Tájékoztatási Hivatala* (Information Office of the Hungarian People's Republic), vol. X, pp. 41, 45; vol. IV, pp. 70-78. *Antiszemita jelenségek és zsidóellenes attrocitások a magyarországi ellenforradalom idején* (Anti-Semitic Phenomena and Anti-Jewish Atrocities During the Hungarian Counter-Revolution). The source of this information is the "Memorandum" *(Emlékirat)* issued by the Central Office of Hungarian Jews (Magyar Izraeliták Országos Irodája-MIOI) compiled by Endre Sós, President, and Dr. Jenő László, executive secretary. *Ibid.,* vol. IV, p. 70. The MIOI "Memorandum" seems to have listed all cases that could be documented in any way since it is clear from the text that one of the main reasons for compiling the document was to justify the high number of Jews among the refugees in 1956. Out of the 21 events listed, two were committed against religious institutions; in two cases, the actions probably had no anti-Semitic motives but were armed robberies of which the victims were Jews; in at least two further incidents it is likely that the Jewish origin of the victims was not the primary cause of the attack; in two cases the person or persons insulted were defended by the population of the village. The "Memorandum" registers one single anti-Semitic manifestation in Budapest, the credibility of which, however, is rather doubtful: allegedly, there was a list compiled about Jews in Ujpest. Two other religious community sources report five further violent anti-Jewish manifestations in Szabolcs County. See László Harsányi, "Adalékok a hajduvárosok zsidóságának történetéhez" (Contributions to the History of the Jews in the Hajdu Towns). *In: Évkönyv 1970* (Yearbook 1970). Edited by Sándor Scheiber. Budapest: Magyar Izraeliták Országos Képviselete, 1970, pp. 116-165 as quoted in Várdy, *op. cit.* Sporadic anti-Semitic remarks in the course of the October 23 demonstrations are reported by one of the interviews conducted with hundreds of refugees by the Columbia University Research Project on Hungary. (Interview no. 207, p. 3, quoted by Bill Lomax, "Az értelmiség forradalma vagy a munkásoké?" (A Revolution of Intellectuals or Workers?). *Magyar Füzetek* (Hungarian Notebooks), Paris, no. 9-10, p. 110. On the unsuccessful attempt to revive the Arrow-Cross Party, see Bill Lomax, *Hungary 1956,* London, 1976, p. 35. David Irving argues that one of the main motives of the October uprising had been the outburst of anti-Semitism, but can only quote a single CURPH interview to justify his statement. He provides several quotations to illustrate the underlying anti-Semitism of the 1950's, however.

40. See *Ellenforradalmi erők a magyar októberi eseményekben, op. cit.,* vol. IV, p. 73; and Márton, *op. cit.,* p. 149.

41. See Fejtő, *op. cit.,* pp. 86ff.

42. See, e.g., the leading role of Jewish intellectuals in the anti-Stalinist movement. In the days of October 1956, the Jewish religious community dismissed its former compromised leaders and its revolutionary committee called for support of the revolution by the international Jewish public. See Márton, *op. cit.,* p. 151.

43. Early in 1973, during a conference dealing with cultural policy issues, a member of the foreign affairs department of the Central Committee of the Pary, using an unusually harsh tone, attacked the cultural policy of the second part of the 1960's for exhibiting "compliance" with Zionism. (The criticized examples of "Zionist content" were the staging of the musical "Fiddler on the Roof" and a Chagall exhibit in Budapest.) The attack was voiced at the peak of the campaign within the Party against the "reform policy" of the late 1960's and it is likely that it reflected not only the personal view of the speaker but that of a certain group inside the apparatus. Nevertheless, its first public appearance ended in defeat: the speech was sharply criticized at the conference and subsequently the speaker was removed from the Party center to an insignificant diplomatic post.

44. This, incidentally, could have resulted from the fact that the sample of the interviews was not representative.

45. J. P. Sartre, *Reflexions sur la question juive.* Paris, 1946. The same view is held by Leszek Kolakowski, *Der Antisemit. Mensch ohne Alternative.* Munich, 1960, pp. 159-169; Ferenc Fehér, István Bibó and the Jewish Question in Hungary: Notes on the Margin of a Classical Essay, *New German Critique,* Milwaukee, Wisc., no. 21, Fall 1980: 3-46. Miklós Szabó, Nemzetkarakter és resszentiment. Gondolatok a politikai antiszemitizmus funkcióiról (National Character and Resentment. Thoughts on the Function of Political Anti-Semitism). *Világosság* (Light), Budapest no. 6, 1981: 358-362.

46. This is assumed by Fehér, *op. cit.,* p. 37.

47. Bibó, *op. cit.,* p. 273.

48. Cf. a personal letter from István Bibó to Gyula Borbándi regarding Borbándi's book about the populist movement, summarized in Borbándi, Bibó István és a népi mozgalom (István Bibó and the Popular Movement). *Új Látóhatár,* Sept. 1980, pp. 155ff.

49. *Ibid.,* p. 155.

50. Mária Márkus, Büszkeség és előitélet (Pride and Prejudice), *Valóság* (Reality), Budapest, Apr. 1976; Péter Józsa, Ideológiai áramlatok városi ifjúságunkban (Ideological Tendencies Among Our City Youth). *Világosság,* Mar. 1979. See also Ágnes Havas, Nacionalista hatások gyermekeinkre (Nationalist Influences on our Children). *Társadalmi Szemle,* Mar. 1967, and Béla Horgas, A film és közönsége (The Film and its Public), *Valóság,* Sept. 1966.

51. See Zsolt Csalogh, *A tengert akartam látni* (I Wanted To See the Sea). Budapest, 1981, pp. 202ff.

52. See Szabó, *op. cit.,* p. 361.

232   THE HOLOCAUST IN HUNGARY — FORTY YEARS LATER

53. The existing system of nomenclature in East European countries even makes the consent of political organs a formal condition for the filling of certain position. See Thomas Löwit, Y-a-t-il des États en Europe de l'Est? *Revue Françaises de Sociologie,* Paris, vol. XX, no. 2, 1979: 431-466.

54. Szabó, *op. cit.,* p. 361.

55. Borbándi, *op. cit.,* p. 156.

56. *Ibid.,* p. 157.

57. Eastern European and Hungarian historical nationalism had already been described by Bibó as a cultural nationalism (in his terms, linguistic nationalism). See his "A keleteurópai kisállamok nyomorusága (The Misery of Small Eastern European Countries). *In: Harmadik út, op. cit.,* pp. 113ff. On the historical types of nationalism and the position of Hungarian nationalism, see Jenő Szücs, *A nemzet historikuma és a történelemszemlélet nemzeti látószöge* (The History of the Concept of Nation and the National Point of View on History). Budapest, 1970, pp. 14-22.

58. Szabó, *op. cit.*

59. This is interestingly analyzed by Várdy, *op. cit.*

60. Bibó, *A zsidókérdés Magyarországon 1944 után,* pp. 310-313.

61. Two representative literary examples of this view are the play by Gyula Illyés, *Sorsválasztók. Dráma* (Selectors of Fate. Drama). Budapest: Szépirodalmi Könyvkiadó, 1982 and the relevant parts of the memoirs of István Vas, *Mért vijjog a saskeselyű?* (Why Does the Vulture Screech?). Budapest, 1981.

62. See Miklós Tamás, Republikánus elmélkedések (Republican Reflections). In: *Bibó-Emlékkönyv, op. cit.* This view is also preferred by Várdy, *op. cit.*

63. Tamás, *op. cit.*

CONTRIBUTORS

Iván T. Berend is Professor and Chairman, Department of Economic History at the Karl Marx University, Budapest. He has held visiting professorships at Oxford, Berkeley, and the Woodrow Wilson Center. He is the author or editor of numerous works, including *Economic Development in East-Central Europe in the 19th and 20th Centuries* (with György Ránki); *The Industrialization and the European Periphery* (with György Ránki); and *The Age of the Great Depression* (in Hungarian).

Randolph L. Braham is Professor of Political Science at The City College of The City University of New York. He also serves as Director of the Institute for Holocaust Studies at the Graduate School and University Center of The City University of New York. He is the author or editor of numerous books and has contributed to others on East Central Europe and the Holocaust. He has also published a large number of notes and articles in various encyclopedias and professional journals. His two-volume work, *The Politics of Genocide,* was published in 1981 by Columbia University Press.

Asher Cohen is Lecturer in Contemporary History at the University of Haifa and Research Director of the Institute for Research of the Holocaust Period. He is the author of several works, including *The Halutz Resistance in Hungary, 1942-1944* (in Hebrew).

István Deák is Professor of History at Columbia University. He held occasional guest professorships at Yale University, UCLA, and the University of Siegen in West Germany. He is the author of several monographs, including *Weimar Germany's Left-wing Intellectuals: A Political History of the "Weltbühne" and Its Circle* and *The Lawful Revolution: Louis Kossuth and the Hungarians, 1848-1849.* Professor Deák is also the co-editor of *Eastern Europe in the 1970's* and of *Everyman in Europe: Essays in Social History.* He published several dozen chapters and essays on Hungarian history, National Socialism, and the history of the Habsburg Monarchy.

233

Elek Karsai is Director of the Central Archives of Trade Unions in Budapest. A recognized authority on the Holocaust in Hungary, he is the author, editor or co-author of numerous works, including *A budai Sándor-palotában történt, 1912–1941, A budai vártol a gyepűig, 1941–1945, "Fegyvertelen álltak az aknamezőkön . . ." Dokumentumok a munkaszolgá-lat történetéhez Magyarországon,* and *Vádirat a nácizmus ellen. Dokumentumok a Magyarországi zsidó üldözés történetéhez* (3 vols.).

Nathaniel Katzburg is Professor of Modern Jewish History and Chairman of the Institute for Holocaust Research at Bar-Ilan University. His publications include *Antisemitism in Hungary, 1867–1914* (in Hebrew), *British Policy in Palestine, 1936–1945* (in Hebrew), and *Hungary and the Jews, 1920–1943.*

András Kovács received his Ph.D. in Sociology from Eötvös Loránd University in Budapest where he also served as Lecturer during the 1974–75 academic year. He also served as a visiting lecturer and research fellow at a variety of institutions of higher learning in Europe and the United States, including the Paderhorn University in the Federal Republic of Germany, the École des Hautes Études en Sciences Sociales in Paris, the Technische Hogeschool Twente in Enschede, and at New York University. He authored a number of studies on the Jewish question in post-World War II Hungary.

Elenore Lester is the author of *Wallenberg: The Man in the Iron Web.* A noted journalist whose articles have appeared in the *New York Times Magazine, Arts and Leisure,* and *Book Review* and other publications, she is currently associate editor of *The Jewish Week* of New York.

Raphael Patai is the author of 35 books, including *Israel Between East and West, Hebrew Myths* (with Robert Graves), *The Hebrew Goddess, The Arab Mind, The Myth of the Jewish Race* (with Jennifer Patai Wing), *The Jewish Mind, The Messiah Texts, Gates to the Old City, The Vanished Worlds of Jewry, On Jewish Folklore* and *The Seed of Abraham: Jews and Arabs in Contact and Conflict.* His books have been translated into ten languages. He taught at the Hebrew University of Jerusalem, the University of Pennsylvania, the Dropsie College, Princeton University, Columbia University, New York University, Fairleigh Dickinson University, and Brooklyn College.

György Ránki is Deputy Director of the Historical Institute of the Hungarian Academy of Science and Hungarian Chair Professor at Indiana University. He has held visiting professorships at Oxford, Paris, and Columbia University. He is the author or editor of numerous works, including *Economic Development in East-Central Europe in the 19th and 20th Centuries* (with Iván T. Berend); *The Industrialization and the European Periphery* (with Iván T. Berend); *Die Deutsche Besetzung Ungarns; History of the Second World War* (in Hungarian); and *Wilhelmstrasse and Hungary. Documents on German Foreign Policy toward Hungary* (in Hungarian).

Ivan Sanders is Professor of English at Suffolk County Community College on Long Island and has taught Hungarian literature at Columbia University. His articles and essays on East European literature have appeared in *The New Republic, The Nation, Commonweal, World Literature Today,* as well as a number of European journals. He has published articles on Jewish topics in *Judaism, Jewish Social Studies,* and *Soviet Jewish Affairs.*

Bela Vago is Professor of Contemporary History and Chairman of the Strochlitz Institute for Holocaust Studies and head of the Historical Documentation Center on East-Central Europe at the University of Haifa. A recognized authority on both the Holocaust and East-Central European history, he is the author or editor of a number of books, including *The Shadow of the Swastika* and *Jews and Non-Jews in Eastern Europe.* His articles appeared in a variety of scholarly journals, including the *Journal of Contemporary History* and *East European Quarterly.*

Raphael Vago is Lecturer in Modern East European History and Acting Director of the Russian and East European Research Center at Tel-Aviv University. His main field of research and teaching is the national problem in East Central Europe. He is the author of "The Destruction of Hungarian Jewry as Reflected in the Palestine Press," which appeared in volume three of the *Hungarian-Jewish Studies* series, as well as of a number of studies which appeared in such journals as *Be'hinot* and *Hungarian Studies Review.*

Elie Wiesel is Andrew W. Mellon Professor in the Humanities at Boston University and Chairman of the U.S. Holocaust Memorial Council. He is the author of a large number of highly acclaimed works that appeared in several editions and translations, including *La Nuit, L'Aube, Le Jour, The Madness of God, Un Juif, aujourd'hui,* and *Le Testament d'un poète juif assassiné.*